Microhistory and the
Lost Peoples of Europe

Selections from *Quaderni Storici*

Edward Muir and Guido Ruggiero, Series Editors

Sex and Gender in Historical Perspective
Microhistory and the Lost Peoples of Europe

Microhistory and the Lost Peoples of Europe

Edited by Edward Muir and Guido Ruggiero

Translated by Eren Branch

The Johns Hopkins University Press
Baltimore and London

The Johns Hopkins University Press
701 West 40th Street
Baltimore, Maryland 21211
The Johns Hopkins Press Ltd., London

∞ The paper used in this book meets the minimum requirements
of American National Standard for Information Sciences—
Permanence of Paper for Printed Library Materials, ANSI Z39.48-1984.

Library of Congress Cataloging-in-Publication Data
Microhistory and the lost peoples of Europe / edited by Edward Muir and
  Guido Ruggiero ; translated by Eren Branch.
      p.   cm. — (Selections from Quaderni storici)
  Includes bibliographical references.
  ISBN 0-8018-4182-8. — ISBN 0-8018-4183-6 (pbk.)
  1. Europe—History—Miscellanea.   I. Muir, Edward, 1946–
II. Ruggiero, Guido, 1944–   . III. Series.
  D21.3.M53   1991
  940—dc20   90-27638

?& Contents

?❧ Introduction: Observing Trifles

by Edward Muir

I've tried to get to the essentials and be as precise as possible, always keeping in mind that if the flour's too refined, the bread loses its flavor.
      —Danilo Dolci, *Creature of Creatures*
Holmes to Watson: "Never trust to general impressions, my boy, but concentrate yourself upon the details."
      —Sir Arthur Conan Doyle, "A Case of Identity"
Holmes to Watson: "You know my method. It is founded upon the observation of trifles."
      —Sir Arthur Conan Doyle, "The Bascombe Valley Mystery"

Sherlock Holmes's knack for noticing the apparently trivial was, of course, the wellspring of his many successes in criminal detection, a trait that makes his solutions, when examined in retrospect, so convincingly simple.[1] Historians have long enjoyed pointing out the similarities between criminal and historical detection,[2] but the comparison has now become central to a debate about historical method that has focused on the genre of microhistory, which evolved in the late 1970s and 1980s. Although it has parallels elsewhere, microhistory was born in northern Italy, especially in Bologna, the same intellectual milieu in which Umberto Eco wrote his best-selling novel, *The Name of the Rose.* It is not an accident, then, that the central character in Eco's novel, a fourteenth-century Franciscan hybrid between William of Occam and Sherlock Holmes, exhibits the same fascination with observing trifles as do the microhistorians, who invoke the famous fictional detective as a methodological guide. Their work responds to the once-dominant preoccupation among historians with quantitative social science, the *longue durée*, and immobile history, and it returns to interpreting utterances and beliefs, to describing brief dramatic events, and to envisioning a past characterized more by abrupt changes than by deep structural continuities.

These changes in the practice of history are analogous to certain developments in other disciplines. Sociologists have moved toward deciphering through microlinguistics short social encounters.[3] Ethologists such as Jane Goodall in her study of chimpanzees insist on the importance of systematic, long-term observation of individual animals in their natural habitat. Goodall's rejection of the laboratory, with its measurements, calculations, and statistical predictions, demonstrates, as Stephen Jay Gould puts it, that "close observation of individual differences can be as powerful a method in science as the quantification of predictable behavior in a zillion identical atoms. . . . When you understand why nature's complexity can only be unraveled this way, why individuality matters so crucially, then you are in a position to understand what the sciences of history are all about."[4] The most important reverberations, however, have been with ethnography. Among anthropologists there is a movement "to stress not just the given nature of society, but also the ways in which human beings continually construct, manipulate, and even recast the social worlds into which they were born and within which they will die."[5] The various disciplinary byways that have led scholars back to individuals making choices and developing strategies within the constraints of their own time and place have been diverse.

In this collection of essays from *Quaderni storici*, the second volume in a series, we propose to follow the path opened by the Italian scholars who coined the term *microhistory* and who have been the most creative in exploring its potentialities. Italian microhistory has made its claim to novelty in two ways. The first has been to argue for a reduction of the scale of historical research in order to isolate and test the many abstractions of social thought. In terms remarkably similar to those of Stephen Jay Gould, Carlo Ginzburg has argued that, "a close reading of a relatively small number of texts, related to a possibly circumscribed belief, can be more rewarding than the massive accumulation of repetitive evidence."[6] The second way has been to offer an alternative method for the evaluation of historical evidence, a method called the *evidential paradigm*, which is similar to the theory of abduction the American philosopher Charles Peirce proposed a century ago as a systematic way to sort out fragmentary clues.

Italian microhistory has evolved in a series of monographs issued by the Turin publisher, Giulio Einaudi,[7] and above all in the journal *Quaderni storici*. Since 1966 *Quaderni storici* has played a singular role in the polycentric, highly ideological Italian university world where young scholars can usually find a position only after years of servitude to an academic "baron" who, at least in the past, was invariably affiliated with one of the major political parties. As Guido Ruggiero pointed out in his introduction to the first volume in this series, *Quaderni storici* has tried to assure a place for experimentation, for minority approaches to scholarship (especially those of women), and for interdisciplinary methodologies; at the same time, it has eschewed any explicit ideological or party affiliation.[8]

In a 1977 *Quaderni storici* article Edoardo Grendi first proposed a research agenda based on microanalysis.[9] Then in 1979 in an essay titled "The Name and the Game: Unequal Exchange and the Historiographic Marketplace," Carlo Ginzburg and Carlo Poni outlined a program for microhistory that might make Italian historical scholarship more independent from the dominating influence of the French *Annales* school. While granting that the quantitative and serial data history characteristic of much of French and American historiography would retain the status of "normal science" in the sense established by Thomas Kuhn, a new type of research, Ginzburg and Poni predicted, would create an ethnographic history of everyday life by devoting itself to extremely circumscribed phenomena such as a single community, a family, or an individual.[10] Italy, they thought, is particularly well suited for ethnographic history because the unmatched richness of documentary material—not only in the archives and libraries, but in land use patterns, the forms of the cities, and the mores of the population—makes the peninsula "an immense archive."

In advocating a finely focused ethnographic history, Ginzburg and Poni concurred with similar developments in certain circles in Britain, France, and the United States. They wanted to develop a method to trace what Natalie Zemon Davis had labeled "the social creativity of the so-called inarticulate."[11] They wanted to escape the traditional overemphasis in Italy on institutional and legal history that preserved Crocean idealism and statism and to redress the newer influences that had led to the cliometric preoccupation with numbers rather than persons and the sociological preference for abstractions as analytical units. In place of these they wanted to substitute a genre that was devoted to social relationships and interactions among historical persons who, in contrast to analytic categories, actually existed and who experienced life as a series of events. Their approach was to be nominalistic, practical, and rooted in "common sense."[12]

Central to their method is tracing the names of individuals. "The lines that converge upon and diverge from the name, creating a kind of closely woven web, provide for the observer a graphic image of the network of social relationships into which the individual is inserted."[13] The ideal result would be a prosopography from below in which the relationships, decisions, restraints, and freedoms faced by real people in actual situations would emerge. Once again, in the fashion of nineteenth-century positivism, individual persons make their own histories, but to the microhistorians the makers of history are seldom "great men" but rather the little peoples lost to European history: in the examples in this collection, a charlatan distiller, the anonymous pillagers of ecclesiastical property, an accused witch, peasants who had disturbing visions, two Jews who destroyed Christian images on their houses, the inhabitants of a small coral-gathering and olive-culture town, and unwed mothers who sought aid in urban hospitals.[14] When the microhistorians have studied great men, such as Galileo or Piero della Francesca, they have focused on obscure clues that have traditionally been ignored or devalued as insignificant.

Although by no means the sole originator of the microhistorical method, Carlo Ginzburg is certainly the best known of the microhistorians, especially outside Italy. Long before the term *microhistory* was coined, Ginzburg explored many of what would become its distinguishing traits in his early studies of witch trials.[15] These studies anticipated microhistorical techniques by treating inquisitors' interrogations of suspected witches as a kind of dialogue in which the most revealing interchanges for the historian are those in which the participants' misunderstandings of each other offer clues to now-lost ways of thinking. His best-known work, *The Cheese and the Worms*, explicitly developed the microhistorical approach by analyzing how a sixteenth-century Italian miller named Menocchio creatively "misread" an odd collection of books, including possibly even the Koran, and interpreted them through the filters of the material culture of his peasant heritage to form a private cosmology so distinctive that it utterly mystified the inquisitors who examined him. Ginzburg uses Menocchio's inquisition trials to trace the reciprocal relationships between popular and elite culture and, on the basis of stray clues found in the miller's testimony, to reconstruct a "millenarian cosmological tradition" that depicted the creation of angels and God out of primal matter just as worms, according to the popular theory of the time, are spontaneously generated out of cheese. The miller's cosmology is presented as a mutant version of a once-pervasive pantheism that still survived in the sixteenth century within nominally Christian society.[16]

The guiding premise in Ginzburg's work has been that through the intense study of a few revealing documents, especially the records of interrogations, one can recapture the interactions between elite and popular cultures. Related themes appear in several of the articles included in this collection, examples of what might be called cultural microhistory. In "The Dovecote Has Opened Its Eyes," Ginzburg and Marco Ferrari show how elements of medical knowledge circulated between literate and nonliterate groups, that is, between print and oral culture, a circulation that has continued into this century in a popular remedy for treating burns. In "Ritual Pillages," a work produced by Ginzburg's seminar at the University of Bologna, the survival into the sixteenth century of the practice of pillaging ecclesiastical and personal property after the death of a bishop or pope shows how a primitive tradition, best explained by reference to the anthropological literature on tribal societies, infiltrated the highest levels of Christian society, despite the protests of numerous Church authorities. Explicitly following Ginzburg's lead into inquisition records, Maurizio Bertolotti in "The Ox's Bones and the Ox's Hide: A Popular Myth, Part Hagiography and Part Witchcraft," examines the interactions between a sixteenth-century witch tutored in an oral tradition and an erudite inquisitor, both of whom shared knowledge of an archaic myth that had been transmitted to them in very different ways and in quite different forms. In a similar fashion Ottavia Niccoli in "The Kings of the Dead on the Battlefield of Agnadello," shows how an ancient myth about the armies of the dead provided the content for some famously disturbing apparitions observed in 1517. She analyzes how the introduction of print complicated the picture of the interaction among cultures and how reports of the apparitions took on different meanings in different social contexts. Despite the evident similarities between ancient myths and Renaissance practices or beliefs, similarities that might have suggested to other scholars some kind of formal analysis, these historians argue that meaning can only be found among the specific social groups and named individuals who accepted the practices and beliefs. Therefore, meaning is entirely contextual.

One of the dominant goals of this form of cultural microhistory has been to write history without the taint of anachronism, a task advocated by most historians but difficult to accomplish. To avoid anachronisms the cultural microhistorians begin with the assumption that the past is utterly alien to the present, that the citizens of sixteenth-century Rome or Bologna were as different from us as are the tribes of the New Guinea highlands. The result is an ambivalent relationship between their historical practice and contemporary politics and ideologies. Ginzburg, in particular, wants to distance himself from the labels, party cliques, ideological factions, petty quarrels, and ephemeral movements that have made Italian intellectual life so reflexive and obscure.[17] The universities—and not only in Italy—have been particularly vulnerable to a kind of self-referential scholasticism, the ruinous habit of ignoring common sense typical of late medieval angelology and more than one contemporary theoretical school. To him the proper goal of the historian is not to explore the historical implications of a contemporary theory or problem, but to write about things that are totally forgotten and completely irrelevant to the present, to produce a history that is "really dead." Many critics have obviously been confused by this idiosyncratic voice of reason. In their insistence on categorizing rather than understanding his thought, some have even accused him of right-wing positions despite his left-wing background, but Ginzburg has refused to be provoked into associating his historical work with any ideology.[18] In contrast to the "unmoving history" of the dominant group in the old *Annales* school or the institutional and intellectual history of Italian scholars on both the Right and the Left who have often presented the past as an unfolding of their own political positions, Ginzburg's history is rent by vast and abrupt changes that produce psychic and intellectual gaps between the past and the present. Historians who worry too much about being relevant to the present, he says, too readily produce anachronistic history, and "anachronism is a kind of conscious or unconscious will to impose your own values and also your own existence on people. So in some way, philology is also related to a kind of respect for the dead."[19]

The philological concern of the cultural microhistorians for the accurate reconstruction of meanings within their original contexts reveals one of the most striking characteristics of their methods: they respect the strictest positivist standards in the collection and criticism of evidence but employ that evidence in highly unconventional ways. Again Carlo Ginzburg serves as the best example.[20] As an explanation for his radical methodological attitude, Ginzburg claims Freud as his intellectual model, despite the fact that his work is often strongly anti-Freudian.[21] It is not Freudianism itself, however, that interests Ginzburg but the distinctive character of Freud's mind: "the peculiar mixture in Freud's intellectual personality of a very positivistic attitude towards truth and that daring attitude about questions, relevancies, methods, and standards of proof."[22]

The cultural microhistorians' distinctive combination of evidential rigor and openness to creative proofs and esoteric topics can be further clarified by comparing their work with the late Michel Foucault's philosophical history.[23] Both the microhistorians and Foucault have written about similar subjects, the objects of persecution such as witches, madmen, and Jews and the institutions of coercion such as inquisitions, hospitals, and prisons. Both have emphasized how modern hegemonic institutions have excluded certain ways of thinking by dismissing them as demonic, irrational, heretical, or criminal, thus narrowing the range of intellectual options available to the culture. Both have consciously inverted the picture of the progressive liberation of modern history, depicting modern cultures as less free in many respects than medieval ones. Yet none of the microhistorians cite Foucault, and Ginzburg, in particular, denies any significant influence from him, calling *Les mots et les choses*, for example, "not so interesting" and "even weak."[24]

Two major aspects of Foucault's views disturb Ginzburg. First, Foucault's theories cannot be verified. According to Foucault's own scheme, standards of verification come from a modern scientific discipline that "refamiliarizes" the past to make it conform to the terms of the present rather than to those of the past. Thus, correctness means conformity to an order of things that has been defined by a discipline or institution. Historical truth is what the discipline of history says it is. For Ginzburg this view is a grand evasion; it may not be easy to respect the dead, but one is not inevitably condemned to violate their graves and distort their beliefs. To Ginzburg correctness can be and must be determined by the concrete, physically real evidence the past presents to us—not by the disciplines, which are artificial constructs. Second, Foucault consciously imposes himself between the past and present in seeking to dissolve the assumed understandings of the coercive disciplines and institutions and thus to "defamiliarize" the past from the present, to make the past radically alien to our contemporary ways of understanding.[25] Although this process seems to be similar to Ginzburg's evocation of dead history, it diverts attention from the object of study to the act of studying and becomes for Ginzburg a kind of intellectual theft in which the integrity of the past is subordinated not so much to the present as to the activity of the scholar.[26]

No matter how critical the microhistorians become about the authority of evidence, no matter how fully they appreciate the interpreter's dilemma in trying to preserve the foreignness of a subject and yet make it familiar enough to be understood, no matter how aware they are of the ways in which texts influence their own meanings, they assume that there is a reality external to those historical texts, a reality that can be known.[27] They certainly accept a kind of historical uncertainty principle, recognizing that history only balances possibilities against probabilities; but they also share an assumption with detectives and ethnologists that clues found in documents, at murder scenes, and in informants' oral accounts point to something other than themselves. Ginzburg wants to employ the primal method of the Paleolithic hunter, that first philologist, who recognized from paw prints that a lion he had never actually seen, heard, touched, or smelled had come his way.[28] The characteristic feature of the hunter's knowledge "was that it permitted the leap from apparently insignificant facts, which could be observed, to a complex reality which—directly at least—could not. And these facts would be ordered by the observer in such a way as to provide a narrative sequence—at its simplest, 'someone passed this way.' "[29] The hunter's position was the inverse of Foucault's: to the hunter the prey was all, he was nothing.

However ancient its roots may be, the microhistorical approach raises questions about selectivity and significance. By what criteria are names to be picked out and how representative of broader social trends and collective mentalities are the subjects' activities and thoughts? What can the few tell about the many, especially when the process of selection is neither random nor statistically rigorous? And how can historians concerned with trifles avoid producing trivial history?

Edoardo Grendi has suggested that a response to these questions should rely on the statistical concept of a normal exception.[30] Since rebels, heretics, and criminals are the most likely candidates from the lower or nonliterate classes to leave sufficient traces to become the subjects of microhistories, their behavior is, by definition, exceptional. However, as Ginzburg and Poni note in "The Name and the Game," certain kinds of transgressions against authority constitute normal behavior for those on the social periphery, the kinds of behavior sociologists call "self help"—that is, those illegal or socially proscribed actions that were normal for those who had no other means of redress.[31] Some transgressors, therefore, might be exceptions to the norms defined by political or ecclesiastical authorities but would be perfectly representative of their own social milieu.

Understanding what behaviors and ideas were beyond the pale might also help to describe better the characteristics of the dominant group that defined what was considered normal.[32] Although most of the essays in this collection study persons who were exceptional in comparison to dominant groups and dominant values, the three examples of what might be called social microhistory show in particular how the behavior of marginal persons can be used to clarify the nature of authority. In his fascinating account of licensed Jewish "iconoclasm" ("Jews, the Local Church, the 'Prince' and the People: Two Late Fifteenth-Century Episodes Involving the Destruction of Sacred Images"), Michele Luzzati reconstructs connections within the Italian Jewish community on the one hand and between specific Jews and various Christian ecclesiastical and secular authorities on the other. By finding out everything he can about every participant in the events, including even the career of the mason hired to destroy the Christian images in a Jew's house, Luzzati shows how much more important are patterns of personal and economic relationships than are the vague abstractions usually invoked in explaining the deteriorating position of Jews in late fifteenth-century Italy.

In a richly complex and sometimes difficult essay ("The Political System of a Community in Liguria: Cervo in the Late Sixteenth and Early Seventeenth Centuries"), Edoardo Grendi develops a social version of microhistory that most fully departs from the cultural orientation of Ginzburg and his associates. Like the others he begins by tracing the names and interactions of his subjects, but in this case the subjects are members of an elite, albeit those in a minor seaside community. Grendi frames his many carefully drawn portraits of individuals with statistics that illustrate the economy of coral gathering and olive-oil production. As a result of his close attention to the actual behavior of individuals and families that can be traced from judicial records, he revises several standard social-science generalizations, showing that factional conflict did not rest on a patronage system but on local solidarity and that economic activity was defined by many forces that were external to the operations of the market. Local connections predominated over all other factors, but in this highly litigious society interpersonal ties were fleeting and transitory. Grendi's work exemplifies how inadequate are institutional studies that rely simply on the elite's self-descriptions of political behavior and economic studies in which global statistics obscure the actual nature of exchanges.[33]

In a similar fashion but for a dramatically different context, Gianna Pomata shows in her "Unwed Mothers in the Late Nineteenth and Early Twentieth Centuries: Clinical Histories and Life Histories" how our understanding of official institutions can be redefined through microhistorical studies of persons who were subject to their influence. For this period in place of the Inquisition whose records are favored by the cultural microhistorians, Pomata looks at hospitals and maternity wards in which the collection of the clinical and life histories of patients was gradually replaced by laboratory analyses and statistical surveys, a process that erased the identities of individual unwed mothers and subjected their bodies to clinical regimentation. Pomata tries to reverse this process, neatly using microhistory to restore to life the experiences of women lost by the same scientific quantifying process that the microhistorians think has eliminated individuals from history.

In addition to seeing their subjects as normal exceptions, the microhistorians consider certain historical documents as examples of a second kind of normal exception. If documents generated by the forces of authority systematically distort the social reality of the subaltern classes, then an exceptional document, especially one that records the exact words of a lower-class witness or defendant, could be much more revealing than a multitude of stereotypical sources.[34] In selecting these exceptional documents and neutralizing the distortions in others, the microhistorians have relied on specific criteria of proof designed to resurrect "forms of knowledge or understandings of the world which have been suppressed or lost."[35] It is here that they most dramatically emulate Freud's daring attitude toward standards of proof that led him to prize obscure clues to things hidden in the human psyche.

Although the characteristic microhistorical attitude toward proof is evident in most of the work presented here, it is again Carlo Ginzburg who has been explicit about its implications. What he has called the "evidential paradigm" suggests that unknown objects can be identified "through single, seemingly insignificant, signs, rather than through the application of laws derived from repeatable and quantifiable observations."[36] He bolsters his use of the evidential paradigm by an analysis of the methods of three disciplines that blossomed during the last decades of the nineteenth century: art history, epitomized by Giovanni Morelli's study in paintings of marginal details such as the shape of ears; psychoanalysis, exemplified by Freud's technique of divining "secret and concealed things" from inadvertent verbal slips and unconscious symptoms; and criminology represented by Francis Galton's 1892 work, *Finger Prints*, and the investigative adventures of Sir Arthur Conan Doyle's fictional hero, Sherlock

Holmes. The methods of artistic connoisseurship, psychiatric diagnosis, and criminal detection have more in common than might at
first appear: Morelli, Freud, and Conan Doyle were all physicians
trained in the late nineteenth century at a time when diagnostic medicine was becoming increasingly influential. The ground these disciplines share was recognized at the time. Freud wrote that Morelli's
stress on minor details was "closely related to the technique of psychoanalysis"; Conan Doyle probably knew about Morelli's techniques
through his artist father and his uncle who was director of the Dublin
Art Gallery, and the physician author's probable model for Holmes,
the medical professor Dr. Joseph Bell, used to lecture on the similarity
between disease and crime and how in making a true diagnosis the
physician must pay particular attention to minute details.[37]

In an impressive display of erudition Ginzburg traces the genealogy
of the evidential paradigm back much further, to Paleolithic hunting
lore that in providing a method for interpreting animal tracks produced
the idea of narrative, to Mesopotamian divination books, to Hippoc-
rates, and in a final sweep, which encompasses too much to add much
clarity, to "physicians, historians, politicians, potters, joiners, mari-
ners, hunters, fishermen, and women in general," all of whom
proceded by building up knowledge of a whole from an examination
of parts.[38] To Ginzburg this is the nub of the matter. The degree to
which an endeavor is occupied with the individual is inversely pro-
portional to its ability to apply the Galilean model, which relies on
the statistical examination of evidence suggested by a hypothesis.
Either understanding of the individual is sacrificed in achieving a math-
ematical standard of generalization or an alternative method must be
accepted that is based on individual cases in a way that "would (in
some way yet to be worked out) be scientific."[39]

Even more than in the other anthropocentric disciplines, history,
according to Ginzburg, "always remains a science of a very particular
kind, irremediably based on the concrete."[40] Historical knowledge,
therefore, is always to some degree conjectural because historians must
work like medical practitioners who cannot actually see most diseases
but must diagnose their presence indirectly on the basis of telltale
symptoms or signs. For example, in his *The Enigma of Piero* Ginzburg
relies on Morellian techniques to isolate a distinctively shaped ear and
demonstrates that the same man's portrait appears in three different
paintings. Sorting out the authentic portraits of Cardinal Bessarion
from the fanciful, Ginzburg compares the subjects' noses.[41] Such trifles

as these generate "conjectural proofs" in two possible ways. First, in a positive operation the historian compares discrete examples of particular details such as noses, ears, or textual citations, using them like a hunter uses tracks or a detective fingerprints to identify a known but unseen animal or person. In this process likenesses confirm the most likely possibility. Second, in a negative operation the investigator systematically eliminates alternatives until only one remains—as Sherlock Holmes does, in perhaps the most frequently cited example of such reasoning, when he points out the curious failure of the watchdog to bark on the night that the racehorse Silver Blaze disappeared from its stable. Holmes eliminates all suspects but one by noting that such a dog resists the temptation to bark only in the presence of its master. In this process the removal of the unlikely isolates the likely.[42]

The proofs found in many of the microhistories have been the object of the severest criticisms of the genre, in part because of a reluctance to recognize or accept the conjectural nature of the endeavor. To understand the microhistorians' task, we need to know what is "conjectural" about these proofs and by what process these historians move from the observation of facts to the production of conclusions. What, in fact, is a conjecture?

The clearest and most consistent analysis of the logical process the microhistorians are trying to follow can be found in the philosopher Charles Peirce's notion of abduction.[43]

> Abduction makes its start from the facts, without, at the outset, having any particular theory in view, though it is motivated by the feeling that a theory is needed to explain the surprising facts. Induction makes its start from a hypothesis which seems to recommend itself, without at the outset having any particular facts in view, though it feels the need of facts to support the theory. Abduction seeks a theory. Induction seeks for facts. In abduction the consideration of the facts suggests the hypothesis. In induction the study of the hypothesis suggests the experiments which bring to light the very facts to which the hypothesis had pointed.

Abduction, moreover, does not prove anything; it "merely suggests that something *may* be."[44] Proof comes from induction. The significance of abduction lies not in its ability to prove that something is operative or actually exists but in the creative potential it represents. According to Peirce, abduction "is the only logical operation which introduces a new idea; for induction does nothing but determine a value, and deduction merely evolves the necessary consequences of a pure hypothesis."[45] It is precisely in their creative innovations based on abduction that the microhistorians have been the most intriguing.

Peirce argued that a method should not be chosen for its security or its guarantee of certain answers but for its potential for fruitfulness or *uberty*, to use his own neologism. In fact, there is an inverse relationship between fruitfulness and security: the greater the potential for *uberty*, the less likely a method will lead to certainty.[46] Abduction, therefore, is the most fruitful and least certain method. "Abduction is, after all, nothing but guessing," and yet Peirce noted that a hypothesis based on observed facts is more often correct than it would be if governed by mere chance, even though such a guess is logically only a maybe/maybe-not proposition. Moreover, no advance in knowledge could be made without abductions.[47] What the microhistorians have done, and most precisely what Carlo Ginzburg has done, is to single out and be explicit about a way of doing history that has, in fact, long governed a great deal of historical practice, whatever its pretensions to scientific status.

Abduction and conjecture, however, have their dangers. Microhistorical arguments, especially those devoted to some form of cultural interpretation, are vulnerable to circularity; because all interpretation "presupposes," as Ginzburg says, "a reciprocal interchange between the whole and the parts," there is both the "healthy circularity of hermeneutic interpretation" and the vicious circle. The best check against the latter is the convergence of several independent lines of investigation, which substantially reduce the possibility of error.[48] But when are similarities true convergences and not just coincidences?

The best answer to this question can be found in the distinction between "to show" *(mostrare)*, which reveals formal analogies in the internal structure of a subject such as similar stylistic traits in paintings by the same artist, and "to demonstrate" *(dimostrare)*, which uses evidence external to the subject such as written contracts to show that the same artist painted two different canvases.[49] The most convincing argument comes when proofs that show and those that demonstrate converge.[50] The final guard against overly elaborated circular arguments comes from what has been called "Ginzburg's razor," one of the strict rules that he wishes imposed on the use of conjectures: "other things being equal, the interpretation requiring fewest hypotheses should generally be taken as the most probable."[51]

In applying "Ginzburg's razor," microhistorians have tried to be very precise about exactly how the sources they use were put together and how the various voices found in them can be distinguished. Ginzburg notes, for example, how inquisitorial records were kept: a notary was charged with the verbatim transcription of what was said, both questions and answers, an obligation that permits the modern scholar to adjust for leading or suggestive questions. But sometimes the notary in laziness or haste switched to the third person and paraphrased the interrogation, making the trial much more problematic as a source.[52] Maurizio Bertolotti shows a similar sensitivity to the presuppositions of both participants in an inquisitorial dialogue, while Ottavia Niccoli unravels multiple layers of opinion and belief and distinguishes among various media of transmission in her account of the spread of news about the Agnadello apparitions. Michele Luzzati in his brilliant close reading of notarial records uncovers changes of opinion by paying particular attention to the erased and crossed-out passages in the revised draft of a notarized contract. Struck by the terrible pathos of her subjects, Gianna Pomata abandons classification and quantitative analysis of the unwed mothers for a careful examination of the supposedly scientific hypotheses that structured the women's clinical and life histories. Her awareness of all the voices in the documents allows her to free the mostly ignorant young women from the constraints of medical practice in order to let them tell their own stories in their own way. The great strength of the microhistories comes from this sensitivity to the nuances of power and the changes of voice in documents.[53] They recognize how there was a series of gaps or disjunctures between what was said and what was recorded, between what the interrogators asked and what the scholar wants to know, and between what the educated notaries or physicians and the bewildered defendants or patients understood about the other. Inquisitors twisted replies to fit their own preconceptions, peasants perplexedly tried to explain themselves and to guess what the officials wanted to hear, and differences in dialect and levels of culture sometimes hopelessly compromised communication but still leave the historian with vital clues.[54]

In the subjects they have chosen, microhistorians have snipped at the fringes of normal historical practice, that vast middle area between *histoire totale* and *microstoria*. Although the fascination with trifles may threaten what in another context Simon Schama has called "the pigmification of historical scale," the ablest practitioners of the microhistorical genre, including those translated here, have been struggling to eliminate the distortions produced by the giantification of historical scale, which has crushed all individuals to insignificance under the weight of vast impersonal structures and forces.[55] To them the idea that microhistory leads to relativism or to an attitude that anything goes—that any little neglected subject is worth examining especially if it is about deviant sex or outlandish religious beliefs—is a serious misreading of their intentions. The purpose of microhistory is to elucidate historical causation on the level of small groups where most of real life takes place and to open history to peoples who would be left out by other methods.

The new historical detectives from Italy may not have found a foolproof method, any more than have real-world as opposed to fictional detectives, but it would be a mistake to dismiss them because they appear to be devoted to little problems. Quite the opposite is the case. They have been struggling with one of the biggest questions: what can we know about the peoples lost to history?

Notes

1. This Introduction borrows liberally from a paper I presented in 1987 as a Mellon Lecture at Tulane University and at a session on microhistory organized by Anne Jacobson Schutte at the Sixteenth-Century Studies Conference in Tempe, Arizona. I wish to thank the many persons who made helpful comments at these presentations and especially those who read early versions of the paper: James Amelang, Linda L. Carroll, Paul Paskoff, Karl Roider, Guido Ruggiero, and Thomas Scheff. I have benefited greatly from their criticisms, and the errors that remain are my own.

2. Robin W. Winks, ed., *The Historian as Detective: Essays on Evidence* (New York, 1970).

3. Thomas Scheff, "Micro-linguistics and Social Structure: A Theory of Social Action," *Sociological Theory* 4 (1986): 71–83. Professor Scheff kindly allowed me to see some of his other work on microsociology prior to its publication.

4. Stephen Jay Gould, "Animals and Us," *New York Review of Books*, June 25, 1987, p. 23, an article that reviews *The Chimpanzees of Gombe: Patterns of Behavior* by Jane Goodall (Cambridge, Mass., 1986).

5. Renato Rosaldo, *Ilongot Headhunting, 1883–1974: A Study in Society and History* (Stanford, 1980), p. 23. The interdisciplinary literature on history and anthropology is now vast: see especially Bernard Cohn, "History and Anthropology: The State of Play," *Comparative Studies in Society and History* 22 (1980): 198–221; idem, "History and Anthropology: Towards a Rapprochement," *Journal of Interdisciplinary History* 12 (1981): 227–52; Natalie Zemon Davis, "The Possibilities of the Past," *Journal of Interdisciplinary History* 12 (1981): 267–75; and Diane Owen Hughes, "Toward Historical Ethnography: Notarial Records and Family History in the Middle Ages," *Historical Methods Newsletter* 7 (1976): 61–71. Recent discussions of the issues from the anthropological side can be found in the extended book review by various authors of Maurice Bloch's, *From Blessing to Violence: History and Ideology in the Circumcision Ritual of the Merina of Madagascar* (Cambridge, 1986) in *Current An-*

thropology 27 (1986): 349–60. Useful recent views from history are Robert Darnton, "The Symbolic Element in History," *Journal of Modern History* 58 (1986): 267–75 and the chapters on "The Historical Anthropology of Early Modern Italy" and "The Sources: Outsiders and Insiders" in Peter Burke's, *The Historical Anthropology of Early Modern Italy: Essays on Perception and Communication* (Cambridge, 1987), pp. 3–24. For a critique by a microhistorian of the ways in which some historians have employed the cultural anthropology of Clifford Geertz, see Giovanni Levi, "I pericoli di geertzismo," *Quaderni storici* [hereafter, *QS*] 58 (1985): 269–77, esp. 275.

6. "The Inquisitor as Anthropologist," in Ginzburg's *Clues, Myths, and the Historical Method*, trans. John Tedeschi and Anne C. Tedeschi (Baltimore, 1989), p. 164, a translation of the collection, *Miti emblemi spie: Morfologia e storia* (Turin, 1986), which does not, however, contain this particular essay.

7. Carlo Ginzburg's study of Piero della Francesca was the first volume in the *microstorie* series published by Einaudi: *Indagini su Piero: Il Battesimo, il ciclo di Arezzo, la Flagellazione di Urbino* (Turin, 1981), trans. Martin Ryle and Kate Soper as *The Enigma of Piero: Piero della Francesca: The Baptism, the Arezzo Cycle, the Flagellation* (London, 1985). Books published for the first time by this series include an analysis of matrimonial strategies in the diocese of Como: Raul Merzario, *Il paese stretto: Strategie matrimoniali nella diocesi di Como (secoli XVI—XVIII)* (Turin, 1981); a dialogue between two historians about recapturing historical consciousness: Pietro Marcenaro and Vittorio Foa, *Riprendere tempo: Un dialogo con postilla* (Turin, 1982); a study of the rebuilding of a Venetian church during the Renaissance: Antonio Foscari and Manfredo Tafuri, *L'armonia e i conflitti: La chiesa di San Francesco della Vigna nella Venezia del '500* (Turin, 1983); a reinterpretation of the charges of heresy against Galileo: Pietro Redondi, *Galileo eretico* (Turin, 1983), trans. Raymond Rosenthal as *Galileo Heretic* (Princeton, 1987); a reconstruction of the systems of kinship and of manufacturing among woolen-cloth workers in the Biellese during the nineteenth-century: Franco Ramella, *Terra e telai: Sistemi di parentela e manifattura nel Biellese dell'Ottocento* (Turin, 1984); a prosopography of the clients of a priest-exorcist in seventeenth-century Piedmont: Giovanni Levi, *L'eredità immateriale: Carriera di un esorcista nel Piemonte del Seicento* (Turin, 1985), trans. Lydia G. Cochrane as *Inheriting Power: The Story of an Exorcist* (Chicago, 1988); an oral history of the experiences of common people as the city of Terni evolved from an agricultural village to a major industrial center: Alessandro Portelli, *Biografia di una città: Storia e racconto: Terni 1830–1985* (Turin, 1985); and an examination of feuding in Liguria: Osvaldo Raggio, *Faide e parentele: Lo stato genovese visto dalla Fontanabuona* (Turin, 1990).

Einaudi's *microstorie* series has also brought parallel examples of foreign scholarship to Italian readers, including Paul Boyer and Stephen Nissenbaum's reconstruction of family factions in the Salem witchcraft trials: *Salem Possessed: The Social Origins of Witchcraft* (Cambridge, Mass., 1974), translated as Microstorie no. 12, *La città indemoniata: Salem e le origini sociali di una caccia alle streghe* (Turin, 1986); Natalie Zemon Davis's book about the celebrated sixteenth-century French case of an imposter who took over the bed and property of a missing husband: *Le retour de Martin Guerre* (Paris 1982), *The Return of Martin Guerre* (Cambridge, Mass., 1983), and as Microstorie no. 9, *Il ritorno di Martin Guerre: Un caso di doppia identità nella Francia del Cinquecento* (Turin, 1984); Anton Blok's study of the evolution of Mafia violence: *The Mafia of a Sicilian Village, 1860–1960* (New York, 1974), translated as Microstorie no. 13, *La mafia di un villaggio siciliano, 1860–1960: Imprenditori, contadini, violenti* (Turin, 1986); and Edward P. Thompson's major articles in historical anthropology translated as Microstorie no. 2, *Società patrizia, cultura plebea: Otto saggi di antropologia storica sull'Inghilterra del Settecento* (Turin, 1981).

Non-Italian examples of microhistory include Jonathan Spence's account of the murder of a seventeenth-century Chinese peasant woman: *The Death of Woman Wang* (New York, 1978); Judith Brown's portrait of a seventeenth-century nun who devoted herself to faked visions and lesbian sex: *Immodest Acts: The Life of a Lesbian Nun in Renaissance Italy* (New York, 1986); Gene Brucker's recounting of a lovers' dispute in Renaissance Florence over the validity of their marriage: *Giovanni and Lusanna: Love and Marriage in Renaissance Florence* (Berkeley, 1986); and Steven Ozment's extended commentary on the letters between a sixteenth-century German merchant and his wife: *Magdalena and Balthasar: An Intimate Portrait of Life in Sixteenth-Century Europe Revealed in the Letters of a Nuremberg Husband and Wife* (New York, 1986). Microhistory has some additional obvious predecessors in the work of Georges Duby, *La Dimanche de Bouvines (27 juillet 1214)* (Paris, 1973); Emmanuel Le Roy Ladurie, *Montaillou: The Promised Land of Error* (New York, 1978); and idem, *Carnival in Romans* (New York, 1979).

8. Cf. Alberto Caracciolo, "Gli indici di 'Quaderni storici': Una rivista modernistica?" *QS* 62 (1986): 613–14.

9. "Micro-analisi e storia sociale," *QS* 35 (1977): 506–20.

10. Thomas, Kuhn, *The Structure of Scientific Revolutions*, 2d. ed. enlarged (Chicago, 1970). On everyday life, see Michel de Certeau, *The Practice of Everyday Life*, trans. Steven F. Rendall (Berkeley, 1984).

11. Natalie Zemon Davis, "The Reasons of Misrule," in *Society and Culture in Early Modern France* (Stanford, 1975), p. 122. Cf. idem, "The Possibilities of the Past," *Journal of Interdisciplinary History* 12 (1981): 267–75.

12. On the use of common sense in history, see Edoardo Grendi, "Del senso comune storiografico," *QS* 41 (1979): 698–720. Cf. Ronald F. E. Weissman, "Reconstructing Renaissance Sociology: The 'Chicago School' and the Study of Renaissance Society," in *Persons in Groups: Social Behavior as Identity Formation in Medieval and Renaissance Europe*, ed. R. C. Trexler (Binghamton, N.Y., 1985), p. 40.

13. For the quotation see Chapter 1. According to Vincenzo Ferrone and Massimo Firpo, who are quite critical of the use of evidence in some examples, microhistories are "an attempt to clarify all the complex density and the thick network of connections and relations that lie tangled together in facts, real situations, events, ideas, images, men, and social groups of the past." "Galileo tra inquisitori e micro-storici," *Rivista storica italiana* 97 (1985): 177–238. Abbreviated and translated as "From Inquisitors to Microhistorians: A Critique of Pietro Redondi's *Galileo eretico*," *Journal of Modern History* 58 (1986): 485–524. The citation is from the English version, p. 521.

14. On the method of concentrating on persons or groups at the periphery of society, Enrico Castelnuovo and Carlo Ginzburg, "Centro e periferia," in *Storia dell'arte italiana*, part 1: *Materiali e problemi*, ed. Giovanni Previtali, vol. 1: *Questioni e metodi* (Turin, 1979), pp. 285–352.

15. See his "Witchcraft and Popular Piety: Notes on a Modenese Trial," in *Clues, Myths, and the Historical Method*, pp. 1–16, and *The Night Battles: Witchcraft and Agrarian Cults in the Sixteenth and Seventeenth Centuries*, trans. John Tedeschi and Anne Tedeschi (Baltimore, 1983), originally published as *I Benandanti: Stregoneria e culti agrari tra Cinquecento e Seicento* (Turin, 1966). All citations are from the English edition. After *The Night Battles*, Ginzburg wrote a more conventional book on the problem of religious dissimulation in the sixteenth century. *Il Nicodemismo: Simulazione e dissimulazione religiosa nell'Europa del '500* (Turin, 1970).

16. *The Cheese and the Worms: The Cosmos of a Sixteenth-Century Miller*, trans. John Tedeschi and Anne Tedeschi (Baltimore, 1980), originally published as *Il formaggio e vermi: Il cosmo di un mugnaio del '500* (Turin, 1976). All citations are from the English edition.

17. The relationship between the evolution of microhistory and the various radical political movements that were so controversial in the 1970s, particularly around the universities of Bologna and Padua, needs further exploration. The Autonomist ideologue, Toni Negri, saw Ginzburg's evidential paradigm as a potential salvation for contemporary society and as a new and revolutionary doctrine. See *Alphabeta* (March 1980). Ginzburg reacted by pointing out that Negri misunderstood his whole position and that far from revolutionary, the paradigm is very ancient. See the debate about Ginzburg's methodological ideas: "Paradigma indiziario e conoscenza storica," *Quaderni di storia* 12 (1980): 3–54.

18. Keith Luria and Romulo Gandolfo, "Carlo Ginzburg: An Interview," *Radical History Review* 35 (1986): 103, and Ginzburg in "Paradigma indiziario," p. 50.

19. Luria and Gandolfo, "Carlo Ginzburg," p. 106.

20. Cf. Keith Luria, "The Paradoxical Carlo Ginzburg," *Radical History Review* 35 (1986): 80.

21. On his positivism, see Anne Jacobson Schutte, "Carlo Ginzburg," *Journal of Modern History* 48 (1976): 298–99, 314n. For his disagreements with Freud, see "Freud, the Wolf-Man, and the Werewolves," in *Clues, Myths, and the Historical Method*, pp. 146–55. By Ginzburg's own account (Luria and Gandolfo, "Carlo Ginzburg," pp. 90–91), the books that have been the most important to him are Federico Chabod's still untranslated masterpiece on the religious life of sixteenth-century Milan, *Lo stato e la vita religiosa a Milano nell'epoca di Carlo V* (Turin, 1977); Marc Bloch's *The Royal Touch: Sacred Monarchy and Scrofula in England and France* (Paris, 1961; London, 1973); and Sir Ernst Gombrich's *Art and Illusion: A Study in the Psychology of Pictorial Representation* (New York, 1960). The art historians of the Warburg Institute, among whom Gombrich is the senior member, deeply influenced Ginzburg during his time as a fellow there. Cf. Ginzburg, "From Aby Warburg to E. H. Gombrich: A Problem of Method," in *Clues, Myths, and the Historical Method*, pp. 17–59. Aby Warburg often quoted Flaubert's "God is in the details," an aphorism echoed in the work of the microhistorians, Ginzburg in particular.

22. Luria and Gandolfo, "Carlo Ginzburg," p. 102.

23. Enrico Artifoni and Giuseppe Sergi, "Microstoria e indizi, senza esclusioni e senza illusioni," *QS* 45 (1980): 1122.

24. Luria and Gandolfo, "Carlo Ginzburg," p. 102.

25. Hayden V. White, "Foucault Decoded: Notes from the Underground," *History and Theory* 12 (1973): 51.

26. Ginzburg reserves his most caustic criticism, moreover, for the post-Foucaultian deconstructionists.

"I am deeply interested in catching the right meaning—I know that is a kind of heresy for a lot of people, that notion of right meaning. But I am deeply against every kind of Derrida trash, that kind of cheap skeptical attitude. I think that that is one of the cheapest intellectual things going on. . . .
. . . "It is a kind of cheap nihilism. I am certainly against it for ideological reasons, but at the same time, I am struck by the fact that it is something so cheap. There is a kind of silly narcissistic assumption. I am deeply against it. I start with a kind of realistic attitude in the sense of a realistic notion of truth. At the same time, I am convinced that you can have a kind of creative misreading of what, for instance, I am trying to write. And I think that maybe the major contradiction is that I am trying to start with that positivistic notion of truth in some way, but at the same time, I am conscious of the fact that there are no rules that can be taken for granted. They have been built by people. So maybe there is a contradiction between that, the fact that I start with that posi-

tivistic notion of truth, but at the same time, I am strongly against any positivistic naïveté about knowledge. Can you look for the implications of power in every kind of intellectual exchange or symbolic exchange without falling in a kind of skeptical trap? This is a problem" (Luria and Gandolfo, "Carlo Ginzburg," pp. 100–101.)

27. Cf. Vincent Crapanzano, "Hermes' Dilemma: The Masking of Subversion in Ethnographic Description," in *Writing Culture: The Poetics and Politics of Ethnography*, ed. James Clifford and George E. Marcus (Berkeley, 1986), pp. 51–52.
28. Carlo Ginzburg, "Spie: Radici di un paradigma indiziario," *Ombre rosse* 29 (1979): 80–107. Also published in *Crisi della ragione*, ed. A. Gargani (Turin, 1979), pp. 57–106, and in Ginzburg's *Miti, emblemi, spie: Morfologia e storia*, pp. 158–209. Translated into English as "Morelli, Freud and Sherlock Holmes: Clues and Scientific Method," *History Workshop* 9 (1980): 5–36, and in *The Sign of Three: Dupin, Holmes, Peirce*, ed. Umberto Eco and Thomas A. Sebeok (Bloomington, Ind., 1983), pp. 81–118. The best translation is the newest, "Clues: Roots of an Evidential Paradigm," in *Clues, Myths, and the Historical Method*, pp. 96–125. Citations are from the *History Workshop* version, pp. 12–14.
29. Ginzburg, "Morelli, Freud and Sherlock Holmes," p. 13.
30. Grendi, "Micro-analisi." Cf. Ginzburg, "Paradigma indiziario," pp. 33–34.
31. Donald Black and M. P. Baumgartner, "On Self-help in Modern Society," in *The Manners and Customs of the Police*, ed. Donald Black (New York, 1980), pp. 193–208. Donald Black, "Crime as Social Control," in *Towards a General Theory of Social Control*, vol. 2: *Selected Problems*, ed. Donald Black (Orlando, Fla., 1984), pp. 1–28.
32. Cf. Ginzburg, *The Cheese and the Worms*, p. xxi.
33. Grendi insists on defining very precisely how social forces or individual choices determine cultural expressions and events. He wants to treat culture as a process, the accumulative data of daily experience. He differs from Ginzburg most of all in his interests since he considers culture less as the object of interpretation than as the medium through which the dynamics of power, the distribution of resources, and the nature of hierarchy can be analyzed. Grendi criticizes Clifford Geertz for his failure to disclose the social and economic dynamics of culture. See "Sei storie Württembürghesi," *QS* 63 (1986): 971–80. A particularly revealing statement of what Grendi thinks is the wrong kind of microhistory can be found in "Storia sociale e storia interpretativa," *QS* 61 (1986): 201–10, his highly critical review of Giulia Calvi's *Storie di un anno di peste: Comportamenti sociali e immaginario nella Firenze Barocca* (Milan, 1984), now available as *Histories of a Plague Year: The Social and the Imaginary in Baroque Florence*, trans. Dario Biocca and Bryant T. Ragan, Jr. (Berkeley, 1989). Her response is "A proposito di 'Storie di un anno di peste,'" *QS* 63 (1986): 1009–18. On the need for a social and economic context to understand culture, see Giovanni Levi, "Villaggi," *QS* 46 (1981): 7–10.
34. Ginzburg, *The Cheese and the Worms*, pp. xxi–xxii.
35. Luria, "Carlo Ginzburg," pp. 84–85. Anne Jacobson Schutte sees this issue as the dilemma that underlies all of Ginzburg's early work. "In Inquisition records or in books written by educated people for popular consumption, for example, how can one identify precisely and determine the relationship among popular ideas in their original form, intellectuals' notions about what the masses believe or should believe, and the common ground of preconceptions shared by exalted and humbler members of a given society?" "Carlo Ginzburg," p. 314.
36. Luria, "Carlo Ginzburg," p. 86. Ginzburg's term in Italian is *paradigma indiziario* ("Spie"), which is almost impossible to translate, as Peter Burke notes, "because *indiziario* refers not only to the phrase *prova indiziaria*, 'circumstantial

evidence,' but also to the various meanings of *indizio*, 'sign,' no less than 'indicator' or 'clue.' " "Carlo Ginzburg, Detective," the introduction to Ginzburg, *The Enigma of Piero*, p. 1. Translation is additionally made difficult by the value of a *prova indiziaria* in Italian jurisprudence, which permits convictions for "moral culpability" and which gives greater weight than Anglo-American law to circumstantial and presumptive evidence. The term *paradigma indiziario* has been variously translated as "conjectural paradigm," "semiotic paradigm," and "aphoristic paradigm" (Ginzburg, "Morelli, Freud and Sherlock Holmes," p. 15); "circumstantial paradigm" (Ferrone and Firpo, "Inquisitors to Microhistorians," p. 490); "divinatory knowledge" (Anna Davin's introduction to Ginzburg, "Morelli, Freud and Sherlock Holmes," p. 6); "an art of suspicion" (Burke, "Carlo Ginzburg," p. 1); and "evidential paradigm" (the Tedeschi translation of "Clues"). Its full meaning includes the connotations of presumption, indication, and intuition. I have chosen *evidential paradigm* since that seems to be Ginzburg's own choice for the equivalent English term.

37. Ginzburg, "Morelli, Freud and Sherlock Holmes," pp. 8, 10 (for quotation). Thomas Sebeok and Jean Umiker-Sebeok, " 'You Know My Method': A Juxtaposition of Charles S. Peirce and Sherlock Holmes," in Eco and Sebeok, *The Sign of Three*, p. 35.

38. Ginzburg, "Morelli, Freud and Sherlock Holmes," p. 15.

39. Ibid., p. 19. The most useful discussion of the evidential paradigm includes comments by several critics and Ginzburg's responses. See "Paradigma indiziario," pp. 3–54. In the case of Redondi's work, at least, the evidential paradigm has been used to privilege a few sources over an enormous body of counter evidence. Pietro Redondi, *Galileo eretico* (Turin, 1983). The most cogent criticisms are those of Ferrone and Firpo, "Inquisitors to Microhistorians," esp. pp. 521–23.

40. "Morelli, Freud and Sherlock Holmes," pp. 15–16.

41. Ginzburg's redating of the Arezzo fresco cycle "depends on a series of very precise factual coincidences" and "upon a chain of conjectures." "However, this uncertainty does not affect the core of the argument, based as it is upon a convergence between biographical, stylistic, and iconographic data, and data concerning the commissioning (direct and indirect) of the cycle." *The Enigma of Piero*, p. 45, cf. pp. 123–24 and 133. Antonio Pinelli points out that Ginzburg's conjectural proofs range from the plausible to mere suppositions. "In margine a 'Indagine su Piero' di Carlo Ginzburg" QS 50 (1982): 692. In other cases, most successfully in *The Cheese and the Worms*, Ginzburg systematically eliminates all possible explanations for the known facts until only one alternative remains, but at one point (p. 66), for example, he acknowledges as "purely conjectural" his assertion that Menocchio must have known about Servetus's *De Trinitatis erroribus* in some indirect way.

Elsewhere he uses the phrase, "elastic rigor." "The existence of a deep connection which explains superficial phenomena can be confirmed when it is acknowledged that direct knowledge of such a connection is impossible. Reality is opaque; but there are certain points—clues, signs—which allow us to decipher it." As the systematic scientific approach declines in its ability to recognize these signs, this "aphoristic" approach gains in interpretive strength. But, Ginzburg asks, "is rigour compatible with the conjectural paradigm?" Since this form of knowledge is so bound up with daily experience, every context appears to be unique. "In such contexts the elastic rigour (to use a contradictory phrase) of the conjectural paradigm seems impossible to eliminate." Ginzburg seems to mean that the approach cannot be reduced to rules because it can be learned only through experience, which then informs intuition. "Morelli, Freud and Sherlock Holmes," pp. 27–29. Cf. Ginzburg, "Paradigma indiziario," pp. 34–37. Peter Burke notes, however, that Ginzburg is willing to impose very firm rules on iconology. "Carlo Ginzburg," p. 3.

42. Arthur Conan Doyle, "Silver Blaze," in *The Complete Sherlock Holmes* (Garden City, N.Y., 1930), p. 347.

43. Eco and Sebeok, *The Sign of Three*, p. vii. In his "Clues" article Ginzburg mentions Peirce and abduction only in a note (n. 33) on Mesopotamian divination.

44. Cited in Sebeok and Umiker-Sebeok, " 'You Know My Method,' " pp. 24–25.

45. Peirce cited in Nancy Harrowitz, "The Body of the Detective Model: Charles S. Peirce and Edgar Allan Poe," in Eco and Sebeok, *The Sign of Three*, p. 181. Although Sherlock Holmes usually calls his logical operations "deductions," Marcello Truzzi argues that, in fact, deductions are rare and that most cases involve abductions. "Sherlock Holmes: Applied Social Psychologist," in ibid., p. 69. Umberto Eco discusses four kinds of abductions. "Horns, Hooves, Insteps: Some Hypotheses on Three Types of Abduction," in ibid., pp. 206–7.

46. Thomas Sebeok, "One, Two, Three Spells U B E R T Y," in Eco and Sebeok, *The Sign of Three*, p. 1.

47. Peirce cited in *The Sign of Three*, pp. 16–17, 49n. Ginzburg expresses frank admiration for audacious abductions (*The Cheese and the Worms*, p. 154n). Conan Doyle in the persona of Sherlock Holmes is less open to this aspect of abduction because he wishes to make his observations closely conform to codes and laws, whereas Peirce emphasized the innovative aspect of abduction. Bonfantini and Proni, "To Guess or Not to Guess," in *The Sign of Three*, pp. 128–29. The principal weakness of Holmes's inferences is that he fails to test the hypotheses he achieves through abduction. Of at least 217 abductions in the Sherlockian canon, the detective searches for external validation in only 28 instances, and not all of these are directly related to the abduction. Holmes's inferences work only because Conan Doyle's fiction permits them to. Truzzi, "Sherlock Holmes," p. 70.

48. Ginzburg, *The Enigma of Piero*, pp. 21–22. He repeatedly shows he is aware of the danger of circular arguments, especially when an interpretation of a painting is adduced as evidence of the painter's state of mind (pp. 1–4) or when one conjectural identity is used to establish another (p. 141). In *The Cheese and the Worms*, however, the argument at some points becomes entirely circular. The coincidence of similar imagery in the Veda and the miller Menocchio's cosmology "may constitute one of the proofs, even though fragmentary and partly obliterated, of the existence of a millenarian cosmological tradition" (p. 58). But in an extended explanatory note on this point (pp. 154–55) Ginzburg states that the existence of an oral cosmological tradition explains Menocchio's own cosmology better than do contemporary philosophical texts. The oral cosmology and Menocchio's beliefs are used to explain one another, but the very existence of the oral cosmology is demonstrated largely by Menocchio's ideas. Acknowledging this circularity and Ginzburg's call for "new criteria of proof" does not necessarily make him wrong and his critic, Paola Zambelli, correct. Nevertheless circularity remains a problem. See Zambelli, "Uno, due, tre, mille Menocchio?" *Archivio storico italiano* 137 (1979): 51–90.

49. Carlo Ginzburg, "Mostrare e dimostrare: Risposta a Pinelli e altri critici," *QS* 50 (1982): 703, 707–10.

50. The best example of a convergence between internal or text-bound evidence and external evidence is Ginzburg's reading of a letter written by Menocchio to the inquisitors asking for forgiveness: Ginzburg establishes the letter's level of literacy through handwriting analysis; examines its content and formal structure; analyzes the use of symmetry, alliteration, and rhetorical devices in its language; and demonstrates that its approach to metaphors is literal. *The Cheese and the Worms*, pp. 87–91.

51. Salvatore Settis, *La Tempesta interpretata* (Turin, 1978), p. 73, cited and translated in Burke, "Carlo Ginzburg," p. 3.

<samp>52. Ginzburg, *The Cheese and the Worms*, p. ix.</samp>
53. Ginzburg, "Prove e possibilità," p. 133. They may be less successful, however, in fully appreciating all the implications of judicial procedure. Cf. Thomas Kuehn, "Reading Microhistory: The Example of *Giovanni and Lusanna*," *Journal of Modern History* 61 (1989): 512–34.
54. Ginzburg, *The Cheese and the Worms*, passim, pp. xiv, 86. Cf. Peter Burke, *Popular Culture in Early Modern Europe* (London, 1978), p. 78.
55. Schama, "The Monte Lupo Story," *London Review of Books*, 18 September–1 October, 1980, pp. 22–23.

Microhistory and the
Lost Peoples of Europe

1 ?✤ The Name and the Game: Unequal Exchange and the Historiographic Marketplace

by Carlo Ginzburg and Carlo Poni

Let us begin with a rather trivial observation. During the past half century, there has been a definite imbalance in the historiographic exchange between Italy and France. Italy has received much more than it has given. We shall not linger over the reasons for this: others have already done so in the course of this conference. We shall limit ourselves to recalling that even in a case like this, the history of historiography, in the traditional sense of the term, shows its own limitations. Only an analysis hinging on the "social use of historiography" (as K. Pomian pointed out in a general way some years ago)[1] is adequate to the task of reconstructing the terms of a relationship that goes well beyond the research of individuals and of research and teaching organizations, to involve basic political choices and, ultimately, whole societies very different from one another.

?✤ The persistence of this basic imbalance, naturally, does not mean that the relationship between Italian and French historians (or, more specifically, the French historians connected with the *Annales* group) has remained unchanged over these fifty years. Those who went before us have shown the forms that this relationship has gradually assumed. It is our conviction that today we are entering into a brand new phase, tied to the emergence, in part still embryonic, of new directions in research. Because these new directions will be our concern here, the discussion will be more prognostic than diagnostic.

Carlo Ginzburg and Carol Poni, "Il nome e il come: scambio ineguale e mercato storiografico," *Quaderni storici*, no. 40 (1979): 181–90.

?₺ We have talked about unequal exchange and the historiographic marketplace. A dependent country, though, does not necessarily mean a poor country, for it is well known that Italy's historiographic dependency goes hand in hand with its extraordinary richness in the very documentary material without which the historian cannot work. (We are thinking here not only of the documents preserved in archives and libraries but also of the countryside, of the shape of the cities, of the people's ways of conducting themselves: all of Italy can be—and has been—seen as one enormous archive.) Years ago Franco Venturi spoke with bitter irony of Italian libraries and archives as terrain that had been subjected to extensive rather than intensive cultivation.[2] Changing the metaphor a little, we could define the Italian archives as precious deposits of primary materials, in large part never mined.

The gap between primary materials such as archival sources and the possibilities for their mining has become particularly apparent during the very period that has witnessed the almost universal triumph of quantitative history. Subjective resistance to that triumph, tied to a cultural tradition still today imbued with idealism, should not be ignored. But limiting ourselves to that resistance alone, as often happens, would be one-sided and, in its own way, idealistic. Quantitative research on any large scale presupposes considerable financial investment and *équipes* of researchers—in a word, an advanced research organization. A study like the one bravely begun and to this day not carried to a conclusion by Elio Conti could be considered representative, especially when put next to that completed and published a few months ago by Christiane Klapisch and David Herlihy on the Florentine tax census of 1427.[3] When employed shrewdly, French-American capital and the computer make possible undertakings that would be impossible for a single individual. (What interests us here is the difference in scale between the two kinds of research, rather than a comparative analysis of the results achieved.)

Research into the history of property and population shows that quantitative history is alive and well. Also very much alive is serial history: the quantitative study of an extended period, which has now shifted from the study of prices (the old point of departure) toward changes in production, analyzed through tithes and account books. Without doubt, we owe valuable results to the powerful investigative tools provided by serial history—for example, the discovery of structural change in demographic crises, from the catastrophic mortality crises of the cruel seventeenth century to the less weightily Malthusian crises of "morbidity" of the eighteenth century.

We are not risking too much, however, if we state that the quantitative study of an extended period can also obscure and distort facts. Prices, food, and mortality are matters that take on significance over the short period especially if we want to analyze the way in which political power reacts to economic fluctuations and food crises, such as through price controls, building up of reserves, requisitions, or buying grain on the foreign market. In looking at an extended period of time, as Steven Kaplan recently pointed out, it is difficult to understand the day-to-day problems of survival. We tend to think in terms of ten-year averages and moving averages reported on semilogarithmic graphs. Lived experience (undoubtedly an ambiguous expression) is largely relegated to the margins. This "long-run approach can generate an abstract, homogenized social history, devoid of flesh and blood and unconvincing despite its scientific cachet."[4]

All the same, we believe that serial quantitative history is by now part of "normal science," in Thomas Kuhn's sense,[5] and that the enormous amount of material preserved in Italian archives must be examined in order to verify the paradigms and rules of the serial approach, in order to articulate, demonstrate, delimit, and manipulate them. (Let us make clear that, in this context, the term *paradigm* has a meaning both weaker and more metaphorical than that given it by Kuhn; historiography remains, despite everything, a preparadigmatic discipline.) A part of the scholarly community must dedicate itself either totally or partially to this kind of research.

❧ Other themes and other kinds of research are, however, already coming to the fore. In particular, we see the emergence in several aspects of historical research characterized by analysis, at extremely close range, of highly circumscribed phenomena—a village community, a group of families, even an individual person. This can be explained for reasons both intrinsic and extrinsic to the discipline. We will begin with the latter, the extrahistoriographic reasons.

In recent years, several very different phenomena, such as the recent wars in Southeast Asia and the Seveso and Amoco-Cadiz ecological disasters, have revived discussion of strategic objectives long discounted and therefore long unanalyzed, whether of socialism or of unlimited technological development. It would not be going too far out on a limb to suggest that the growing fortunes of microhistorical reconstructions are tied to growing doubts about the established procedures of macrohistory. Precisely because we are no longer so sure that the game is worth the candle, we are persuaded to reanalyze the rules of the game. We are tempted to compare the optimism, whether for reform or revolution, of the fifties and sixties with the radical skepticism of the late seventies, a skepticism destined probably to grow more intense in the coming decade. That microhistorical investigations often take as the object of their analyses the themes of the private, the personal, and the lived experience, the same themes forcefully proposed by the women's movement, is no coincidence, since women constitute, without doubt, the group that has paid the highest price for the development of human history.

The increasingly close connection between history and anthropology is both symptom and instrument of this awareness. (In this case, too, we have a relationship of imbalance, in spite of the growing interest in history on the part of such anthropologists as J. Goody.)[6] Anthropology has offered historians not only a series of themes largely overlooked in the past—from kinship relationships to material culture, from symbolic rituals to magic—but also something of much greater importance: a conceptual frame of reference, whose outlines we are only now beginning to make out. The demise of the ethnocentric illusion (which, paradoxically, coincided with the unification of the global market) has made untenable the idea of a universal history. Only an anthropology saturated with history or, what is the same thing, a historiography saturated with anthropology will be adequate to the task of rethinking the multimillennial endurance of the species *Homo sapiens.*

Thirty years ago, in an article later reprinted as an introduction to the *Anthropologie structurale* collection, Claude Lévi-Strauss wrote that "the famous statement by Marx, 'Men make their own history, but they do not know that they are making it,' justifies, first, history, and, second, anthropology. At the same, time it shows that the two approaches are inseparable."[7] The desired convergence of history and anthropology still has many obstacles in its path: first among them is the difference between the documentations used by the two disciplines. The complexity of social relationships, reconstructible by the anthropologist through fieldwork, contrasts sharply with the one-sidedness of the archival sources that must serve as field material to the historian. Each of these sources, born of a specific social relationship and, more often than not, sanctioned by an institution, can offer legitimacy for the researcher's specialization. One is a historian of the church or of technology, of business or of industry, of population or of property, of the working class or of the Italian Communist party. The motto for this kind of historiography could be, "Don't let your left hand know what your right hand is doing." This fragmentation reflects the fragmentation of the sources. The church records introduce us to individuals at birth or death, as parents or children; the property registers, to individuals as owners or tenants; the criminal records, to individuals as plaintiffs or witnesses in a trial. This way, however, we risk losing the complexity of the relationships that connect any individual to a particular society. This is true even of those sources richer in unpredictable data, such as criminal or inquisitional proceedings, which, particularly the latter, are the closest thing we historians have to the modern anthropologist's field study. But if the area of research is sufficiently circumscribed, then the individual documentary series can transcend time and space in a way that permits us to find the same individual or group of individuals in different social contexts. The thread of Ariadne that leads the researcher through the archival labyrinth is the same thread that distinguishes one individual from another in all societies known to us: the name.

᠅ The use of names to open up new fields for historical research is not new. Nominative demography (Henry's study of Crulai, for example)[8] has led to a noted shift of perspective in the area of historical demography and to a new object of investigation: the reconstruction of families. But nominative methodology can be carried well beyond the strictly demographic sources. In the church records of rural parishes in sharecropping areas—the district around Bologna comes immediately to mind—next to the names and surnames of the "manager" (*reggitore*) and of the members of his family, there are also the names of the farmhouse and of the cultivated land (Red House, White House, the Palace, etc.). Taking this place-name as guide, it is not hard to find in the property registers (and thus in another archive) an important piece of information: the extent of the farmland. Next to the name and to the land dimensions in the register, we find the name of the landowner. From here, from this name, we can go back to the private archive for that property in which, if we are lucky, we can find in the administrative registers the annual farm accounts and, together with the name of the sharecropper and of the land that he farms, also the annual account of crop production, divided according to crop types (grain, hemp, corn, vine, timber) with the halving of the gross product and the account of the farm debt for each land-holding and for each tenant-farmer family. In other words, we find a series of facts (usually, but not always, covering a brief period) with which it is possible to reconstruct the interconnections among diverse conjunctures.

The journey of investigation, obviously, can begin at any point in the chain. The best point of departure is probably not the archive of the parish but that of the large property. The latter includes the names of peasants and the names of places that we can seek with greater hope of success in other archival sources, such as parish and property registers, in which, in principle, there should be listed the names of all the families and all the landholdings. Applying an analogous procedure to notarial records, it is possible to reconstruct the matrimonial strategies among families that were allied or related. The course of this research can be carried even further by going to episcopal ecclesiastical archives and there looking for dispensations allowing marriage between blood relatives. Once again, the guiding thread is the name.

As we have already indicated, this game of rebuff and rebound does not necessarily close the door to serial investigation, if it is useful. A series, particularly if it has not been manipulated, is always an expendable good. But the center of gravity for the kind of micronominative research proposed here resides elsewhere. The lines that converge upon and diverge from the name, creating a kind of closely woven web, provide for the observer a graphic image of the network of social relationships into which the individual is inserted.

Studies of this kind are also possible in the case of individuals belonging to those social strata characterized by greater geographical mobility. Here, certainly, we must proceed a little more tentatively, entrusting ourselves to the particular case at hand and to good luck. But once again the name serves as a valuable compass. Let us take Costantino Saccardino, a distiller and professional jester, tried for heresy by the Inquisition of Bologna and condemned to death together with three followers in 1622.[9] The trial proceedings, unfortunately lost, created a notable echo: civic chronicles in manuscript as well as printed narratives provide further details of the event and its protagonist. It turns out that Saccardino had lived in Venice, and a probe into the archives of the Venetian Inquisition brings to light a group of denunciations with which he was charged. One brief mention shows

Saccardino in Florence, serving the Medici in the role of jester, and, in fact, his name can be found among the recipients of payments by the court in the first decade of the seventeenth century. From a bibliographical check one discovers a small treatise on medical arts that he published, concluding with a list of clients cured and healed, similar to other records drawn up by Bolognese notaries that mention these clients by name. This list is confirmed by an examination of the notarial sources preserved at the State Archive of Bologna. One document, however, refers to a corresponding record drawn up some years before by a notary in Ferrara. Bit by bit, a biography, albeit fragmentary, emerges from the network of relationships that circumscribe it.

※ For all their dissimilarities, the two studies we have outlined have two elements in common: their reference to the lower strata of society and their use, as guiding thread, of the name. Several years ago, describing the state of prosopographical studies, Lawrence Stone distinguished two currents: one, qualitative, concentrated on the study of elites (political, cultural, etc.) and the other, quantitative, aimed at investigating broader social groups.[10] Our present proposal would combine the nonelitist perspective of the second current with the particularized analysis of the first to achieve a prosopography from below (analogous to that proposed by E. P. Thompson), one opening out into a series of case studies but never excluding, as we have said, serial research.

It is obvious that a prosopography from below should take as its objective a series of case studies. An investigation that is both qualitative and exhaustive will be able to take under examination only entities that are numerically circumscribed—elites, in other words. The problem, then, will be to choose from the mass of available data those cases that are relevant and significant.

Are they significant in the sense of statistical frequency? They will not always be, because there also exists what Edoardo Grendi has called, with an apt oxymoron, the "normal exception."[11] We can assign at least two meanings to this expression. First, it designates documentation that is only apparently exceptional. Stone pointed out the singular fact that the only subordinate groups about whom it is sometimes possible to collect a good deal of information are all "minority groups, which are by definition exceptional since they are in revolt against the *mores* and beliefs of the majority."[12] But an examination of criminal trials before 1800 (before, that is, the figure of the professional criminal had been established in the modern sense of the term) leads the researcher to less pessimistic conclusions. The overwhelming majority of these trials concern very common and often unimportant crimes, such as brawling, petty thievery, and so forth, carried out by absolutely unexceptional individuals. It is no paradox to affirm that in preindustrial societies a certain type of transgression constituted the norm, in fact, even if not in law.

But the "normal exception" can also have another meaning. If the sources are silent about or systematically distort the social reality of the lower classes, then a truly exceptional (and thus statistically infrequent) document can be much more revealing than a thousand stereotypical documents. As Kuhn has shown, it is the marginal cases that bring the old paradigm back into the arena of discussion, thus helping to create a new paradigm, richer and better articulated. These marginal cases function, that is, as clues to or traces of a hidden reality, which is not usually apparent in the documentation.

Coming from very different backgrounds and working on very different themes, both authors of the present essay have found themselves recognizing the decisive importance of those traces, those clues, those details previously overlooked, which upset and throw into disarray the superficial aspect of the documentation.[13] Beyond this, it is possible to reach a deeper, invisible level, the one comprising the rules of the game, "the history that men do not know they are making." At this point we recognize the echo of lessons, at the same time different and connected, taught us by Marx and Freud.

ꝸ Microhistorical analysis therefore has two fronts. On one side, by moving on a reduced scale, it permits in many cases a reconstitution of "real life" unthinkable in other kinds of historiography. On the other side, it proposes to investigate the invisible structures within which that lived experience is articulated. The implicit model corresponds to the relationship between *langue* and *parole* formulated by Ferdinand de Saussure. The structures governing social relationships are, like those of *langue*, unconscious. Between the form and the substance there is a gap that science has the obligation to fill. (If reality were transparent, and therefore immediately knowable, said Marx, critical analysis would be superfluous.) We propose, therefore, to define microhistory, and history in general, as the *science of real life* [*scienza del vissuto*], a definition that seeks to comprehend the reasoning of both the supporters and the enemies of the integration of history with the social sciences, and for this, no doubt, it will not be pleasing to either side. The term *structure* is ambiguous. Although historians have identified it primarily with extended duration, perhaps the moment has come to emphasize instead, within the notion of structure, that characteristic of system that, as Roman Jakobson has shown, includes synchrony as much as diachrony.

⁊ In no case can microhistory limit itself to verifying, on its own scale, the macrohistorical (or macroanthropological) rules that have been elaborated elsewhere. One of the first discoveries of the student of microhistory is the rare and sometimes nonexistent relevance of the analyses (to begin with the chronological ones) elaborated on the macrohistorical scale. From this the comparison takes its decisive importance. In this connection we can note that comparative history, unpopular in Italy for reasons known to all of us, is, in spite of everything, on the rise in France.

⁊ The history of Italy is a polycentric history, as demonstrated by, among other things, the series of documents preserved in the archives of the peninsula. It is our belief that today microhistorical investigations constitute the most appropriate way to mine this extraordinary accumulation of primary material, a method more appropriate and more accessible also to craftsmanlike ways of gathering.

In this sense, perhaps, we can be allowed to look forward in the coming years to an exchange between Italian and French historiography that is less unequal than in the past and that will strengthen further the collaboration between the two.

Notes

Reproduced here, with some variations, is a paper read before the conference on "The *Annales* and Italian Historiography," held in Rome in January 1979.

1. K. Pomian, "L'histoire de la science et l'histoire de l'histoire," *Annales: Economies, Sociétés, Civilisations* 30 (1975): 952.

2. F. Venturi, *Settecento riformatore: Da Muratori a Beccaria* (Turin, 1969), pp. xvii–xviii.

3. D. Herlihy and C. Klapisch-Zuber, *Les toscans et leurs familles* (Paris, 1978). [Now in an abbreviated translation as *Tuscans and Their Families: A Study of the Florentine Catasto of 1427* (New Haven, 1985). Since the publication of this article Elio Conti has completed *L'imposta diretta a Firenze nel Quattrocento (1427–1497)* (Rome, 1984).]

4. S. E. Kaplan, *Bread, Politics and Political Economy in the Reign of Louis XV* (The Hague, 1976), pp. xx–xxi.

5. T. Kuhn, *The Structure of Scientific Revolutions*, 2d ed. (Chicago, 1970).

6. J. Goody, *The Domestication of the Savage Mind* (Cambridge, 1977).

7. C. Lévi-Strauss, *Structural Anthropology* (Garden City, N.Y., 1967), p. 24.

8. L. Henry, *La population de Crulai, paroisse normande*, Travaux et documents de l'INED (Paris, 1958).

9. For a brief look ahead to the research referred to here, see C. Ginzburg and M. Ferrari, "La colombara ha aperto gli occhi," *Quaderni storici* 38 (August 1978): 631–39. [Translated in this collection as "The Dovecote Has Opened Its Eyes."]

10. L. Stone, "Prosopography," *Daedalus* 100 (1971): 46–79.

11. E. Grendi, "Microanalisi e storia sociale," *Quaderni storici* 35 (May–August 1977): 512. [Cf. the discussion of Grendi's article in the Introduction to the present volume.]

12. Stone, "Prosopography," p. 59.

13. See C. Ginzburg, "Spie. Radici di un paradigma scientifico," *Rivista di storia contemporanea* 7 (1978): 1–14 [an enlarged version appeared in *Ombre rosse* 29 (1979): 80–107; in *Crisi della ragione*, ed. A. Gargani (Turin, 1979), pp. 57–106; and in Ginzburg's *Miti, emblemi, spie: Morfologia e storia*, (Turin, 1986), translated as "Morelli, Freud and Sherlock Holmes: Clues and Scientific Method," *History Workshop* 9 (1980): 5–36 and also published in *The Sign of Three: Dupin, Holmes, Peirce*, ed. Umberto Eco and Thomas A. Sebeok (Bloomington, Ind., 1983), pp. 81–118. However, the best translation is as "Clues: Roots of an Evidential Paradigm," in Ginzburg's *Clues, Myths, and the Historical Method*, trans. John Tedeschi and Anne C. Tedeschi (Baltimore, 1989), pp. 96–125.] Also see C. Poni, "Innovazione contadina e controllo padronale," presented to the Arbeitsprozesse colloquium, Gottingen (June 22–28, 1978).

2 ?⥈ The Dovecote Has Opened Its Eyes

by Carlo Ginzburg and Marco Ferrari

Today we are all aware that access to and control of the channels of communication have political importance. Although the evidence for this claim is obvious, it is not inappropriate to recall its implications in a discussion of the connections between the literate and the illiterate and between written culture and oral culture (the two pairs are *not* synonymous) in Italian society in the fifteenth and sixteenth centuries. During this period, as has recently been observed,[1] individuals belonging to less privileged social strata abound in the ranks of authors, thus diluting the homogeneity of those ranks. Even if the quantitative dimensions of this phenomenon escape us, it will still be worthwhile to examine its qualitative implications through the examination of a single case. We mean qualitative in the sense of cultural and political implications. Did access, however limited, to the publishing of printed books on the part of social strata different from the traditional ones (though we will need to define exactly which strata were actually involved) result in the production of different messages, reaching a different public? Did it establish a different connection between authors and readers? The following analysis provides one answer to these questions, extremely circumscribed and not generalizable, and confirming that in the period indicated the connection between the culture of the subordinate class and the culture of the dominant class was complex, comprising two-way exchanges as well as one-way repression.[2]

Carlo Ginzburg and Marco Ferrari, "La colombara ha aperto gli occhi," *Quaderni storici*, no. 38 (1978): 631–39.

⅋ In November 1622, four men were hanged at Bologna in the market square, in front of a large crowd. For three years, according to the accusation, they had secretly defiled with excrement the sacred images of the city and had attached posters filled with blasphemies and obscure threats against the political and religious authorities. One of these predicted the imminent destruction of papal power by the Elector Palatine, a prediction destined for rapid disappointment. Only the promise of a great reward combined with the secret accusation by a comrade permitted the Holy Office to capture the conspirators: Costantino Saccardino, a Roman, his son Bernardino, and the two de' Tedeschi brothers, employed at the tax office for mills. It became clear right away that most important in the cast of characters, the true head of the conspiracy, was Costantino Saccardino. Converted Jew, professional clown in the service first of the grand dukes of Tuscany and later of the Bolognese *anziani*, Saccardino owned a shop for the distillation of water and had earned considerable fame as a healer. Some years earlier he had been denounced to the Venetian Holy Office and was subsequently prosecuted and jailed in Bologna as a heretic.[3]

Unfortunately, the records of Saccardino's two inquisitorial trials (1616 and 1622) cannot be found. The indictments returned against him can be reconstructed only in a fragmentary way and only on the basis of indirect evidence, such as denunciations and reports published after his death. The available documents, however, do give us a glimpse of several directions for investigation.

Saccardino's two professions, as clown and distiller, are only apparently dichotomous, in reality revealing a coherent persona, that of the charlatan. In some famous pages of the *Piazza universale delle professioni del mondo* (*The Universal Presentation of the Professions of the World*), Tomaso Garzoni clearly indicates that the *commedia dell'arte* was born not at court as has sometimes been maintained, but in the public piazza.[4] It is in the town square, whose carnivalesque culture has been analyzed by Bakhtin,[5] that the masked figures (Brighella, Frittellino, Dr. Graziano, and others) take life, through the movements and the rigmarole of the charlatans, in order to attract the attention of a diffident and bewildered public. And Saccardino, the seller of miraculous remedies who became the masked figure of Dr. Graziano at the banquets of the Bolognese *anziani*,[6] was an accomplished charlatan. Perhaps even the blasphemous and scatalogical form of the conspiracy that cost Saccardino his life can be traced to that carnivalesque culture, founded upon obscenity and excrement, that has been analyzed by Bakhtin in his already classic book and, more recently, by Piero Camporesi.[7] Similarly the nocturnal plot of Saccardino and his companions invites a thorough exploration of the nexus between festival and rebellion,[8] between carnival and subversion.

Even Saccardino's single extant piece of writing, the *Libro nominato la verità di diverse cose, quale minutamente tratta di molte salutifere operationi spagiriche et chimiche* (*Book Called the Truth of Diverse Things, Which Treats in Detail Many Healthful Procedures, Both Spagyrical and Chemical*), is in certain respects a product of superior charlatanry. (So far only one copy of this work, published at Bologna in 1621, has been discovered, preserved at the University Library of Bologna.)[9] This work concludes with a detailed catalog of people cured by Saccardino and references to the notaries who can vouch for the actual healing of the sick. But the glorification of the author's powers frames a veritable encyclopedia of popular medicine.

✺ The book written by Costantino Saccardino belongs to a genre of literature that we can term *books of secrets*.[10] These are books in the vernacular, containing prescriptions and practical advice not only on medicine but also on alchemy, astronomy, veterinary science, physiognomy, the art of perfumery, and so forth. Such works are presented as practical medical encyclopedias, highly popularized, based in great part on ancient and medieval texts (pseudo-Aristotle, Dioscorides, and Avicenna), and directed toward a very large public. We can distinguish between two forms: books of secrets true and proper, published generally between the middle of the sixteenth and the middle of the seventeenth centuries, rather lengthy (around three hundred pages), usually in octavo; and charlatan pamphlets, composed of few, usually unnumbered pages, particularly frequent between the end of the sixteenth and the middle of the seventeenth centuries, in octavo or smaller formats. Alongside these two we can juxtapose the fly sheets, of which we have at least one example.[11]

The authors of and the public for the real books of secrets were socially and culturally distinct from those for the pamphlets of secrets. The authors of the first are physicians, professors, and nobles. Among them we find, for example, Benedetto Vittori, professor of medicine, logic, and philosophy at Padua and friend of Pope Julius III; Pietro Bairo, graduate in medicine from Turin and lecturer at the same university, principal physician (*protomedico e archiatra*) of Carlo II and

Carlo III of Savoy; Leonardo Fioravanti, graduate in medicine at Bologna, where subsequently he was made knight; Domenico Auda, head pharmacist at the Hospital of Santo Spirito in Rome; and Isabella Cortese, Venetian noblewoman.[12] In contrast, we do not have biographical information on the authors of the pamphlets except in a few cases: their nicknames, however, reveal that they belonged to the professional stratum of charlatans and clowns. It will be enough to mention Tommaso Maiorini called *Policinella*, Francesco called *il Biscottino* ("the Little Biscuit"), Pietro Muzii called *il Zanni bolognese* ("the Bolognese Buffoon"), *l'Americano* ("the American"), Tommaso Francolino called *l'Ortolano* ("the Greengrocer"), Claudio Amelli called *il Gran Piemontese* ("the Great Piedmontese"), Domenico Fedele called *il Mantoanino* ("the Little Mantuan"), Biagio called *Figadet*, Felice Boldini called *il Marchesino d'Este* ("the Little Marquis of Este").[13] The authors' diverse social backgrounds certainly corresponded to the diversity of their reading public. In format and size, the pamphlets were intended to be sold in the piazze, in markets, and at fairs during the charlatans' performances; the frontispieces of the books of secrets, on the other hand, were addressed to "men and women of high understanding . . . physicians . . . every sort of industrious artisan . . . every virtuous person."[14]

The authors of the pamphlets, inasmuch as they were charlatans and professional clowns, could become intermediaries between the culture of the people and middle-high culture. This, apparently, was also the case for Saccardino, distiller and clown, poised between the courts and the square. His *Libro*, containing only about thirty pages and issued by the shop of a pamphlet printer, makes use of the preface to Dioscorides by Dr. P. A. Mattioli and the little treatise *Della fisica* by the already mentioned Fioravanti.[15] The use of these texts presupposes in Saccardino a level of knowledge superior to that of his colleagues Biscottino or Policinella. But Saccardino's singularity comes above all from his creative use of his sources. Starting with its subtitle, the *Libro* promises "useful discussions exposing many frauds that, on account of self-interest, occur often, as much in medicine, as in medicinal substances." In fact, the passages from Dr. Mattioli were inserted into a violent polemic against Galenic medicine, opposed on one side to the experimental "spagyric" or alchemical art of Paracelsian derivation, and on the other to popular medicine. Fioravanti had stated that medicine "is distributed among all the people of the world, . . . the irrational animals have one part, the peasants have another, the women another, and the rational doctors another."[16] This ascending hierarchy is picked up and reversed by Saccardino: the animals know how to cure themselves, likewise the women, the peasants, and the mountain dwellers, while the "rational doctors," full of arrogance and ostentation, cling to their "logic" in order to squeeze money out of the "poor sick patients," reducing them to desperation.[17] The opposition between what today we might call quacks and official medicine, which appears in the titles (even if not in the texts) of such charlatan pamphlets as *Con il poco farete assai* (*With a Little You Will Do a Lot*) or *Il Medico dei Poveri o ver lo stupore dei Medici* (*The Doctor to the Poor or Truly the Astonishment of the Doctors*), becomes explicit and bold in Saccardino's *Libro*. From this opposition, we can cull expressions attributable to a tradition of a Paracelsian type. But regarding the diffusion of Paracelsus's ideas and writings in Italy we know, for now, very little.[18]

Saccardino's scavenging of the texts he uses is even more notable considering the remarkable viscosity of this literature of "secrets." One example will suffice. From Dioscorides, to the books of professors like Falloppia, to the pamphlets of charlatans like the Bolognese Buffoon, the prescriptions for curing burns are based on substantially the same ingredients: oil or grease, wax, and egg white.[19] In other cases, this continuity does not exclude burlesque variations to be found in the charlatan pamphlets but in this case the continuity ought to be explained, in part because it also seems to appear in popular medicine based exclusively on oral tradition. Only thirty years or so ago in the province of Foggia, as we learn from an oral report, the *sparapizzi*— that is, the manufacturers of fireworks—still used as a treatment for burns an ointment composed of wax and oil.[20] It is obviously absurd to presume that the formula for this ointment had come down to the *sparapizzi* through an unbroken written tradition, almost two thousand years old and leading back finally to Dioscorides. It is more probable to presume the existence of two parallel medical traditions, one written and one oral, differentiated socially but substantially similar in content. These two parallel traditions came into contact with each other with particular intensity during specific historical moments: besides the well-known example of Paracelsus, who declared polemically that he had been taught by old women of the people,[21] we can recall the statement by Alessio Piemontese (alias Gerolamo Ruscelli) that he had sought the secrets of medicine "not only from the great men as doctrine and from great nobles, but also from poor women, from artisans, from peasants, and from every sort of person."[22] In this case there was a kind of circularity from low to high; when, on the other hand, the charlatans inserted prescriptions, taken from the books of secrets, into pamphlets to be sold in the public squares, the circularity was inverted, going from high to low.

෫ Saccardino's boldness and originality in elaborating the materials from "high" culture were not limited to the art of medicine. From a collection of inquisitorial denunciations we learn that for years Saccardino had traveled through Venice, Ferrara, and Bologna proselytizing among groups of artisans (butchers, printers, and others). To these people he repeated again and again that religion, and hell in particular, were only a fraud: "Those who believe it are blockheads. . . . The princes want to make them believe it, in order to have their own way, but . . . by now the whole dovecote has opened its eyes."[23] This was the same thesis upheld during those same years by the erudite libertines, but with the difference that one term (that of class) was inverted: according to the scholarly libertines, the knowledge of the fraudulence of religion must be limited—or else risk the collapse of the social structure—to an intellectual and political elite. The huge lie of religion was, in their eyes, indispensable for holding the common people in check.[24] Saccardino replayed the same thesis, inverting the political sentiment: the "dovecote" (unmetaphorically, the common herd, the most humble part of the social structure) had to refute religion as a lie used by the princes to maintain their own privileges. In this case we can accurately speak of "popular libertinism."[25] It is not a matter of an unwarranted juxtaposition. The proof that Saccardino had come to know (through channels yet to be discovered) the ideas and the writings of the scholarly libertines is provided by his repeated statements on the origin of the human species. Repeating Fioravanti's statements to the letter, Saccardino refers in his *Libro* to the spontaneous generation of certain animals (mice, moles) from the earth.[26] But in the speeches that he was used to making in the streets and shops of Ferrara and Bologna, he pushed this to a radical extrapolation: the first men were not created by God but were born from mud as toads and mice are born from the mud of summer, as a consequence of the heat. During those same years, the same thesis was maintained by Giulio Cesare Vanini; it then became a libertine commonplace. The point of departure for both men (explicit in Vanini's case, implicit in Saccardino's) was a famous page in Diodorus Siculus.[27]

Even a case like that of Saccardino, which is susceptible to generalization in only the most limited way, serves to remind us of the untenability of every reductionist vision of the culture of the subordinate (in this case, urban) classes.

Notes

1. See A. Petrucci's introduction to the collection, edited by him, *Libri, editori e pubblico nell'Europa moderna: Guida storica e critica* (Bari, 1977), pp. xxvi–xxviii.
2. See C. Ginzburg, *Il formaggio e i vermi. Il cosmo di un mugnaio del '500* (Turin, 1976) [*The Cheese and the Worms: The Cosmos of a Sixteenth-Century Miller* (Baltimore, 1980)].
3. See R. Campeggi, *Racconto de gli heretici iconomiasti giustiziati in Bologna* (Bologna, 1622–23). Based almost exclusively on Campeggi is the discussion by L. Montanari, "Contestari d'altri tempi," *Strenna storica bolognese* 24 (1974): 135–61. Passages from the *Racconto* are reproduced in the anthology, *La storia moderna attraverso i documenti*, vol. 1, ed. A. Prosperi (Bologna, 1974), pp. 220–21.
4. See T. Garzoni, *La piazza universale di tutte le professioni del mondo* (Venice, 1588), pp. 741–48 ("De' formatori di spettacoli in genere, et de' Ceretani, o ciurmatori massime. Disc. ciii").
5. See M. Bakhtin, *L'oeuvre de François Rabelais et la culture populaire au Moyen Age et sous la Renaissance*, French trans. (Paris, 1970) [*Rabelais and His World* (Cambridge, Mass., 1968)].
6. See Campeggi, *Racconti*, p. 69. For contrast, however, also see F. Giorgi, *Un buffone degli Anziani di Bologna nel secolo XV* (Bologna, 1929), taken from *L'Archiginnasio* 24 (1929): 13.
7. See Bakhtin, *L'oeuvre*, and P. Camporesi, *La maschera di Bertoldo: G. C. Croce e la letteratura carnevalesca* (Turin, 1976).
8. See Y.-M. Bercé, *Fête et révolte. Des mentalités populaires du XVIe au XVIIIe siècle* (Paris, 1976).
9. Cataloged: Aula V, Tab. I, K. II (4). The copy was traced by Rossana Verrillo in the course of a seminar held at the University of Bologna in 1975–76 and 1976–77 under the direction of one of the present authors (and with the collaboration of the other). On the frontispiece of the copy preserved at the University Library of Bologna, there is a note concerning ownership: "del Marescalco" (an individual not yet identified). In the same hand and accompanying the name of the *Libro*'s author are the following words: "Which poor man was burned to death with his young son in the year [date missing], and he kept shop near to the *pelradaro* in the little store where he displayed a Madonna, beautifully adorned." The *pelradaro* is the barber. The handwritten note seems inspired by compassion, if not downright sympathy, for Saccardino: the man who had been condemned for having profaned sacred images kept a "Madonna beautifully adorned." For another piece of writing published by Saccardino, we have, for the moment, only the title: *Sonetto in morte del Serenissimo Ferdinando Medici Gr. Duca di Toscana dedicato al suo Serenissimo Figliuolo Cosimo Medici Gran Duca di Toscana dall'umilissimo servo di S.A. Costantino Saccardini detto il Dottore* (Florence, 1609). See G. Cinelli Calvoli, *Biblioteca volante . . .* continued by Dionigi Andrea Sancassani, 4 (Venice, 1747), p. 192.
10. For a historical framework for this kind of literature, see N. Z. Davis, "Printing and the People," in *Society and Culture in Early Modern France* (Stanford, 1975), pp.

189–226, 326–36. For a bibliography, see J. Ferguson, *Bibliographical Notes on Histories of Inventions and Books of Secrets* (Glasgow, 1882).

11. See A. Corsini, *Medici ciarlatani e ciarlatani medici* (Bologna, 1922), fig. 4.

12. B. Vittori, *Prattica dell'esperienza . . . nella quale si contengono maravigliosi rimedii da lui istesso, e da molti altri eccellentissimi medici esperimentali in tutte l'infermità, che occorrer possono nel corpo humano . . .* (Venice: Bolognino Zaltieri, 1570); P. Bairo, *Secreti medicinali . . . ne' quali si contengono i rimedi che si possono usar in tutte l'infermità che vengono all'huomo, cominciando da capelli fino alle piante de piedi. Et questo libro per l'utilità sua si chiama Vieni meco,* (Venice: F. Sansovino, 1561); L. Fioravanti, *Del compendio dei secreti rationali . . . libri cinque. Nel primo de' quali si tratta de' secreti più importanti nella professione medicinale. Nel secondo vi si insegnano molti secreti appartenenti alla cirugia, e si mostra il modo di esercitarla. Nel terzo si contengono i secreti più veri e più approvati nell'arte dell'alchimia. Nel quarto si scrivono molti belletti, che usano le donne per apparer belle. Nel quinto si comprendono i secreti più notabili in diverse arte e esercitii . . .* (Turin: l'heredi del Bevilacqua, 1580); D. Auma, *Breve compendio di maravigliosi segreti approvati e pratticati con felice successo nelle indispositioni corporali . . . ,* 5th ed. (Rome: a spese di Gregorio e Giovanni Andreoli librari in Parione, 1663); T. Cortese, *I secreti . . . ne'quali si contengono cose minerali, medicinali, arteficiose, e alchimiche, e molte de l'arte profumatoria, appartenenti a ogni gran signora* (Venice: Giovanni Barileto, 1561.

13. T. Maiorini, detto Policinella, *Frutti soavi colti nel giardino delle virtù, cioè trenta secreti bellissimi, con una regola per sapere tutto il tempo dell'anno* (Bologna: per gli heredi del Cochi, 1642). Francesco detto Biscottino, *Giardino di varii secreti, havuti da diversi signori, dove si contengono varie sorti di giuochi, secreti, e burle . . .* (Milan, Genoa, and Lucca: per li heredi del Marescalco, n.d.); P. M. Mutii, detto il Zanni bolognese, *Nuovo lucidario de secreti . . . non più uditi né stampati* (Bologna: per Alessandro Benacci, 1585); Americano, *Il vero e natural fonte, dal quale n'esce fuori un fonte d'acqua viva di mirabili e salutiferi secreti . . . dove leggendo ne caverete quell'acqua viva desiderata della sanità. Altri secreti si riserva il sopraddetto al lui di gran valore; il quale egli offerisce a chi si diletta, e prezza la virtù, e a chi sì dimostra generoso nello spendere, sì come merita* (Rome, Brescia, and Bologna: presso B. Cochi, 1608); Tomaso da Francolino, detto l'Ortolano, *Tesoro di secreti naturali . . .* (Rome, Venice, Milan, Siena, and Bologna: presso Bartolomeo Cochi, al Pozzo Rosso, 1617); C. Amelli, detto il Grasso Piemontese, *Fioretto bellissimo con il quale si potrà pigliarsi trattenimento in qual si voglia honorata conversatione, ove si contengono giochi bellissimi e secreti curiosi . . .* (Bologna: per il Sarti sotto alle Scuole, alla Rosa, n.d.); D. Fedele, detto il Mantoanino, *Con il Poco farete Assai* (Rome, n.d.); Biagi, detto Figadet, *Tesoro di secreti raccolti da diversi valenti huomini che ne hanno fatto isperienza . . .* (Bologna: appresso Bartolomeo Cochi, al Pozzo Rosso, 1617); F. Boldini, detto il Marchesino d'Este, *Il medico de' poveri, o sia il gran stupore de' medici, epilogato in diversi secreti naturali, che alcuno non ne fa stima, cavati da quelle herbe, piante, radiche, fronde, fiori e frutti, create dalla Provvidenza di Dio per beneficio de' mortali, esperimentati da me . . . operatore spagirico, e ricavati anco da virtuosi singolarissimi, che in simil professione si essercitano per la salute del genere humano . . . Et in fine tutte le astuzie ciarlatanesche in materia della sua esperienza* (Venice, Padua, and Ferrara: per Bernardino Pomatelli Imp. Epis., n.d.)

14. T. Rosselli, *De secreti universali . . .* (Venice: il Barezzi, 1644).

15. P. A. Mattioli, *Il Dioscoride . . .* (Venice: V. Valgrisi, 1548), and Saccardini, *Libro,* pp. 18–19; L. Fioravanti, *Della fisica . . .* (Venice: per gli heredi di Melchior Sessa, 1582), book I, chaps. ixxx–xcv, and Saccardini, *Libro,* chaps. xi–xxv, xxvii.

16. L. Fioravanti, *Reggimento della peste* (Venice: per gli heredi di Melchior Sessa, 1571), p. 8v.

17. Saccardini, *Libro*, pp. 10, 14.

18. It should be noted that "Filippo Aureolo Teofrasto Paracelso" is one of the few names introduced by Saccardino in a long catalog of "ancient and modern names of brave and most famous philosophers and simplifiers [*semplicisti*]" (*Libro*, p. 19) derived almost wholly from Mattioli's dedication to Dioscoride.

19. See Mattioli, *Il Dioscoride*, p. 131 (blossoms of rockrose mixed with wax); p. 147 (ground olives); p. 223 (egg white); p. 253 (pork fat); p. 633 (fronds of elder tree); G. Falloppia, *Secreti diversi e miracolosi* . . . (Venice: appresso Marco di Maria, 1563), p. 92 (egg white, oil, pork fat, new wax, and elder tree juice); P. M. Mutii, detto il Zanni bolognese, *Nuovo lucidario*, p. 5r (suet and oil).

20. This communication comes from Mrs. Archina Decembrino (Manfredonia), whom we thank very much.

21. See G. Bonomo, *Caccia alle streghe* (Palermo, 1959), p. 363.

22. Alessio Piemontese (i.e. Gerolamo Ruscelli), *De segreti* . . . (Venice: ad istanza di Aloise Zio, 1564), introduction.

23. See the Archivio di Stato di Venezia, *S. Uffizio*, b. 72 ("Costantino Sacardino"). There is a reference to this document, in a different context, in C. Ginzburg, "High and Low: The Theme of Forbidden Knowledge in the Sixteenth and Seventeenth Centuries," *Past and Present* 73 (November 1976): 35–36 [republished in idem, *Clues, Myths, and Historical Methods* (Baltimore, 1989), pp. 60–76].

24. See R. Pintard, *Le libertinage érudit dans la première moitié du XVIIe siècle*, 2 vols. (Paris, 1943).

25. G. Spini also discusses "popular libertinism" ("Noterelle libertine," *Rivista storica italiana* 78 [1976]: 792–802) in connection with Domenico Scandella called Menocchio, the Friulian miller who is protagonist of *Il formaggio e i vermi* [*The Cheese and the Worms*]. This conjecture, however, is completely unfounded. A comparison between the ideas and social ambience of Menocchio and those of Saccardino (not to mention the respective dates) clearly shows where it is legitimate to speak of "popular libertinism."

26. See Fioravanti, *Della fisica*, pp. 112–14.

27. See Archivio di Stato di Venezia, *S. Uffizio*, b. 72 ("Costantino Sacardino"), deposition of the Venetian butcher, Nicolò Stella (April 6, 1617): "He told me moreover that nature produced men who are various and different from one another, just as the earth produces different plants, and that God does not meddle with these things"; R. Campeggi, *Racconto de gli heretici*, p. 88: "But strange and ridiculous was the opinion concerning the origin of men (denying that Adam and Eve had been the first persons) that he [Saccardino] held in his confused and corrupt intellect. . . . He affirmed that men, like so many toads or frogs of August were born from the fat earth with the help of the sun's rays." The same idea was formulated during the same years by Vanini, in his *De admirandis Naturae arcanis* (1616): see L. Corvaglia, *Le opere di Giulio Cesare Vanini e le loro fonti*, vol. 2 (Città di Castello, 1934), pp. 178–79. Saccardino could have read the passage of Diodorus Siculus, recalled by Vanini, in the popularization printed by Giolito (Diodoro Siculo, *Historia overo libraria historica* . . . [Venice, 1575], 1: 7–8).

3 ⅋ Ritual Pillages: A Preface to Research in Progress

by the Bologna Seminar, coordinated by
Carlo Ginzburg

The events that took place in Rome at the end of August 1559 are well known.[1] As soon as the news had spread that Pope Paul IV Carafa was nearing the end of his life, a crowd "overwhelmed by frantic gaiety"[2] attacked the Palace of the Holy Office on the Via Ripetta, destroying a great part of the archives that were kept there, freeing the prisoners, and setting fire to the building. Two days after the pope's death, the crowd broke up his statue in the Palace of the Conservators. The head of the statue was exhibited in public, deco-rated like a Jew with a yellow cap—the ignominious mark that Paul IV had imposed on the Jews—and in the end was thrown into the Tiber. An official proclamation was issued, which in the name of the Roman people ordered the destruction everywhere of the insignia of the Carafa. Riots, pillages, and murders followed upon each other without pause for three days. For some time groups of armed men roved through the city, committing acts of murder and violence.[3]

Overall, these violent episodes can be seen as the dramatic expres-sion of tensions and rancor provoked by the pontificate of the Carafa pope. Shortly before dying, Paul IV had stripped his own nephews of all political and administrative responsibilities and had sent them into exile.[4] But the old pope, who was eighty-three when he died, was considered principally responsible for these same nephews' ar-rogant behavior. The anti-Spanish policy, which had contributed to a rekindling of the long war between France and the Hapsburgs, and the fanatical persecution of heresy were largely unpopular. There was

Seminario bolognese coordinato de Carlo Ginzburg, "Saccheggi rituali: premesse a una ricerca in corso," *Quaderni storici*, no. 65 (1987): 615–36.

widespread intolerance toward the pope, in spite of contemporary testimony suggesting that the disorders might have been stirred up by the Farnese, the principal opponents of the Carafa.

September 5 marked the beginning of the conclave called to elect the successor to Paul IV. Among the cardinals deemed electable, Ercole Gonzaga, son of Isabella d'Este, seemed to have the greatest probability of becoming the new pope. This refined humanist, for many years bishop of Mantua, had the support of France and Spain, as well as of many minor Italian courts. But the Farnese's hostility toward him turned out to be decisive. On Christmas morning of 1559, the unusually long conclave finally ended: Ercole Gonzaga, along with a majority of the cardinals, voted in favor of Gian Angelo Medici, who took the name of Pius IV.[5]

The conclave was still in session when, on October 20, Guglielmo Gonzaga, duke of Mantua and nephew of Ercole, wrote to Camillo Suardo and Galeotto del Carretto, *podestà* and commissioner [*commissario*] respectively of Sermide and Revere, two small villages situated on the outskirts of Mantua, on the right bank of the Po. In the two letters, the duke of Mantua spoke of having heard that Ercole ("our most illustrious monsignor uncle") had been elected pope. The news was still to be confirmed, wrote the duke—though, as was to become clear, it was actually an unfounded rumor. The duke foresaw, however, as he had written the day before to Galeazzo Anguissola, the *podestà* of Ossiglia, that "some insolent and rash persons . . . might give themselves license" to pillage Ercole's property. Officials, therefore, were called upon to issue a proclamation that would compel those who had already stolen the duke's property to give back their ill-gotten gains. If they refused, they would have to be dispatched to Mantua, under threat of suitable punishment.[6] In reality the duke's letter was a prophecy after the fact: both in Sermide and elsewhere the plundering had already begun the day before. On October 19, Camillo Suardo, *podestà* of Sermide, had written to the duke of Mantua informing him that as soon as the news of Ercole's election had spread, riots had broken out in front of the church and around the pawnshops of the Jews.[7] Twenty persons armed with guns and led by a certain Mario Miari, a one-time bandit from Ferrara, had tried to attack the Jewish moneylenders: the mayor himself had protected them, putting the pillagers to flight. Even the tenant farmers from the Benedictine abbey in Felonica, a part of Ercole's benefice, were victims of pillaging.[8]

৪৯ On the one hand, we have very well-known events, set against the background of the capital of Christianity; on the other, we have noted obscure episodes in the life of little towns in the Po Valley. The connection between these developments, separated by an interval of a few months, can be sought in a series of practices much more ancient, which R. Elze has subjected to a close study.[9] Limiting ourselves for the moment to the ecclesiastical hierarchy, we find on the one hand for centuries and centuries the custom of despoiling the corpse and pillaging the goods of dead bishops, cardinals, and popes; and on the other, that of pillaging the palaces of newly elected popes (and sometimes of other cardinals) as well as the cells that they had occupied during the conclave.[10]

The most ancient testimony concerns the custom of pillaging the personal property of bishops at the time of their death. According to documents from the Council of Calcedonia (451), those who disgraced themselves by this offense were clerics.[11] A century later, in Spain, the phenomenon took on a more complex aspect: the Council of Ilerda (524) lamented the frequent (and therefore not exclusive) presence of clerics at the pillages; the Council of Valencia (546) asserted that, besides the clerics, the relatives of the dead bishop took part in the pillages. Both the clerics and the relatives were enjoined to forebear from stealing not only the furnishings kept in the bishop's house or in the church, but also money, utensils, vases, grain, flocks, and cattle.[12] The expansion of this custom to the diocese of Rome resulted in the possibility of new and incomparably richer booty: in 885, as appears in the biography contained in *Liber pontificalis*, Pope Stephen V, entering the Lateran Palace after having been elected, discovered that the *vestiarium* had been robbed of jewelry, gilded clothing, ornaments, vases, and even the very precious gold cross donated by Belisarius. The wine cellar and the granary had been emptied: in order to provide support for the poor, the pontiff had to draw on the patrimony of his parents.[13] Less than twenty years later, the council called together at Rome by Pope John IX to rehabilitate the memory of Pope Formosus (904) censured the custom of sacking after the death of the pontiff not only the Lateran but also the whole city and its environs, observing that this very wicked custom, practiced also in other dioceses at the death of the bishop, was by this time well established (*inolevit*).[14]

The reference to proliferating targets for pillage and the absence of the specifics mentioned in the earlier councils, such as clerics and relatives of the dead bishop, lead us to suppose that by now the pillagers constituted a heterogeneous mob. The same emerges from later evidence, whether it refers to Rome or to the other dioceses. In 1051 Pope Leo IX sent a very harsh letter, drawn up perhaps by Peter Damian, to the inhabitants of Osimo, who had broken into and looted the residence of the dead bishop, cut down the vines and shubbery, and set fire to the houses of the peasants. According to the pope's definition, these were acts of bestial ferocity, which implied that they had been provoked (although not justified) by some wrong committed by the bishop in his lifetime. They were not exceptional, however, considering that they had their source in "perverse and detestable customs of certain common people."[15] At the death of this same Leo IX, the Romans, "according to the usual custom," invaded the Lateran (as a biographer wrote soon after), seizing all the furnishings.[16] It emerges from the formulations of the apostolic chancery of the thirteenth century that these acts of violence ended up becoming almost institutionalized: individuals specified only as "citizens" commonly took possession of the personal property of a dead bishop, preventing the successor from assuming office until he had promised to observe the tradition.[17] The extension of the pillage to the residence of the newly elected pope perhaps began near the end of the fourteenth century, although a bull promulgated in 1516 by Leo X speaks simply of a custom established "for some time" among the populace of Rome.[18] In his own memoirs Aeneus Silvius Piccolomini recalled how, after his election in 1458 to the pontifical seat, the servants of the cardinals, following a "vile custom," robbed the cell he had occupied during the conclave, taking possession of the small amount of silverware, books, and clothes; in the meantime a vulgar mob (*vilissima plebs atque infamis*) sacked the palace, removing the marbles and breaking them to pieces.[19]

Even this brief recapitulation provides a glimpse of a phenomenon (or a series of interlaced phenomena) disconcerting by its amplitude, diffusion, and continuousness. From the time of the Council of Calcedonia, certainly, the custom of pillaging the goods of the dead bishop was changing, above all in Rome. But in all the cases mentioned so far, the target of the pillages—which, as we have seen, were often accompanied by destruction—was personal property. A different phenomenon, though also tied to the occurrence of a vacancy in episcopal power, was the confiscation by the feudal nobility of the real estate of the dead bishop. During the twelfth century, in the climate of the

Gregorian reform, these acts provoked growing resistance on the part of the ecclesiastical hierarchy. "No prince, no governor of a castle, no layman may venture to violate, either totally or partially, the goods of the bishop [at his death]," wrote, for example, Pope Hadrian IV (dead in 1159) to Berengarius, archbishop of Narbonne, censuring what he defined as "a wicked custom, which for some time has gained a footing against God and your church."[20] Near the end of the thirteenth century, the attitude of the Curia became openly aggressive in regard to secular power: the Apostolic Camera extended its own claims, at least in theory, to the personal goods of all clerics (cardinals as well as bishops) independent of whether they had left a will.[21]

To legitimize this practice, the notion of the "right of spoils" (*jus spolii*) was elaborated—even though the expression seems to have entered into use only at the end of the fifteenth century. Elze cautiously proposes the hypothesis that the *jus spolii* may be derived historically from the pillage of personal property perpetrated by clerics, by relatives of the bishops, or by anonymous mobs at the death of bishops or popes.[22] Certainly the mobs of pillagers were convinced that they were exercising a right that, although rejected in principle, was at least partially tolerated in fact by both lay and ecclesiastical authorities. "It could easily be true that there were some insolent and reckless [persons], who gave themselves license to rob and pillage the rooms of His Most Reverend Lordship (*Sua Signoria Reverendissima*)" wrote the duke of Mantua in the letter already cited. More than six centuries earlier, the Roman Council of 904 had spoken of the abuse, of the *praesumptio* of such deeds. What were the roots of this obscure, persistent, customary right to pillage that was claimed on such specific occasions?

᳸ According to the chronicler Wiponus, the inhabitants of Pavia, accused of having destroyed the royal palace after the death of Henry II in 1024, justified themselves to his successor, Conrad II, saying "we cannot be accused of having destroyed the residence of the king, seeing that the king had died." A ship survives the death of its helmsman, Conrad II had retorted: "The king was dead, but the kingdom still endured" (*si rex periit, regnum remansit*). This memorable exchange was probably embellished, at least formally, by the chroniclers; nevertheless, the substance of the argument attributed to the inhabitants of Pavia perhaps casts light by analogy on the pillages that followed the death of bishops and of popes.[23] For those who experienced the relationship with the authorities as a totally personal bond, it was obvious that the goods of the dead should be considered as *res nullius*, things at the mercy of the first comer, especially when, as in the case of the churchmen, any distinction between personal property and that of the *ecclesia*, that is to say of the community, appeared problematical.[24] Even in Venice, the custom of abandoning the ducal palace to a pillaging mob immediately after the death of the doge lasted until 1328.[25]

The pillages that, after the conclusion of the conclave, struck the palace of the newly elected cardinal (or, by an error too frequent not to have been deliberate, those of other cardinals)[26] seem, at first glance, to represent a different phenomenon, if only because they involved the goods of a living person. A series of checks made in chronicles, documents, and criminal proceedings shows that similar events took place even outside of Rome. The pillages and the riots provoked by the false news of Ercole Gonzaga's election were not a freak occurrence: we can juxtapose them to other similar events, largely foreseeable both in form and aim, both expected and, within certain limits, even tolerated by the authorities. Such appear to be, for example, the pillages that took place at Mantua in 1522 (sparked by false news of Sigismondo Gonzaga's election to the pontificate) and at Bologna in 1590, in 1621, in 1740 (after the election, respectively, of Urban VII, Gregory XV, Benedict XIV). In each case the newly (or allegedly) elected cardinal was also the local archbishop, with the single exception of Urban VII (Giovan Battista Castagna). But even he, after receiving his doctoral degree at Bologna, returned there as governor in 1576–77 and then as legate in 1584–85. It seems permissible to conclude, at least provisionally, that even outside of Rome pillages took place on the occasion of papal elections, but only, if not necessarily, in localities to which, by reason of birth or of career, the new electee had been previously connected. Such circumstances unleashed the kind of behavior that followed the election at Bologna in 1740 of Benedict XIV (Prospero Lambertini): the festive mob, first having, "under the guise of being transported by jubilation," assaulted and devastated the guard corps situated in the Piazza Maggiore, then turned toward the Lambertini Palace, "assuming it to be," according to the *Diario* of the Bolognese Senate, "on such an occasion, their own."[27] But why did they consider it "their own," and why did they do so at that time?

The decree *De non spoliando eligendum in Papatu*, passed in the forty-first session of the Council of Constance (1417), stated that "some persons, harking back to a licentious abuse, claim falsely that the objects and the goods of the newly elected, who had attained, so to speak, the summit of wealth [*quasi culmine divitiarum adepto*], belong to whoever takes them."²⁸ The condemnation of this practice was taken for granted: the *spolium* carried out under these circumstances was an abuse, not a right. But the almost parenthetical aside, *quasi culmine divitiarum adepto*, clearly restores a true or presumed justification attributed to the authors of the pillages. We can translate it in these terms: the violent appropriation of the new pope's goods confirmed the image of a harmoniously hierarchical society, in which the inequalities of wealth were to be brought back within defined limits. The analysis of some concrete cases of pillage does not contradict this interpretation, but rather enriches it with new elements.

᷍ On October 20, 1559, Camillo Suardo, *podestà* of Sermide, hurried to the Abbey of Felonica where pillaging had begun as soon as the false news of Ercole Gonzaga's election as pope had arrived. As Suardo himself reported in a letter to the duke of Mantua, two hundred armed men greeted him with evident hostility. The steward who had rented the abbey recounted that the consul and the senior officials of Felonica, at the head of a very numerous group, had forced him to hand over the keys; they had completely emptied the granary and the hayloft; they had carried away about five hundred sheep, eighty horses, twenty cows, linen, beds, sheets, kitchen utensils, with a total value of twenty-five hundred scudi. But a different picture emerges from the interrogations conducted by a magistrate at the request of Suardo. After a quarrel among the nobles of the place, the pillagers had reached an agreement on the criteria of distribution. It would be done "by the head and not according to the tax assessment," by subdividing the booty into four parts: one to the townsfolk, one to the nobles, one to the parish priest, and one to the steward. As Suardo concluded, the behavior of the alleged victim, that is to say the steward, had been "neither gracious nor good."

Upon interrogation by the magistrate, Giovanni Francesco Andreasi, the consul of Felonica, justified the community's and his own behavior on this occasion. Hearing the news of Ercole Gonzaga's election, people from nearby Sermide and from Ferrara had threatened to pillage the abbey. But

such gain, being necessarily awarded to the citizens of some commune and removed from no one individual, as was the custom when the Supreme Pontiff were elected, went more honorably to these men than to any other and even more so because in case of restitution these townfolk could be held responsible for loss, as they would be whether they had committed it or others, even foreigners, had. Therefore, for the profit and the honor of this Commune, they had committed [the pillage].

The booty consequently remained in the control of the commune, which was ready to restore it in case the news of the election turned out not to be true.[29]

In reality, there was no restitution: the attempts of the duke to regain possession of the abbey's stolen goods proved fruitless, due certainly, at least in part, to the lack of cooperation by the local authorities. On April 20, 1560 (six months, that is, after the pillage), Raniero Ranieri, the Mantuan judge assigned to take up the Felonica case, wrote to the duke proposing a general acquittal, partly because "the said Magnificent *Podestà* did not deny at the time that the said Abbey, as property of the pontiff, could with good reason be plundered; on the contrary in the midst of the gaiety, he had to speak words of at least tacit consent."[30] In fact, apart from the initial altercation with the steward, the pillage took place in a very orderly fashion. The whole community had participated in it, not only for a rational calculation ("gain"), but for considerations of a symbolic nature ("honor"). To permit foreigners to take possession of the new pope's goods would have been in every sense an affront to all. Through the rite of pillage, local identity was reaffirmed, and the social hierarchy of the community was reestablished.

෧ But sometimes the violence of the pillages that followed papal elections was more than symbolic. On September 16, 1590, as soon as the news of the election of Urban VII (Giovan Battista Castagna) spread through Bologna, a hundred or so people, for the most part "little children" all shouting "to the Jews, to the Jews!" headed toward the ghetto, where the Jews had returned three years earlier. The synagogue on the Via dell'Inferno was pillaged; the windows broken out; and books, furnishings, and benches thrown into the street. An alms box ended up in the hands of four passersby—an innkeeper, a macebearer of the *anziani*, and two weavers—who, after some uncertainty, handed it over to the vice-legate, Camillo Borghese, the future Paul V. Three of them were arrested and forced to return the booty, a small sum of ten *bolognini*, to the representatives of the Jewish community. But in the meantime, to the shouts of "Long live Castagna, long live the pope!" another crowd, composed of young people and adults (perhaps two hundred, perhaps four hundred strong) ran along the Via Santo Stefano. After having thrown stones at the bakery of San Biagio, they besieged the bakery of Santo Stefano, breaking down the door and taking possession of everything that was within including bread and money. "[Only] three ounces for a *bolognino*! We want to discount it now! The baker has not closed up! Pillage, pillage!" they shouted. Some of those responsible were identified and brought to trial.[31]

Thus the invisible line that, in the eyes of the authorities, separated tolerable violence from unacceptable violence had been overstepped. But the targets chosen by the pillagers were not casual, just as it was probably not casual that the harvest had been bad that year. One will remember that in 1559 even at Sermide the *podestà* had to protect the banks of the Jews from the mob's assault; the same thing took place in Mantua in 1522, when false news of the election of Sigismondo Gonzaga spread.[32] The violence of the pillagers was probably called forth by the special bond, forged of oppression and protection, that linked the pope (or, in France, the king) to the Jews. They could be considered "people of the pope" and in a certain sense his property: that being the case, their goods were at the mercy of the firstcomer. But even the selection of the bakery to be sacked was not casual: the one annexed to the Abbey of Santo Stefano had for centuries enjoyed special pontifical privileges, which had been reconfirmed in 1587 and 1588 when the abbot commendator was Alessandro Peretti, nephew of the reigning pope, Sixtus V. This was the only Bolognese bakery that had the right to sell better-quality, higher-priced white bread, theoretically reserved for students and for the sick. "Traitor, who wants to give only three ounces of bread for a *bolognino*!" shouted the pillagers (one *bolognino* generally bought from four to six ounces of common bread). Because Cardinal Castagna did not have a palace in Bologna, it was impossible for the mob to exercise its customary rights on the palace of the newly elected pontiff. So, instead, they broke loose against substitute targets but still chose ones connected to the power of the pontiff.

≈ Without doubt the violence perpetrated against the Jews and against the bakery of Santo Stefano with its special privileges provided an outlet for feelings of latent aggression and a general rejoicing that assured a temporary immunity from further violence. This element emerges clearly in the tumultuous events that took place in Bologna on February 11 and 12, 1621. The news of the election of Gregory XV (Alessandro Ludovisi) arrived in the late afternoon of February 11. Among the crowd that had gathered in the Piazza Maggiore was a Veronese gentleman named Domenico Brugnoli. While he was chatting with some friends, a masked man attacked him and shot him once with a pistol. In the trial that followed it turned out that the ambush had been ordered by Giulio Sanuti, a Bolognese noble who, having heard about the new pope, had decided to take advantage of the confusion to vindicate an old affront. (For this Sanuti was first sent into exile and then pardoned.)[33] In another part of the city a goldsmith entered a girl's house in order to abduct her, taking advantage of the fact that in those hours (as recollected afterward by the victim) "everything was topsy-turvy."[34] The next morning the peasants who arrived at the market were held up and robbed and the bakeries plundered, amid jokes and laughter.[35] The chief of police [bargello] decided to restore order and entered the square with twelve guards. A group of boys began to throw rocks and, since there had been a great snowfall, even snowballs. As the crowd grew, someone began to shout "Death to Sfreghino!" (the nickname of a particularly hated guard). One man tried to tear off the gold chain that the chief of police wore around his neck. One of the guards fired his gun, gravely wounding an artisan who died a few hours later. At this point the mob broke loose. In the days that followed various people interrogated by the judges of the Tribunal of the Torrone recalled having seen the vice-legate appear fleetingly on a balcony and make a gesture, which was interpreted as an authorization or an incitement. The house of the police chief and the guards was attacked and plundered. Everything was taken away including horses, jewelry, clothing, pictures, furniture, doors, and windows. One witness recounted that all that remained in the empty rooms was a heavy smell of spilled wine. For the chief of police and the guards there remained nothing to do except to present a minute inventory of all that they had lost.[36]

Meanwhile the raging mob looked for other targets. An attack on the ghetto was not a possibility because the Jews had been expelled from Bologna in 1593. Fifty people or so headed for the Borgo Santa Caterina, an infamous quarter and home to Vittoria Piccinini, a Modenese courtesan widely known to be the lover of the chancellor. Behind the windows of nearby houses some prostitutes witnessed the scene. Some of the attackers, with faces blackened with soot, broke down the door of Vittoria's house. Leading them was Giacomo Vaccari, proprietor of a spice shop near the square. With sword drawn he shouted, "Long live the pope! They have murdered some of our own people! Everyone grab something! Everyone!" For months and months the judges of the Torrone continued to follow the trail of the clothing stolen from Vittoria Piccinini.[37]

?> The brief summary of these cases suggests certain considerations. That no pillage is exactly the same as another is of little import, since we are dealing with events that by definition depend on contingencies; however, the similarities that emerge notwithstanding everything seem attributable to the specific circumstances in which these events took place. The violence of the pillagers was focused on the property of the new pontiff or on a group somehow protected by him (the Jews, for example). Their declared pretext of exercising a customary right, at the same time deep-rooted and transitory, connected to a totally exceptional situation, inspired actions and behavior with a recognizable ritual component.

Terms like *rite* and *ritual* are among the most inflated in the language of the social sciences. Alongside the accepted literal meaning of *cult ceremony* we find a series of usages that become increasingly metaphorical, all the way to the *courtship rituals* that the ethnologists attribute to certain animal species.[38] A metaphorical element, even though obviously weaker, is also carried by the expression *ritual pillages*. Of course rite here does not imply a set arrangement, to be followed with scrupulous exactitude but rather an open outline of behaviors, a scenario like those of the *commedia dell'arte*. We could compare the pillages to a "counterdrama" improvised on the "stage of the street."[39] Certainly these events developed in a way that discloses a symbolic component, not reducible to the pure and simple desire for gain. As we have seen, the fathers of the Council of Constance recognized in the pillagers' claim to the goods of the newly elected pope a form of reimbursement, more or less symbolic, with regard to whoever had arrived at the summit of power.

In a famous study E. P. Thompson defined as "moral economy" the complex of values that legitimized, in the eyes of their perpetrators, the bread riots that took place in England in the eighteenth century.[40] Similarly the phenomena that we have been considering seem infused with the same kinds of values. But why these values should have manifested themselves in precisely these circumstances still remains to be explained. Did the death of the bishop or of the pope have, in the eyes of the pillagers, something in common with the election of the latter?

Elze has emphasized that both cases involve a passage to a new condition, to a new identity, symbolized absolutely in the case of the papal election by the assumption of a new name. Nevertheless he has not interpreted the pillages that often accompanied these events as "rites of passage."[41] Other historians more inclined to use anthropological categories would not hesitate to move in this direction, a direction, however, that implies a difficulty often concealed by the somewhat demagogic antithesis between "traditional" history and "new" history. How far is it permissible or useful to employ in the historical analysis of specific situations categories developed in detail within totally different cultural contexts? The subject we are discussing throws some light on the implications of this question.

The category of "rites of passage" is generally associated with the book that A. Van Gennep published in 1909 with the same title (*Les rites de passage*). The book was the result, its author declared some time later, "of a kind of inner illumination that suddenly dispelled a sort of darkness in which I had been floundering for almost ten years."[42] But the reality was a little different. Van Gennep's "illumination" would not have been possible without his reading the study by R. Hertz, which appeared in 1907 in *Année sociologique* with the title "Contribution à l'étude sur la représentation collective de la mort."[43] On one page of *Rites de passage* Van Gennep cryptically alluded to this debt: the whole matter, which he himself had previously considered (in *Tabou et totémisme à Madagascar*, 1904) as a general collection of negative practices directed to circumscribing the impurity of the corpse, now appeared to him as "a marginal state" through which the survivors, and perhaps the dead person himself, were first separated and then reintegrated, respectively, in the society of the living and in the world of the dead. In a note Van Gennep referred to the ethnographic studies conducted by J. A. Wilken in Indonesia, the conclusions of which had been "generalized" by Hertz.[44] The reader of the note could not suspect the breadth of the generalization proposed by Hertz: to the rites of double burial he had juxtaposed those connected to initiation, birth, and marriage, and finally concluded that "to the social consciousness, death is only a particular instance of a general phenomenon."[45] We shall see shortly what this extension had suggested, but for now we can observe that the analysis of death, the passage *par excellence*, led Hertz to formulate clearly within the compass of rite the separation-marginality-aggregation sequence, later taken up and systematized by Van Gennep.[46]

This sequence, according to Van Gennep, should have a transcultural validity, being tied to the necessary stages of life (birth, social puberty, marriage, etc.); thus, from knowledge of the end one could derive by analogy the means, that is the rituals, that were employed.[47] But is it an analogy purely of form or also of content? A page in Hertz's study suggests that the second, certainly the more perplexing, is also a possibility. "The death of a chief," Hertz emphasizes, "causes a deep disturbance in the social body which, especially if it is prolonged, has weighty consequences. It often seems that the blow which strikes the head of the community in the sacred person of the chief has the effect of suspending temporarily the moral and political laws and of setting free the passions which are normally kept in check by the social order."[48] In a long note Hertz refers to testimony of missionaries or voyagers reporting on heterogeneous cultural locales: the islands of the Pacific (Fiji, the Sandwich and Caroline Islands) and the archipelago of the Marianas and Guinea. With respect to this last, he cites a passage from Bosman (1704): "'As soon as the king's death is public, everybody steals from his neighbor as best he can . . . without anyone having the right to punish, as if justice died with the king.' The thefts cease as soon as the successor is proclaimed."[49] It is impossible not to think of the pillages that follow the death of the bishops or the popes. But another reference to the study of the Rev. L. Fison on the funeral customs of the Fiji Islands (1880) uncovers an analogy still more surprising. At the death of the leader, the people run through the city, slaughter the animals, rob, and burn the houses, but this custom (widespread also in Central Africa "and elsewhere") is falling into disuse, as shown by the fact that in one area indiscriminate robbery strikes only the personal property of the deceased, while in another it is practiced only by the relatives of the deceased. According to Fison, in an interpretation not reported by Hertz, the vacuum of power led to the resurfacing of "the old communal idea": in the area of Navatu, this idea was expressed in a nonviolent form, through an exchange of mutual gifts.[50]

⁊❦ Many historians would not consider for even a moment the possibility that customs documented at Rome or at Bologna in the tenth or in the sixteenth centuries could be clarified by a comparison with customs prevalent in the Fiji Islands. Others would accept a comparison between facts so disparate only for "touristic" ends in order to observe a familiar documentation from an unfamiliar angle. Only a few, probably, would push through to the point of interpreting the eventual convergence between the two sets of facts as a single phenomenon, based on transcultural elements.[51] In every case the comparison with the ethnographic facts, either in its most prudent version, which simply seeks a hint for new questions, or in its most daring version, which does not exclude the possibility of discovering new answers, demands a preliminary critique of the evidence.

One fact immediately catches the eye. Hertz, who admittedly worked at second hand, obtained from his sources descriptions saturated with evaluations. He not only borrowed facts, then, but assimilated interpretations. The observation on the "temporary suspension of moral and political laws" following the loss of the sacred person of the leader took up and reelaborated Bosman's observation that it was "as if justice had died with the king." The apparently neutral allusion to the existence in certain societies of a "period of anarchy" after the death of the leader retraced literally Fison's sentence about the "wildest anarchy" that takes over in such circumstances. One could object that here *anarchy* is simply a synonym (with connotations that, at least for Fison, are clearly negative) for social disorder. But the comparison that follows immediately afterward in Hertz's note—"a kind of saturnalia"—was more compelling, because it carried with it a series of implicit references to rituals of social inversion, to recurring transgressions, and so forth. It happens that the same comparison had been proposed in a book, *The Legends and Myths of Hawaii* (1888), that carried on its frontispiece the name of His Majesty Kalakaua, king of Hawaii, and of the American diplomat R. M. Daggett. The latter (the self-styled editor but actually the author of the book)[52] affirmed that "at the death of the king, during the period of mourning, which sometimes lasted for weeks, the population indulged in an unbridled saturnalia of license and rashness. Any law might be openly violated, any crime might be openly committed."[53] Elsewhere Daggett juxtaposed the legends of the creation widespread in Hawaii with the Hebraic ones (not ruling out a remote common origin) and discovered in the indigenous mythology figures parallel to Helen, Paris, Agamemnon.[54]

Hertz, who does not cite Daggett, could have formulated the comparison with the saturnalia in a totally independent manner. Similarly, the reference to the "carnival and to the Saturnalia" made by M. Sahlins in regard to other rites practiced in the Sandwich Islands does not necessarily echo Hertz.[55] But Daggett's example emphasizes, almost to the point of caricature, the obvious paradox implicit in any interpretation, even in any description: an unknown reality can be approached only through necessarily approximate and potentially deformative models drawn from a known reality.[56] The projection of cultural models familiar to the observer is, in an early stage, necessary to organize the facts, if not absolutely to perceive them. In approaching civilizations of other continents, European travelers and scholars often make use, sometimes without realizing it, of the knowledge and categories derived from Greek and Roman antiquity (the term *rite*, for example) as indispensable instruments of orientation.[57] In this way the premises were set for a projection in the opposite direction, that is to say, for the consideration of Greek or Roman antiquity from an anthropological perspective. Even the global and transcultural consideration of the rites associated with birth, marriage, and death as purification rites had been suggested to Hertz in a note in *Sibillinische Blätter* in which H. Diels, in a dispute with Wilamowitz, interpreted elements of Greek and Roman religion from an implicitly anthropological point of view, derived from Usener, their common teacher.[58] Recently H. S. Versnel made use of Hertz's study in order to interpret as manifestations of the anomie, called forth by a chaotic situation, the scenes of transgressive desperation (stoning of temples, exposing of newborn infants, etc.) that, according to Suetonius, followed the death of Germanicus (A.D. 19).[59]

?❧ Between Daggett's exaggerated ethnocentrism and Hertz's cautious suggestion of connections drawn from Greek or Roman religion, there is, naturally, a profound difference. In the second case one can speak of true and proper comparison: the initial interpretive model is corrected on the basis of new elements drawn from specific documentation. For example, the association between the death of the king and the death of justice, which had been suggested to Bosman by his observation of the funeral rites in Guinea, becomes reformulated by Hertz with regard to the Sandwich Islands through the notion of

taboo, which Frazer had juxtaposed to the Latin term *sacer*, emphasizing the ambivalence of both.[60] The trangressions, including pillages,
that follow the death of the leader are comparable with those that
follow the violation of a *taboo*: "The death of a chief is a veritable
sacrilege, for which his entourage must bear the punishment."[61] But
this is not an interpretation offered by the natives, but rather by Hertz.
One of his sources, the Protestant missionary W. Ellis, who, scan-
dalized by what he saw, left a reticent description of the "enormi-
ties"—self-mutilation, fires, pillages, sometimes murders, "every sort
of vice"—committed in the Sandwich Islands at the death of the
leaders, asked the natives, whose language he had learned, why they
behaved in this way: the grief was such that it reduced them to madness, they answered.[62] It is, comments the anthropologist W. Davenport, a matter of rationalization: "The license also seems to have
symbolized the temporary state of anarchy and suspension of the
divine mandate to rule."[63]

It was symbolic but for whom? For the actors in the rite or for
their observers, direct or indirect? After all, the points of view of the
former and that of the latter are by no means inevitably coincident.[64]
Through the comparison it is possible, in principle, to reconstruct a
significance no less authentic than that embodied in the lived experience, which in its turn is identical with neither the conscious experience nor the experience that has left a documentary trail. In the
direct or reelaborated ethnographic evidence, of rituals of funeral
transgression, the distinction between these interpretive levels often
appears anything but clear.

⅋ The same difficulty arises when we interpret the "ritual pillages"
as rites of passage. To our eyes this category is the only one that
unifies, beyond the morphological analogies, the series of phenomena
we have taken into consideration. Whether and how the series came
to be perceived by the pillagers is an open question. It is worthwhile
to note, however, that recourse to the rites of passage seemed at first
to imply the risk of a mechanical projection on to Rome or Bologna
of the data that had emerged from Guinea or the Pacific Islands. Now
we have seen a different risk taking shape: of uncontrollable contamination, rather than of ethnocentrism in reverse. These data, indeed,
do appear imbued with elements derived from cultural horizons very
much closer to us, which have inevitably, even if partially, conditioned
the perception of direct or indirect observers: the "justice that dies

with the king" of Bosman, the "old communal idea" of Fison, the saturnalia of Hertz, the "suspension of the divine mandate to rule" of Davenport. Can reports like these, in which description and interpretation interlace so closely, throw some light on the phenomena that formed our starting point?

Perhaps they can illuminate a great deal but more by contrast than by similarity. The grief and the despair that infused the funereal transgressions of the Sandwich Islands or those totally exceptional ones aroused by the death of Germanicus turn out to be totally extraneous to the pillages that followed the death of a bishop or a pope. Certainly the "frantic gaiety" manifested by the Roman mob at the death of Paul IV had contingent motives. But this same term *gaiety* came to designate commonly the festivals, often accompanied by pillages, with which the enthronement of the new pontiff or of lay princes was celebrated. In the Italy of the medieval period and the early modern age, manifestations of violence and manifestations of joy turn out to be closely associated.

The symmetry between the two types of pillages (those for the death of the pope and those for his election) undoubtedly constitutes a distinguishing feature of the phenomena that we are discussing. The banal wisdom of the proverb, "a pope is dead, another is made," alludes to a phenomenon not at all banal—the perpetuation of the institution precisely where, by definition, the biological continuity was broken. At Rome, the power vacuum created by the vacant seat offered the possibility for two consecutive pillages, one hard upon the other. Outside of Rome the occasions were rarer, but when they presented themselves they were exploited conscientiously, in Bologna as well as in the little villages around Mantua.

⁓ Violence against defined targets, in great part tolerated by the authorities and sometimes, as in Felonica, carried out by the entire community, gave shape to situations obviously not identifiable with chaos or with anomie. In the violent affirmation of the right to pillage—at the same time customary and transitory—values and tensions suddenly came to the surface that had been latent in normal times and that, for that reason, had generally been undocumented. From this fact we can see the symptomatic value of a marginal phenomenon like the pillages that we have defined as ritual. The research, of which we are presenting the first results, can be compared with an experiment that explores the reactions of an organism in an exceptional situation.[65]

Notes

1. These pages, written in anticipation of a more extensive work, come out of an investigation begun in 1983, in which the following individuals took part: Valeria Balbi, Dora Anna Barelli, Silvia Campanini, Silvia Evangelisti, Lorena Grassi, Mirella Plazzi, Raffaella Sarti, Anna Maria Semprevivo, Maria Teresa Torri, and, serving as coordinator, Carlo Ginzburg. The text that follows has been edited by the last, on the basis of the group's discussions.

2. The expression comes from Philibert Babou d'Angoulême, ambassador to Rome, in a letter to the cardinal of Lorraine. See G. Ribier, *Lettres et Mémoires d'Estat, des Roys, Princes, Ambassadeurs . . .*, vol. 2 (Paris, 1666), pp. 827–28.

3. See, in addition to L. von Pastor, *Storia dei papi . . .*, Italian trans., vol. 6 (Rome, 1943), pp. 584ff. [*The History of the Popes*, vol. 14 (London, 1924), pp. 415–16], P. Nores, "Storia della guerra degli Spagnuoli contro papa Paolo IV," *Archivio storico italiano*, 1st. ser., 12 (1847): 276–78; G. Duruy, *Le cardinal Carlo Carafa . . .* (Paris, 1882), pp. 304–5.

4. The principal events are set forth by R. De Maio, *Alfonso Carafa* (Vatican City, 1961), pp. 63ff.

5. See H. Jedin, "Il figlio di Isabella d'Este: Il cardinale Ercole Gonzaga," in *Chiesa della fede, Chiesa della storia*, Italian trans., with preface by G. Alberigo (Brescia, 1976), pp. 499–512.

6. Archivio di Stato di Mantova (hereafter, ASM), *Archivio Gonzaga, Libri del Copialettere*, b. 2945, libro 349, pp. 182r–182v.

7. One of these men was named Rafael Vigevano: see S. Simonsohn, *History of the Jews in the Duchy of Mantua* (1962; rpt. Jerusalem, 1977), p. 223, n. 87. The man who kept the bank in Revere was, rather, Vita (Haim) Massarano, whose sister had married the celebrated man of letters and philosopher Azarià de Rossi (p. 218). See also E. Castelli, "I banchi feneratizi ebraici nel Mantovano (1386–1808)," *Atti e memorie dell'Accademia Virgiliana di Mantova* 31 (1959): 235–40 (on Revere), 250–55 (on Sermide). On this latter place, see V. Colorni, "Gli ebrei a Sermide. Cinque secoli di storia," in *Scritti in memoria di Sally Mayer (1875–1953)* (Jerusalem, 1956), pp. 35–72.

8. ASM, *Archivio Gonzaga, Corrispondenza fra Mantova e i Paesi dello Stato*, b. 2567 (October 19, 1559). On Felonica, see the entry in the *Dictionnaire d'histoire et géographie ecclésiastiques* (Paris, 1912).

9. See R. Elze, "'Sic transit gloria mundi': La morte del papa nel Medioevo," *Annali dell'Istituto storico italo-germanico in Trento* 3 (1977): 23–41; Cf. idem, *Päpste-Kaiser-Könige und die mittelalterliche Herrschaftssymbolik*, ed. B. Schimmelpfennig and L. Schmugge (London, 1982).

10. Concerning all this, see the documentation collected by G. Moroni, *Dizionario di erudizione storico-ecclesiastica*, vol. 11 (Venice, 1841), s.v. "Cella," pp. 66–68; vol. 20 (Venice, 1843), s.v. "difensori, o difensore," p. 45; vol. 50 (Venice, 1851), s.v. "Palazzo, o Palagio," pp. 198–99; vol. 69 (Venice, 1854), s.v. "Spogli ecclesiastici," p. 4. There is abundant literary evidence, beginning with Boccaccio's novella about Andreuccio da Perugia (*Decameron*, second day, novella 5). See also D. Gnoli, *La Roma de Leon X* (Milan, 1938), p. 81 (on the plundering of the corpse of Cardinal d'Estouteville). The attack on the residence of the newly elected pope has been rightly associated with the destruction of the baldacchino of the bishop (or the pope) in the ceremony that followed their election: see G. Belvederi, "Cerimonie nel solenne ingresso dei Vescovi in Bologna durante il Medio Evo," *Rassegna Gregoriana* (March–May 1913): 172.

11. See G. D. Mansi, *Sacrorum Conciliorum nova, et amplissima collectio*, vol. 7 (Florence, 1762), col. 390 (hereafter abbreviated, Mansi).

12. Mansi, 8: 614–15, 619ff. See also Mansi, 8: 836 (conc. Aurelianese, a. 533); 10: 541–42 (conc. Parisiense, a. 615; conc. Cabilonense, a. 650 circa); 11: 28–29 (conc. Toletanum, a. 655).

13. See *Le Liber Pontificalis*, ed. L. Duchesne, vol. 2 (Paris, 1955), p. 192. Besides ecclesiastical vestments, jewelry and money were stored in the *vestiarium* (according to Du Cange, s.v.). The pillage of the *vestiarium* by Isaac, exarch of Ravenna, in 640 immediately after the election of Pope Severinus, seems instead to be an episode of another kind, because it was tied to specific political circumstances, even if it was facilitated, probably, by the seat being vacant. See *Le Liber Pontificalis*, pp. 328–29; O. Bertolini, *Roma di fronte a Bisanzio e ai Longobardi* (Rome, 1941), pp. 322ff.; Idem, "Il patrizio Isacio esarca d'Italia (625–643)," *Scritti scelti di storia medioevale*, vol. 1 (Livorno, 1968), pp. 65–68. For a different opinion, see G. A. Ghisalberti, *Il diritto di regalia sui benefici ecclesiastici in Italia (spogli e vacanze)* (Pavia, 1914), pp. 8–9.

14. See Mansi, 18: 225–26.

15. See C. Baronius, *Annales Ecclesiastici*, vol. 17 (Lucca, 1745), pp. 59–60; F. Dressler, *Petrus Damiani Leben und Werk* (Rome, 1954), p. 105. See also V. Petra, *Commentaria ad Constitutiones Apostolicas seu Bullas singulas Summorum Pontificum*, vol. 1 (Rome, 1705), pp. 156ff. S. Prete writes, without basis, about the "popular reaction to the contemptible spectacle of unscrupulous trafficking in the goods of the church," in "S. Pier Damiani, le chiese marchigiane, la riforma del secolo XI," *Studia Picena* 19 (1949): 123; the identification of the bishop of Osimo with Gislerius (p. 124), if correct, necessitates a modification of the date of the latter's death—1057—proposed by L. Bartoccetti, ibid. 15 (1940): 108.

16. ". . . Romani, aestimantes illum [i.e., Leo IX] mortuum esse, Lateranense adeunt palatium, quatinus more solito omnem illius diriperent suppellectilem." See S. Borgia, *Memorie istoriche della pontificia città di Benevento*, vol. 2 (Rome, 1764), p. 327, in note.

17. See G. Mollat, "A propos du droit de dépouille," *Revue d'histoire ecclésiastique* 39 (1933): 316–43, in particular p. 323. Concerning participation by clerics in these events, see the much later pages (not referring to Rome) of the Neapolitan jurist, S. Mattei, *Saggio di risoluzioni di diritto pubblico ecclesiastico*, vol. 1 (Turin, 1745), pp. 1–96, in particular p. 16: "whoever would like to see a lively picture of militant licentiousness in the pillage of enemy cities should go back to the death of the bishop in order to observe those one would have thought were sober, continent, etc., attain the greediness of a whale." This description, even if written with polemic intention, seems reliable.

18. See [Vanel], *Histoire des Conclaves depuis Clément V jusqu'à présent*, 3d ed., vol. 1 (Cologne, 1703), pp. 15–16, on the conclave of 1378, in which Pope Urban VI was elected. This work, which contains numerous references to pillages, draws largely on manuscript chronicles: for example, the pages on the events following the death of Sixtus IV (pp. 55–56) translate the *Diaria Rerum Romanarum* of Stefano Infessura. See the edition by O. Tommasini (Rome, 1890), pp. 161–62. The bull of Leo X is reproduced in *Bullarum privilegiorum ac diplomatum Romanorum pontificum amplissima collectio*, vol. 3, part 3 (Rome, 1743), pp. 423–24. See also the decree "Contra invadentes domos cardinalium" of the Fifth Lateran Council, in *Conciliorum oecumenicorum decreta*, ed. G. Alberigo et al. (Bologna, 1973), pp. 649–50.

19. See *Pii II Commentarii rerum memorabilium quae temporibus suis contigerunt*,

vol. 1, ed. A. van Heck (Vatican City, 1984), pp. 106–7. The two passages are mistakenly conflated in [Vanel], *Histoire des Conclaves*, 1: 47–48.

20. See Mansi, 21: 826–27. See also ibid., 20: 818–19 (conclave of Clairemont, 1095); 21: 227 (conclave of Toulouse, called in 1119 by Pope Calixtus II): "Primitias, decimas, oblationes, et coemeteria, domos etiam et bona caetera deficientis episcopi, et clericorum, a principibus vel quibuslibet laicis diripi et teneri, penitus interdicimus."

21. See G. Mollat, "Dépouille (droit de)," in *Dictionnaire de droit canonique* (Paris, 1935). By the same, "A propos du droit" and "L'application du droit de dépouille sous Jean XXII," *Revue des sciences réligieuses* 19 (1939): 50ff.

22. See Elze, "Sic transit," pp. 31–34.

23. Ibid., pp. 35–36; to the bibliography cited, add A. Solmi, "La distruzione del palazzo regio in Pavia nell'anno 1024," *Rendiconti del R. Istituto Lombardo di scienze lettere e arti* 57 (1924): 351–64; M. Bloch, *La société féodale. Les classes et le gouvernement des hommes* (Paris, 1940), p. 196 [*Feudal Society*, vol. 2: *Social Classes and Political Organization* (Chicago, 1961), p. 409].

24. See F. Porchnow, *Das Spolienrecht und die Testierfähigkeit der Geistlichen im Abendland b.z. 13 Jh.* (1919).

25. See E. Muir, *Civic Ritual in Renaissance Venice* (Princeton, 1981), p. 269.

26. See ibid., p. 29, n. 19. D. Cantimori dwelt on this theme in his Neapolitan seminar on the *De cardinalatu* of Paolo Cortese: see S. Bertelli, "All'Istituto Italiano per gli studi Storici," *Belfagor* 22 (1967): 318–19.

27. Archivio di Stato di Bologna (hereafter, ASB), *Assunteria di sede vacante. Diari di sede vacante 1730–1775*, fasc. 1740; *Senato, Diario (1714–1749)*, n. 12, *Giornale di quanto si è fatto dal Senato . . .* , bound in separately numbered section, fol. 1v.

28. See Mansi, 27: 1170; see also H. B. P., *Traicté sommaire de l'élection des papes*, 3d ed., expanded (Paris, 1605), pp. 14–15.

29. ASM, *Archivio Gonzaga, Corrispondenza fra Mantova e i Paesi dello Stato*, b. 2567 (September 20 and 21, 1559).

30. Ibid., b. 2568 (April 20, 1559).

31. ASB, *Tribunale del Torrone*, b. 2338, fols. 207v–238v, 254v–264v, 282v–289v.

32. ASM, *Archivio Gonzaga, Copialettere*, b. 2927, libro 269 (January 5 and 9, 1522).

33. ASB, *Tribunale del Torrone*, b. 5111, fols. 94r–103v, 167r–183v, 252r–272v, 299r–348v.

34. Ibid., b. 5100, fols. 191r–193v, 374r–399v, 404r.

35. Ibid., b. 5120, fols. 85r–86v, 349r-v.

36. Ibid., b. 5110, fols. 103r–108v, 113r–123r, 125r–130v, 140r–152v, 172r–173r, 194r–197v, 201r–204r, 223r–v, 232r–235r, 236v–240v, 243v–244v, 246r–253v, 280r–289v, 297r–314v, 322v–325v, plus four loose pages and one fly sheet; b. 5120, fols. 19r–27r; 31r–45v; 58r–v.

37. Ibid., fols. 123v–125r, 163r–v, 204v, 221r–224r, 231v–232r, 235r–236r, 240v–246r, 251r.

38. See *Ritualization of Behaviour in Animals and Man*, ed. J. Huxley, Philosophical Transactions of the Royal Society of London, vol. 251, no. 772 (London, 1966).

39. See E. P. Thompson, "Folclore, antropologia e storia sociale," in *Società patrizia, cultura plebea*, Italian trans. (Turin, 1981), p. 318 [originally published as "Folklore, Anthropology and Social History," *Indian Historical Review* 3, no. 2 (January 1978): 247–66]. There are useful observations of a general nature under the heading "Rito" by V. Valeri, in *Enciclopedia Einaudi*, vol. 12 (Turin, 1981), pp. 210–43.

40. See E. P. Thompson. "L'economia morale delle classi popolari inglesi nel secolo XVIII," in *Società patrizia*, pp. 57–136 [originally published as "The Moral Economy of the English Crowd in the Eighteenth Century," *Past and Present* 50 (1971): 76–136].

41. See Elze, "Sic transit," pp. 28–29.

42. See N. Belmont, *Arnold van Gennep*, English trans. (Chicago, 1979), p. 58. [The original French text is from 1974.]

43. See R. Hertz, *Sulla rappresentazione collettiva della morte*, introd. P. Angelini (Rome, 1978). [Hertz's "A Contribution to the Study of the Collective Representation of Death," is in *Death and the Right Hand* (Glencoe, Ill., 1960), which also contains his "The Pre-Eminence of the Right Hand: A Study in Religious Polarity."] Regarding Hertz, see also R. Needham's preface to the collection, edited by him, *Right and Left: Essays on Dual Symbolic Classification* (Chicago, 1973).

44. See A. Van Gennep, *Les rites de passage* (Paris, 1909), pp. 210–11 (*I riti di passaggio*, Italian trans., introd. F. Remotti [Turin, 1981]; pp. 128 and 201, nn. 1 and 2).

45. See R. Hertz, *Sulla rappresentazione*, p. 89 [*Death and the Right Hand*, p. 81]. This very definite affirmation contradicts the judgment of N. Belmont, according to whom the credit should go to Van Gennep, and not to Hertz, for having shifted the emphasis from the similarities of content to similarities of form among various rituals (*Arnold Van Gennep*, pp. 64–65). Actually, as is stated immediately afterward, Hertz takes both into account.

46. The priority of Hertz has already been indicated by H. S. Versnel in a very rich essay that will be discussed more at length in the definitive version of this research (thanks to Xavier Arce for the reference): see "Destruction, Devotio and Despair in a Situation of Anomy: The Mourning for Germanicus in Triple Perspective," in *Perennitas. Studi in onore di Angelo Brelich*, ed. M. Piccaluga (Rome, 1980), pp. 541–618, esp. p. 581, n. 182 (and, further, n. 55). E. E. Evans Pritchard instead limits himself to emphasizing the usefulness of a comparison between the two scholars (see the introduction to R. Hertz, *Death and the Right Hand*, trans. R. Needham and C. Needham [Glencoe, Ill., 1960], pp. 15–16). According to M. Gluckman, who finds *Les rites de passage* "rather boring," Van Gennep departed from the territorial passages to construct a model valid for all the rites of passage. See "Les rites de passage," in *Il rituale nei rapporti sociali*, ed. M. Gluckman, Italian trans. (Rome, 1972), pp. 19, 21, 25, 29 [*Essays on the Ritual of Social Relations* (Manchester, 1962)]; see also F. Remotti, in Van Gennep, *I riti di passaggio*, p. xviii. As we have seen, however, Van Gennep's account of his "discovery" does not coincide with its genesis.

47. See Van Gennep, *I riti di passaggio*, p. 5 [*Rites of Passage*, p. 3]. Belmont (*Arnold Van Gennep*, p. 45) states instead that for Van Gennep the "rites of passage" comprise a schema that is purely methodological and seeks to give order to the confused mass of ethnographic data.

48. See Hertz, *Sulla rappresentazione*, pp. 58–59 [*Death and the Right Hand*, p. 49].

49. Ibid., p. 106, n. 127 [in English, pp. 129–30, n. 127]. The citation has been rechecked and integrated with the French translation (*Voyage de Guinée*, [Utrecht, 1705]) to which Hertz refers. On the text of Bosman (which is used by Bayle), see A. M. Iacono, *Teorie del feticismo* (Milano, 1985), pp. 13ff.

50. See L. Fison, "Notes on Fijan Burial Customs," *Journal of the Anthropological Institute* 10 (1880): 137–49, esp. 140–41, which refer also to T. Williams, *Fiji and the Fijans* (this last citation has not been checked).

51. This is a matter of one of the interpretive lines (the third, psychosociological and anthropological) followed by Versnel, *Destruction*.

52. R. Daggett, a picturesque figure who was a gold hunter and journalist, on the advice of his editor, friend, and ex-colleague, Samuel Clemens, alias Mark Twain, had, for publicity purposes, transformed the presumed informer Kalakaua into coauthor (the book, nevertheless, was a fiasco): see F. P. Weisenburger, *Idol of the West: The Fabulous Career of Rollin Mallory Daggett* (Syracuse, 1965), pp. 156ff.

53. *The Legends and Myths of Hawaii: The Fables and Folklore of a Strange People*, by His Hawaiian Majesty Kalakaua, edited with an introduction by Hon. R. M. Daggett (New York, 1888), p. 59. [The editors have been unable to check the original English of this quote. Thus, what appears is a translation from the Italian.]

54. Ibid, pp. 33–35, 69ff., 117ff.

55. See M. Sahlins, *Historical Metaphors and Mythical Realities: Structure in the Early History of the Sandwich Islands Kingdom* (Ann Arbor, Mich., 1981), p. 19. A specific juxtaposition to the saturnalia, with other bibliographical references, is in H. S. Versnel, *Destruction*, pp. 587ff.

56. See the illuminating pages of E. H. Gombrich, *Art and Illusion: A Study in the Psychology of Pictorial Representation* (New York, 1960), pp. 63–90.

57. See A. Momigliano, "Il posto della storiografia antica nella storiografia moderna," in *Sui fondamenti della storia antica* (Turin, 1984), p. 52.

58. See Hertz, *Sulla rappresentazione*, p. 124, n. 315 [*Death and the Right Hand*, p. 149, n. 315], which refers to H. Diels, *Sybillinische Blätter* (Berlin, 1890), pp. 48–49, n. 2, observing: "It is a matter, however, of seeing why in these three moments of life a purification should be necessary." The passage of Hertz (although not its source) is mentioned by Versnel, *Destruction*, p. 581, n. 182. On the difficult relationship between Usener and Wilamowitz, see the beautiful page of A. Momigliano's "New Paths of Classicism in the Nineteenth Century," *History and Theory* 21, no. 4 (1982), Beiheft 21: 35–36; on p. 37, Diels is defined as "perhaps, among Usener's students, the one most dear to him."

59. See Versnel, *Destruction*.

60. See Hertz, *Sulla rappresentazione*, p. 106, n. 127 [*Death and the Right Hand*, p. 129, n. 127], and *Encyclopaedia Britannica*, s.v. "Taboo," reprinted in J. G. Frazer, *Garnered Sheaves* (London, 1931), p. 92.

61. [For the quotation see Hertz references in previous note.] The destruction of the system of the *kapu* (*taboo*) in the Hawaiian Islands in 1819 was provoked by the conscious prolongation of the ritual transgression that followed the death of the king: see Sahlins, *Historical Metaphors*, p. 65 (with further bibliography).

62. See W. Ellis, *Polynesian Researches*, 4th ed., vol. 4 (London, 1859), pp. 175ff. See also the lengthy introductory essay by C. W. Newbury, prefacing the French translation: *A la recherche de la Polynésie d'autrefois*, 2 vols. (Paris, 1972).

63. See W. Davenport, "The 'Hawaiian Cultural Revolution': Some Political and Economic Considerations," *American Anthropologist* 71 (1969): 10, which also cites among its sources *The Legends and Myths of Hawaii* by Daggett.

64. See K. L. Pike, *Language in Relation to a Unified Theory of Structure of Human Behavior*, 2d ed. rev. (The Hague, 1967), pp. 37ff., on the distinction between "etic" and "emic" points of view (respectively external and internal to a particular linguistic or cultural system; the two terms are modeled on "phonetic" and "phonemic"). The author observes (p. 39) that the distinction was in a certain sense anticipated by E. Sapir, to whom the book is dedicated.

65. See E. Grendi, "Microanalisi e storia sociale," *Quaderni storici* 35 (1977): 512; C. Ginzburg and C. Poni, "Il nome e il come: scambio ineguale e mercato storiografico," ibid. 40 (1979): 187–88. [The latter is reprinted, in English translation, in the present volume.]

4 ?& The Ox's Bones and the Ox's Hide: A Popular Myth, Part Hagiography and Part Witchcraft

by Maurizio Bertolotti

For these things were done, that the Scripture should be fulfilled: "A bone of him shall not be broken."

—John 19:36

To us, Zilia is little more than a name. All that remains from the proceedings brought against her in 1519 by the Inquisition of Modena is the brief deposition given by a witness, a certain Giovanni da Rodigo, before Father Bartolomeo da Pisa of the Order of Preachers.

Giovanni describes a ritual that is not mentioned elsewhere in the surviving court records of Modena: a woman, taken once to the witches' sabbat (*ad cursum*) by Zilia's mother, recounted that among the things they ate on that occasion was an ox, whose bones were then gathered into the hide, "and the mistress of the sabbat, arriving at last, beat on the ox's hide with a staff, and the ox appeared to come to life again."[1]

At this point in the interrogation, which went according to the usual pattern, suddenly there is a note of surprise. At Giovanni's revelations, the priest is unable to hide his confusion, and he asks the witness whether the person who told him these things, a certain Mariotto, "told them seriously or more as a joke" (*diceret hec serio vel potius ioco*).[2]

As we shall see, Giovanni da Rodigo's account, as well as the priest's reaction and the reasons behind it, holds great interest for the historian of popular religion.

?& It turns out that the priest we have seen questioning Giovanni da Rodigo[3] was none other than the Dominican Friar, Bartolomeo Spina, author of the famous *Quaestio de strigibus*.[4] Spina held the office of

---

Maurizio Bertolotti, "Le ossa e la pelle dei buoi: un mito popolare tra agiografia e stregoneria," *Quaderni storici*, no. 41 (1979): 470–99.

vicar to the inquisitor of Modena and Ferrara (then Antonio Beccari)[5] from 1518 to 1520, during which time he conducted numerous trials, most of them concerning cases of witchcraft.[6]

The *Quaestio de strigibus*, published in 1523, was written during the stormy days when our vicar was going after witches.[7] This work can help us to understand the reasons behind the question that Fra Bartolomeo put to Giovanni da Rodigo: we can in fact find a specific reference there to the mysterious ritual of the resurrection of the oxen. In the trial *contra Ziliam*, it is stated that, "when they were in place she saw . . . many others there, and they both ate and drank, and among other things they ate a cooked ox all of whose bones they threw onto the ox's hide, and the mistress of the sabbat, arriving at last, beat on the ox's hide with a staff and the ox appeared to come to life again." The *Quaestio de strigibus* reads, "For they say that after they had eaten some fat ox meat, . . . the mistress . . . ordered all the bones of the dead ox to be collected on its stretched out hide, and folding it on four sides over the bones, and beating it with the staff, she rendered the ox alive as before."[8]

The correspondence between these two texts is almost perfect, indicating that the source for Spina's account was the interrogations that he was in the process of conducting in the Monastery of San Domenico. We can rule out, furthermore, the possibility that Spina might have taken these reports from an earlier demonologist. I could find no references to this belief in any work concerning witchcraft prior to the treatise by Spina, with the exception of the *Lamiarum sive striarum opusculum*, written about 1460 by Girolamo Visconti, a Dominican from Lombardy, and the *Tractatus de strigibus* by Bernardo Rategno, written in 1508. Granted that Fra Bartolomeo might have known these two works (and that is not demonstrable given the fact that in the *Quaestio* only the *Malleus maleficarum* is cited), the discrepancies among these texts only confirm the argument that he was drawing on experience as his source. Visconti's account, in fact, lacks the detail of the ox's hide on which Fra Bartolomeo's witches gather the bones after the banquet, while we find the added detail that the witches ate children as well as oxen.[9] Rategno makes one fleeting reference, denying reality to the idea "that they eat the calves who afterward rise up again through the power of Demons."[10] He makes no mention at all of the *domina cursus*.

All of this confirms what had already emerged from the verbal record of the trial—that is, that the ritual of the oxen's resurrection had aroused in Spina a very particular interest. What is surprising, though, is the fidelity of his account, accustomed as we are to assuming that the testimony of written sources can provide only a distorted picture of the culture of the subordinate classes, especially if we are dealing with sources hostile in spirit to their subject.[11]

🪶 Our object now will be to examine the context surrounding the passage quoted from the *Quaestio*.

In the first two chapters of his work, Spina lines up a series of arguments in support of the thesis, which he was preparing to refute "on the false side of the question" (*pro parte quaestionis falsa*), that the experiences recounted by the witches were merely imaginary.[12] With the exception of the passage from the *Canon Episcopi*, whose interpretation was the particular focus between 1400 and 1600 for the polemic concerning the reality of witchcraft and witches' sabbats,[13] the arguments referred to by Spina all take their source and substance from the accounts of the witches. These pages, therefore, are a precious source for our knowledge of witchcraft in Emilia during the early sixteenth century.

However, it appears incredible, explains Fra Bartolomeo, that the witches could have feasted during their nocturnal banquets on great rounds of cheese and fat oxen stolen from the households of the noble and the rich since nothing in fact was ever missed in those households. Furthermore, the witches themselves add that upon returning from their meetings they felt just as afflicted and hungry as they did on the nights when they did not attend. But even more incredible is the witches' persistent assertion that the *domina cursus*, who presides over their gatherings, should not only have restored the baskets of bread and flasks of wine to their original fullness but should also have brought the oxen back to life. We are dealing with miraculous works that can be accomplished only by God or by means of divine power. It is a sin to attribute them to the devil, and so it seems we must infer, concludes Spina, that "all these things happen through illusion."[14]

In effect both Rategno and Visconti had arrived at this same conclusion: for the former, however, the recognition that both the meal and the resurrection of the calves were illusions produced by the devil still did not call into question the reality of the witches' meeting;[15] Visconti, on the other hand, denied the existence of the witches, their maleficent activities, and their pact with the devil.[16]

If, however, we consider the writers involved in the witchcraft polemic that began in Emilia around 1520,[17] we cannot identify with the same certainty exactly who used this story of the oxen as a demonstration of the fantastic, illusory nature of the nocturnal meetings: neither Ponzinibio, who aims his critiques at the theory of a real demonic transport, nor Alciato makes reference to the oxen.[18] On the other hand, there is a mysterious but pertinent allusion by Pietro Pomponazzi in the *De incantationibus*. In a passage in his chapter 8, Peretto begins talking about cases of men being resurrected, cases passed down from sacred and pagan stories. Then, however, he inadvertently goes on to discuss animals that have died and been resuscitated, reminiscent of the oxen of the popular belief: "For if that was truly seen by some and not merely recounted as a fiction, such animals must not have been really dead, just as is often seen in our times . . . if it was a true resurrection, it was not, however, by demons, but in fact by God himself."[19] This last phrase is significant: indeed it is true that Pomponazzi did not believe in miracles by God, either, but in his eyes the position of Catholic theology (which on this occasion he repeats voluntarily, writing that "no created power can bring someone directly back from death, this truly belongs only to God")[20] had the additional merit, in contrast to the opinion of the "crowd" (*volgo*), of circumscribing the stormy eruption of personal forces, whether angelic or demonic, within the impersonal order of nature.

Many of the items contained in the exordium to the *Quaestio* are also referred to by Giovan Francesco Pico della Mirandola, in his dialogue *Stryx sive de ludificatione daemonum*.[21] He recalls, among other things, that, during their sabbat, the witches eat and drink and kill oxen, and he does not miss pointing out, in this regard, the trick (*praestigium*) involving the folded-up hide of the ox they had already eaten that rises onto its feet (*complicatae pellis comesti iam bovis et exsurgentis in pedes*).[22] It is Dicaste himself, the inquisitor of the dialogue, who with one terse phrase demolishes the credibility of the oxen's resurrection: "They appeared to be mockeries concerning the oxen."[23]

The judgment of this strenuous defender of Catholic orthodoxy reinforces our opinion that even those most convinced of the reality of witchcraft probably did not believe or at least doubted the ritual of the oxen's resurrection. It is reasonable to suppose then that in the exordium to the *Quaestio*, which, more than other places, seems to reflect Spina's inquisitorial experience, he should have poured out his own doubts as well as those circulating within the environment of the Inquisition's tribunal.

?❧ It is plausible that the witches' accounts of their meetings (the *cursus*) should have puzzled the inquisitors of Modena, if we consider that for them this constituted a "discovery," a new fact to be added to the current case histories of individual sorceries (*maleficia*): "*Most astonished by the novelty of the material*, they very insistently asked me to put in writing the things that concern *this strange matter*," recalls Fra Bartolomeo referring to the legal experts whom he had called together before passing sentence against a Ferrarese woman guilty of having participated in a witches' meeting.[24]

This material about the *cursus* is new and strange for our learned doctors, and even more so for Spina, who lived his first "pastoral" experience in Modena after completing a brilliant career as teacher of theology, all within the walls of Dominican schools and monasteries.[25] Accustomed to being around teachers and students of the *scientia consequentiarum*, of a religion nourished by Thomistic rationalism, how could he not be surprised to discover a world of religious ideas and magical actions apparently so foreign to the schemata of metaphysics and Christian ethics? The devil must therefore have seemed much more threatening and various than what Spina had known in the *De Malo* of Aquinas, and perhaps even than what he had known in the course of the "heretic" Pomponazzi's polemic on the immortality of the soul. ("The Devil singled you out, among all the others, as his most appropriate channel for spreading his poisons through the weak souls of all his followers," he apostrophized in his *Flagellum*.)[26]

Before 1518 then, Spina had not concerned himself with witchcraft.[27] Once arrived at Modena, in order to confront his new task he certainly had to take cognizance of the *Malleus maleficarum*, as well as of the papal documents of Innocent VIII and Julius II on the *secta maleficarum*. These texts, however, which Spina certainly knew since he quotes them, do not mention the witches' nocturnal meeting, the "sabbat"; they concentrate rather on the individual *maleficia*, which Spina excludes deliberately from the purview of his own research.[28] That the whole world was stained by such crimes was an established fact for Spina, one that had already been fully investigated (*exploratissimum*). He was interested instead in *new* material about the *cursus*.

But why new, if so many writers in the course of the fifteenth century had already discussed the witches' nocturnal rituals? This problem deserves special study. On the one hand it seems untenable that the already classic image of the diabolical sabbat was not known in the environment of the Holy Office of Modena, when we find it already affirmed at a popular level in a series of celebrated trials in northern Italy in the fifteenth and sixteenth centuries.[29] On the other hand we wonder why Spina did not ever quote Nider or Mamoris or Jaquier, who, if he had read them closely, could have provided help for his task. And if, in particular, he knew the *Opusculum* of Visconti or the *Tractatus* of Rategno, then he must also have known the story of the oxen. It is, therefore, hard to explain Spina's incredulous surprise at the revelations of Giovanni da Rodigo, surprise expressed in the eloquent question, "but did Mariottus say this seriously or more as a joke?"

Now, in light of the information outlined in the preceding pages, we can appreciate the full extent of that question: Fra Bartolomeo's surprise, in the context of a new fact that cannot be categorized among the known doctrinal schemata, is a measure of the abyss that separated Catholic knowledge from the culture of the peasants. At this point in the discussion, however, it is still not possible to identify precisely which was the decisive mainspring that set off Fra Bartolomeo's reaction.

In the *Quaestio*, the note of surprise gives place to an effort to explain "rationally" the "phenomenon" of the resurrection of the oxen. Certainly Spina does not hesitate to recognize in the *domina cursus* of the Modenese witches yet one more transfiguration of the eternal enemy, and the reality of the "witch's testimony" (*delatio a daemone*) and of the nocturnal meetings seems to him proved by incontrovertible evidence.[30] Yet the detail of the oxen's resurrection continues to create difficulties even once it has been incorporated into the schema of the Inquisition's demonology.

Fra Bartolomeo gives a whole chapter to this thorny problem, presenting an opinion not unlike that of his predecessors: the resuscitation of dead animals is not granted to demons, but only to God, and therefore it is necessary to recognize such feigned rebirths as illusions produced by the evil one with his false and powerful art. Our author then reviews the possible means by which the trick might have been accomplished, supposing among other things that the demons might have formed an aerial body in the likeness of the ox and that they might have inserted it under the hide of the dead animal.

This hypothesis would explain the occurrence often referred to by the witches: the oxen thus resuscitated and led back to their stalls would die within a period of three days, "as if they were shriveling up hourly into nothing."[31]

Such meticulous and detailed explanations do not occur in Visconti and Rategno. Spina's particular originality, however, resides in the fact that he not only wonders *how* the demons accomplish these false resurrections, but he also attempts to understand *why*. In fact he goes on to say that the devil enjoys showing his power in this God-like way and that he wants to be considered and adored by everyone as if he were God. This is the Devil as "monkey of God" (*simia dei*), of course, though in our case the more apt epithet would be "monkey of the saints." Spina explains in fact that the devil, with these "performances" of his, would like to imitate Saint Germain's earlier miracle, when he resuscitated a calf served to him by a poor family who had welcomed him as a guest, ordering that the bones be collected into the hide and then touching them with his staff.[32]

%> Consider the following statements: by Spina, "whether he said this seriously or as a joke"; by Pomponazzi, "if that be not said as a fiction"; by Pico, "they appear to be mockeries concerning the oxen." Joke, fiction, mockery: both supporters and skeptics of the reality of witchcraft, in spite of their differing world views, are united in a reaction of spontaneous incredulity at the idea of the resurrection of animals. Even for us this popular myth is bound to remain an inexplicable oddity, unless perhaps we go along with Propp and try to retrace its possible historical roots, if any.

It is Vladimir Propp who has given us the key to resolving our problem. In his 1934 article "The Magic Tree on the Tomb," he traces the origin of the motif, present in various folktales, of the burial of bones and the subsequent growth from the corpse of a magic tree back to a magical custom typical of hunting societies.[33] Among the hunter populations of the subarctic tundra (in Asia, Europe, and North America), the custom persisted of collecting the bones of an animal that had been killed, carefully avoiding breaking or losing any of them, and then burying them. This custom was based on the belief common to hunters that the dead animal's soul could return to the bones if they were preserved intact, and that the animal could thereby be reborn.[34] If we see here a deep root for the folktale motif that Propp studied, then we can also see the root for the motif that we encountered in the court proceedings against Zilia. Furthermore, it is already clear that the meaning or goal of the magic custom referred to was to guarantee the abundance of wild game. Once again, therefore, the study of popular witchcraft, in its original aspect and distinct from the schemata imposed on it by the Inquisition, brings us to the submerged continent of cultures founded on motifs of collective prosperity.[35]

Corresponding to the magic customs that unfolded with each hunt, there existed among some peoples periodic ceremonies, centered on the sacrificial killing of some animal such as a bear or a deer.[36] Influencing these ceremonies was the myth of the "Lord of the Animals," an ambivalent divinity to whom hunters all attributed the power of overseeing the fortunes of hunting activities, and whose benevolence they strove to achieve by respecting defined norms and ritual behaviors. If the Lord is satisfied by the hunter's treatment of the animal, he will cause it to be reborn from its bones, or in any case he will later provide an abundance of game.[37]

When we juxtapose these magic customs and rites practiced by the hunting cultures with the motif of the oxen's resurrection embedded in the proceedings against Zilia, we find a precise correspondence of meaningful elements: killing of the animal, preservation of its bones, and its resurrection through the work of the divinity. This is different and historically more conspicuous than the merely typological analogy between the magic of the cultures studied by ethnologists and that of European witchcraft.[38] This correspondence points to a *historical* connection between a specific popular belief that is incorporated into witchcraft in the Christian era and the hunting cultures that developed in the European region in the archaic era. The existence of this connection, in which we can trace the formation of one component of popular ritual witchcraft, can be confirmed using the instruments of philological criticism. In the following pages, we will set out all the elements at our disposal, which, even if they do not allow us to reconstruct such a historical event in its entirety, will in any case help to cast some light upon it.

From the fourth century on, as has been pointed out, the clerical culture appropriated and distorted many elements from the folklore tradition.[39] Our first line of exploration, therefore, should consider the hypothesis that the clerical culture served to transmit the motif of the oxen's resurrection from the pre-Christian tradition to the Emilian peasant culture of the sixteenth century. The impetus for this comes from Spina's mention of a miracle of Saint Germain, which corresponds perfectly to the magic act accomplished by the *domina cursus*.

Germain, bishop of Auxerre at the beginning of the fifth century, is the saint we are looking for. His earliest and most reliable biographer, Constantius of Lyon,[40] who himself reports miracles influenced by "folkloric" elements, does not mention our miracle.[41] Four-hundred years later, in the second half of the ninth century, the monk Heiric of Auxerre composed both a *Vita Germani* in hexameters and the *Miracula Germani* in prose, in which legend takes clear precedence over history, allowing the reader to see a definite substratum of folklore.[42] In the eighth chapter of Book I, he recounts how Germain, while on a trip to Britain, asked if he could take shelter from the cold at the king's palace. The latter ("who was uncivilized in spirit and by birth") refused to give Germain hospitality. But one of the king's rustics, struck by Germain's dignity and presence, welcomed him into his house and prepared for him the only calf that he possessed. When supper was over, Germain ordered "that he arrange the bones of the calf carefully gathered on the hide before its mother in the stall," and the calf was brought back to life. The next day, the saint overthrew the king, replacing him with the rustic, whose descendants reigned thenceforth over the British nation.[43]

How did this miracle find its way into the work of Heiric?

❦ Heiric states that he learned of the miracle from an old hermit of English origin named Mark, who had assured him that the miracle "is included in the Catholic documents in Britain."[44] Thus, even before Heiric could have written his work, a legend of Saint Germain that included the miracle of the oxen was in circulation in England.

Ranulf Higden, a Benedictine monk living in the fourteenth century at the Monastery of Saint Warburg of Chester, succinctly recounts in his *Polychronicon* this episode from the life of Germain. Higden informs us that the episode was also contained in the "historia" of Gildas.[45]

The work to which Higden refers was not actually written by Gildas, even though in a series of manuscripts it appears under his name.[46] This work is the *Historia Brittonum*, a chronicle of the history of the island from the landing of Caesar until the end of the seventh century and usually attributed to Nennius. According to Ferdinand Lot, the original nucleus of this chronicle is the work of an anonymous

northern writer and goes back to the second half of the eighth century.[47] The author who goes under the name of Nennius is instead a
native of Wales, who around 826 must have rearranged and interpo-
lated the original text.[48]

This author, who says that he took his reports from a *Liber Sancti
Germani*, recounts the episode in a version almost identical to that
appearing in the work of Heiric; however, he omits the detail of the
bones being collected in the hide, while he adds that, before supper,
"Saint Germain advised them not to break a single one [of the calf's]
bones."[49] Lot classifies as interpolations by Nennius all the parts of
the *Historia Brittonum* that feature Saint Germain, but he rules out
the possibility that Nennius might have taken them from a *Liber Sancti
Germani*, whose existence he doubts, preferring to assume that they
were invented. As for the testimony of Heiric of Auxerre, the French
historian supposes that the Anchorite Mark might have read Nennius
and that in this way the miracle passed from the *Historia Brittonum*
to the *Miracula Germani*; during this oral passage the legend may
have been embellished or altered. On the basis of these suppositions,
he concludes that, "it seems clear to me that the author of the *Liber
Sancti Germani* and Nennius are one and the same."[50]

The data from anthropology, which in this case brilliantly help
philology, belie this judgment. The careful collecting of the bones,
an element present in the account of Heiric and absent from the
Historia Brittonum, cannot in fact be considered an extemporaneous
embellishment by the writer of Auxerre; instead, as we know, it is
an essential element of the mythical idea of the resurrection of the
animals by their Lord. Similarly essential is the element, absent in
Heiric, that is mentioned in the English text: Saint Germain orders
the other people eating not to break even a single bone. This corresponds precisely with the taboo present in the hunters' rites.

Both Heiric's informant and the author of the *Historia Brittonum*
had access to a common source, or, more precisely, to a *Liber Sancti
Germani*, which presumably contained the most complete version of
the miracle and in which Germain's action must have repeated faithfully the salient features of the ancient hunting rite.

Saint Germain and his missions on the island played a role in the
conversion of the Celts of Britain, already well underway in the fourth
century,[51] and it was Patrick, a disciple of Germain, who was the
protagonist of Ireland's later conversion.[52] Conditions existed, in other
words, that explained why the figure of the saint of Auxerre would

have become popular among the insular Celts. They explained also why that figure would have been seen by clerics engaged in the work of conversion as the most appropriate one to subsume within himself those elements of an autochthonous culture that the effort of cultural adaptation, imposed by the exigencies of conversion, allowed to filter into the context of the new religion.[53] Thus it was possible for the British legend of the saint to be born and to include, perhaps even before the eighth century, the ancient motif of the oxen's magical resurrection. The interesting problem remains of whether during late antiquity and the high Middle Ages the Celts preserved the ancient hunting rite or a myth connected to it. We do not have the information necessary to clarify this.

⅋ We can reconstruct the missing link in our chain on the basis of data that come to us from the Germanic culture and, in particular, from its northern sources. In the *Edda*, the famous work of Norse mythology composed by Snorri Sturluson in the first half of the thirteenth century and, more precisely, in the section entitled "Gylfaginning," it is recounted that the god Thor, together with Loki, left on a voyage to the land of the giants of Utgardhr.

> During the evening Thór took the goats and slaughtered them, then had them skinned and put into a cauldron. When they were cooked, Thór and his companion sat down to supper and Thór invited the farmer and his wife and children to the meal. The farmer's son was called Thjálfi and his daughter, Röskva. Thór spread the skins out away from the fire, and told the farmer and his household to throw the bones on to the skins. Thjálfi, the farmer's son, took firm hold of a thigh-bone of one of the goats and split it with his knife, breaking it for the marrow. Thór stayed there that night, and just before daybreak got up and dressed, took the hammer Mjöllnir, raised it and consecrated the goatskins. Then the goats stood up. One of them was lame of a hind leg; Thór noticed that and declared that the farmer and his household had done something silly with the bones; he knew that a thigh-bone was broken. There is no need to make a long story about it; everyone can guess how terrified the farmer would be when he saw Thór letting his eyebrows sink down over his eyes.[54]

The correspondence is perfect between the significant elements of the magic act carried out by Thor and those of the miracle of

Saint Germain related to us by the *Historia Brittonum* and by Heiric and which must have appeared in the original British legend of the saint. The most surprising element, however, is the formal similarity between the two episodes: in both cases we have a voyage in the course of which our heroes are given hospitality by a peasant. There are differences too, of course, and we will look at those further on. Meanwhile we might ask ourselves how a myth belonging to hunting peoples could have been passed within the mythology of the Norse god Thor.

In the sources of the Norse religion, all relatively late, Thor, like Odin, appears as a divinity of composite aspect, in whom characteristics are superimposed that probably had originally belonged to different divinities.[55] The dominant attributes, however, seem to be those characterizing him as a Uranic being with meteorological functions, so much so that he carries the same name as the thunder. Adam of Bremen thus describes the character of the god: "Thor, they say, rules in the air, where he governs the thunder and lightning, the winds and showers, fair weather and the fruits of the earth." The reference to the "fruits of the earth" implies that, at least at the time of Adam (eleventh century), Thor was seen as related to the fertility of the fields. One turned to him, that is, when starting to plough a new field, and, although Thor's functions are not finally limited to this specific arena, some scholars have chosen to see the god as the protector of peasants, in contrast to Odin, the protector of nobles.[56]

This agricultural characterization of the god, apparently taking us far from the religions of hunters, could, all the same, be the result of a historical-cultural transformation, the product of convergences and superimpositions.

On the other hand, as Pettazzoni, a well-known historian of religions, has shown, the figure of a heavenly god—who appears as the supreme being characteristic of a civilization of livestock raising in contrast to the Mother Earth, the supreme being of an agricultural civilization—has some intrinsic connections to the Lord of the Animals, the divinity belonging to hunters. *Tore*, god of the Efe; *Khmyum* of the western pygmies of Gabon; *Bayagaw* of the pygmies of Luzon; *Kande Yaka* of the Vedda of Ceylon; and *Watauineiwa* of the Yamana of Tierra del Fuego (as well as others that could be cited) are all gods in whom the characteristics of the Lord of the Animals, who presides over the abundance of game and over the fortunes of the hunt, are connected with the meteorological attributes of a being more properly

Uranic, the governor of good weather and bad, lord of the wind, of tornadoes, and of hurricanes.[57]

To project these data from distant cultures onto the dawn of the Nordic peoples' religions, according to a model of comparison that is properly ethnological, and from this to presume an originally hunting character for Thor, does not seem correct from a historical point of view.[58] An observation of Pettazzoni's, however, is useful to understanding our problem: if the association of the heavenly Father with the Lord of the Animals can be considered in certain cases "the result of an historical-cultural convergence and superimposition" of distinct religious formations, then it can in other cases be seen as the result of an "ideological development along internal lines," traceable to the importance, recognized by many peoples, of the weather conditions to the goals of the hunt.[59]

Were Thor's goats domestic or mountain goats? The latter hypothesis would confirm the relation of Thor to *fajrguni*, a Gothic word meaning mountain originally, possibly the mountain of Donar (Old High German for Thor).[60] This would allow us to see in Thor a primitive aspect of the "Lord of the Mountain," an epithet equivalent, among certain peoples, to Lord of the Animals.[61]

In conclusion, let us recall that, in the Celtic Olympus, though not in its highest position, we find a god Taranis or Tanarus, names also etymologically connected with "thunder"—a god of lightning, therefore, for whom, again by analogy to the Germanic Thor, the oak was sacred.[62] Moving from this evidence to the conclusion that the Celtic Thor was present in Britain in our myth, involves a step that is not absolutely justified. Yet it is not absurd to suppose that the myth spread from the continent (perhaps crossing on the ships of the Saxons) to the island, where it would have become fixed thanks to the similarity between Thor and Tanarus.

❧ Our myth did not disappear in its passage from a hunting economy to an agricultural one, partly because of the animals' continued importance where pastoral activity is carried on alongside of cultivation. It does not seem accidental in this regard that Thor should have been welcomed during his voyage by a peasant. The detail should be considered in the light of what was said earlier about Thor's partial characterization as a god of the fields and protector of peasants. His hammer, Mjöllnir, carries pertinent and conspicuous associations with fecundity: as we have seen, it brought the butchered goats back to life; furthermore, in nuptial rites the hammer of Thor was placed on the bride's lap in order to assure her fertility. Such elements hark back to the symbolic connection between the hammer and lightning, the latter, like rain, incorporating the idea of a fecundative force, both sign and means of rebirth.[63]

We should note that the Christian version of the myth, which is how the miracle of Saint Germain should be considered, reflects a complete assumption of that myth into the culture of the farmer-husbandman, evident in the substitution of the calf for the goats. The episode from the *Edda* perhaps exemplifies one phase of the passage.

On the other hand, the Christian version of the myth lacks the important detail of the hammer whose touch carries the power of resurrection. While this probably indicates a scruple particular to the Christian conception (according to which the saint is not the direct author of a miracle but only the intermediary for God's work), it also allows for the combination of the most openly magical elements of the event. Yet perhaps such a combination was not yet complete in the original British legend of the saint, and perhaps the staff of Saint Germain had in effect inherited the power of Mjöllnir. The fertilizing power of Germain's "staff" (*baculus*) is attested to by two miracles recounted by Heiric: planted in the ground during a sermon, it flowered and was transformed, in one case, into a robust hazelnut tree, in the other, into a leafy beech-tree. The sites of the miracle became the destination of religious pilgrimages and took on names commemorating the event ("that same place was popularly named for Saint Germain's beech-tree").[64]

⅋ The miracle of the beech-tree is interesting in another regard as well. The oak tree or *Quercus* was, as we know, sacred to Thor. Like the beech, it is also a member of the family of *Fagaceae*, and its Indoeuropean name, *bhagos*, gives proof of its original confusion in terminology with the beech or *Fagus*. The Greek *fēgos* means oak and *Fēgonaios* was an epithet of Zeus, just as *Baginatis* was the epithet of the Celtic Zeus, the Tanarus mentioned earlier.[65] Whether oak or beech, the tree sacred to the Germanic and Celtic god of lightning is undoubtedly the same one to appear later connected to the cult of Saint Germain.

This does not appear to be a coincidence: Vincent of Beauvais, speaking in his *Speculum historiae* about Germain's ordination into the priesthood (which coincides with his elevation to bishop) recounts that particularly dear to the young lord was a pear tree, from whose branches "he would hang the heads of wild animals he had caught, in order to inspire admiration for such a great hunt."[66] Here we see a reflection of the pre-Christian cult of trees, or even more precisely of the custom, typical of hunting cultures, of hanging on trees parts of animals that had been killed.[67] The fact remains, however, that Amatoire, then bishop of Auxerre, recognized the pagan character of Germain's behavior and ordered the tree cut down and burned. At the latter's violent reaction to this, Amatoire revealed the design of God, who had chosen Germain as the new bishop of the city.[68]

The data offered by Heiric and Vincent reflect two distinct phases in the history of the conversion, marked respectively by two distinct attitudes on the part of the clerical culture toward the folklore tradition. In the first phase, characterized by the necessity for cultural adaptation on the part of the missionaries, rather than cutting down the trees sacred to Thor, they are dedicated to Saint Germain. Religious legends are born from this to justify the veneration of the plant. For the pagan place-names, Christian names are substituted. In successive phases, the church intensifies the work of conversion, looking to eradicate even those elements of the peasant tradition that, through an opportune transformation, had been preserved in the context of the new religion.[69] In the history of Germain's clerical promotion, recorded in the *Speculum*, we recognize an allegorical representation of the passage from "paganism" to Christianity, meant to serve as an edifying account and used to convince the "hard" peasants, guilty in their turn of having "folklorized" the figure of the saint of Auxerre.

❧ If we recognize in the figure of Thor a successor to the ancient Lord of the Animals, we can also be allowed to see in Saint Germain a Christian replacement for Thor.[70] In the intermediate passage of our hunting myth into Christian culture, however, the figure undergoes a change in meaning.

In the *Edda* account, the peasant's fright when confronted with the ire of Thor reenacts the terror of his hunter ancestors, when they were guilty of having violated one of the taboos connected with the hunting activity. There is, on the other hand, no trace of either the hunter's primordial fear or the ancient divinity's ambivalence (still present in Thor) in the Christian legend.[71] There the positive and propitiatory nature of the saint triumphs, whole and unmitigated, while the resurrection of the calf figures as the prize for the pious charity of the humble man, contrasted to the greedy indifference of the powerful man. The superimposition of the new conception upon the old, however, is not so complete in this case as to obliterate the outlines of the archaic sacred connection, by which the timely offer (the single calf!) assures abundance and prosperity.

This remains true even when our myth is taken over by the pressure of social developments and by the advancing social classes[72] and inserts itself, as happens with Nennius, into the legend of the peasant origin of the king of Powys (Wales): it does not seem at all farfetched to conclude that the idea of natural rebirth becomes extended, in such a case, to that of historical rebirth, implicit in the image of a new royal progeny, an allegory, in its turn, of the earthly triumph of the new religion, since the new kings are Christians, whereas the deposed sovereign "was of a barbarous people and spirit" (Heiric). We have the impression, in short, that the myth, because of its internal symbolic energy, does not submit passively to being transferred to another context, and that it tends rather to impose its own significance onto the elements with which it comes in contact during the course of its historical development.

All of this is confirmation, if there were ever need of any, that the conversion was not a one-way process, from above downward. In the historical occurrence of the motif of the resurrrection of the oxen, there develops another circularity that moves from below upward.

?❧ In the thirteenth century, with Vincent of Beauvais and Jacobus de Voragine, the biography of Germain loses its more historical components and connotations that had been emphasized so vividly in the ancient text of Constantius; it instead becomes set in the form of a *florilegium* of miracles. Both the *Speculum* and the *Legenda aurea* preserve the miracle of the resurrection of the animals,[73] and it was probably from this latter source, or from a subsequent vulgarization of it,[74] that Spina learned of the miracle.

In the *Legenda aurea*, Germain appears as the protagonist of another episode, not mentioned in the sources before the thirteenth century and, in our connection, rather interesting. He reveals to his hosts the diabolical nature of the "good women who walk about at night" and for whom, in the hope of propitiating them, the hosts had set places at the table.[75] The account is important for the history of witchcraft, since it documents the diffusion through medieval Europe of the belief in nocturnal walks led by a female divinity: with such names as Abundia-Satia, Holda, Perchta, Diana-Ecate, and others, she reappears in different areas of north-central Europe from the fifteenth through the seventeenth centuries. Sometimes the souls of the dead participate in the meetings and processions over which she presides; other times the prosperity of the community and agrarian fertility in particular seem to depend on the meetings. It is onto this main trunk of autonomous peasant beliefs that, at the end of the fifteenth century, witchcraft true and proper began to graft itself[76]— one thinks, for example, of the vignette from the first chapter of the *Quaestio*.

The "great wave of folklore of the twelfth and thirteenth centuries, which crests in Jacobus de Voragine's *Golden Legend*,"[77] thus also adds a new episode to the legend of Germain, which undergoes a drastic contraction in Voragine's hands. Equally significant is the fact that the miracle of the calf survives through this. The two episodes, on closer look, express the same mythical idea: that of the visit by a divinity, who must be propitiated with well-timed offers in order to assure prosperity. This observation helps us to understand why, several centuries later, the two elements are found to coexist in the single mythology of popular witchcraft.

The irony of history has required that in the *Legenda aurea* Germain is heir to the divinity on whom prosperity depends (as in the miracle of the calf) and, at the same time, that he be the one who unmasks its diabolical nature (as in the episode of the "good women"). This is the same redoubling of historical functions that we traced in regard to the motif of the cult of the tree and that can be explained only in terms of the two motifs having made their entrance into Christian culture in different eras, marked by different attitudes on the part of the clerical culture toward the folklore tradition.

?❧ Going back to the query with which we began, we can now say with certainty that the presence of our motif in the context of witchcraft was not the result of some late "influence" from the ecclesiastical tradition down to the culture of the subordinate classes.

In the text of Heiric of Auxerre, and therefore also in the later ones deriving from it, the necessary link between the preservation of the bones and the resuscitation of the animal is not absolutely clear: there Germain limits himself to gathering the bones together at the end of the supper, whereas in the version of the *Historia Brittonum* he commands explicitly *before dinner*, that the bones should not be broken. In the fifteenth century this important detail is still present and alive in popular culture, as Visconti testifies when in the passage already cited from his *Opusculum* he recounts that "the mistress of the game advised them to save the bones."

A proof that is still more persuasive comes from Propp. Among the Lopars (inhabitants of the peninsula of Kola), "if by chance a bone [of a deer] was eaten by a dog, the dog was killed and the deer's bone was substituted with the corresponding bone from the dog."[78] There is no trace of this kind of behavior in the Christian testimony we have reviewed. But then in a trial held in 1390 by the Milanese Inquisition, the accused Pierina de' Bugatis, describes the resurrection of an animal in terms similar to those already noted: "And if any of the bones is missing, they put into its place something made of the wood of the elder-tree."[79] At this point it is important to recognize that there existed a popular tradition of the myth distinct from the clerical one. In the fifteenth and sixteenth centuries, as we shall see shortly, this tradition obviously had not only taken root, but was alive and spreading through all of northern Italy, from Piedmont to the Trentino, from Lombardy to Emilia.

The two traditions of the myth, the clerical and the popular, perhaps originating from the common mythological stock of the Nordic gods[80] and having independently traversed the history of the western Middle Ages, meet up and recognize each other in the *Quaestio de strigibus*. The recognition happens by chance, if you will, but in circumstances worthy of our notice.

We should point out that Spina included in his account of the miracle a detail that was absent from the entire hagiographical tradition of the motif and therefore also absent from the source from which he took it: that is the detail of the *baculum* whose touch has the power to resurrect the calf ("when thus with his staff he struck the hide, the calf that had previously been eaten suddenly rose up alive"). This gives the impression that Spina was quoting from memory, especially since the legend of Saint Germain must have been very familiar to him, in that several times in the *Quaestio* he mentions and discusses the episode of the "good women."[81] But if this is true, then it is also true that the history of the miracle was already known to him at the time when he heard Giovanni da Rodigo's account of the resurrection accomplished by the Lady of the Game. The striking correspondence must have been immediately apparent to Spina, a correspondence so precise as to surprise even the cleverest expert in the mimetic arts of

Satan. He may well have been left disconcerted, incredulous, and disquieted to discover in the demon the perfect double of the saint, in the "other" culture the perfect double of their own: "Was Mariotto saying this seriously, or as a joke?" the priest then asked.

⊰ The power of the *domina ludi* to bring men prosperity and abundance is still the strongest element in the beliefs of Pierina de' Bugatis, the woman tried by the Milanese Inquisition in 1383 and then in 1390, with the variation that the benevolence of the Lady is made to depend on the diligence shown by the women she visits as they attend to domestic cares.[82] This power is expressed in the resurrection of the animals that had been eaten by her followers.

But how do we reconcile the propitiating significance evident in the magic of the animals, which corresponded more closely to the original value of the ritual, with the information given by Spina that, according to the witches of Modena, the oxen thus reborn would die in the course of three days? It must then have been a matter of a fictitious rebirth, in anticipation of definitive death, so that in the work of the Lady we are tempted to recognize an evil deed rather than a gesture of benevolent munificence. On the other hand, the fact that Fra Bartolomeo does not even hint at any connection between this detail of the *cursus* and the references in the papal bulls to the deadly incantations by the witches against the "oxen, sheep, and cattle" implies that in the confessions a nexus of this kind was not absolutely clear.

A trial, carried out in 1474 against four women of the Canavese, shows instead that the myth of the oxen's resurrection had, because of witchcraft, actually ended up taking on a maleficent connotation: not only does it recur here in the context of numerous mortal incantations against cattle (a good ten separate accusations have to do with this crime), but it becomes completely reduced to one element in a rite whose maleficent finality is explicit and unequivocal. The *inquisitio* of the Holy Office of Turin repeats that the accused had

> gone at nighttime to circulate near Turin in the Avilian Field where many people from the witches' sect used to gather. . . . After having done their usual dances, several went nearby into the midst of a herd, where they took two cows that were then skinned *and bewitched and enraptured in such a way that they would have to die soon within a certain time.* After having eaten the meat, one pro-

claimed that everyone who had any bones should present them; when these were wrapped up in the hides of the steers, the witches said: "arise, Ranzola," and the steers came back to life.[83]

❧ Thirty years later, in Trentino, they were not yet at this point. A group of women, tried in 1505 by a civil tribunal of the Val di Fiemme, recounted that at the witches' sabbat they ate cows and calves. At the center of their meeting was the devil: it was he who, once the banquet was over, would have the bones brought together and would call the animals back to life; they would be returned to their stalls once they had been assigned a period of time for their death (*datogli el termino della morte*). During that period, the animals would shrivel up and die.[84]

It is true that in the accounts from the Trentino each banquet, without exception, would conclude with a similar deathly sentence, but this does not turn out to have been the central motive and inspiration for the rite; nor was the bewitching of the animals the reason for attending the witches' sabbat, as it clearly was according to the *inquisitio* of the Turinese tribunal. Only once does a specifically malevolent intention emerge as the motive for going, when Margherita dell'Agnolo recounts that "they had deliberated as to whether to make a real storm or real hoarfrost [*brina*]";[85] but, by contrast, it also happened that her companions had sometimes invited her with very different arguments: "let's go, we want to eat a cow at Castelrutta."[86] Stealing the animals to be eaten at the sabbat is never an act of evil intention for these women: *they do not do it to betwitch them.* If death occurs, it happens by force of a fatal consequentiality: "But all those that are thus eaten, are all in danger and make a bad death."[87] In this light, assigning them a period of time for their death figures more as a prediction than as a decisive cause; we might say that it resembles the attempt to justify a posteriori an event otherwise inexplicable.

❧ The trials in the Canavese and the Trentino seem therefore to reflect two phases in the deterioration of the maleficent aspects of our myth's original meaning. The difference that we have brought to light, however, might also lead back to the different character of the two series of documents in our possession: in the first case, an accusatory act in which the judges' interpretation holds sway; in the second case, the transcription of the depositions, which gives us the thoughts of the

accused in a less-mediated form. It is probable that if the judges of
the Val di Fiemme had drawn up an *inquisitio* like that of the Turinese
tribunal, they too would have ended up assigning to the ritual of the
animals and to participation in the sabbat the same maleficent inten-
tionality that, by contrast, is not at all evident in the accounts of the
women from the Trentino. This assumption of ours can be demonstrated indirectly.

We still have a transcription of the interrogation to which another
woman, Antonia Comba, was subjected by the Turinese judges. We
learn from this record that people dance, eat, and drink at the sabbats
and that people eat the meat of sheep and of oxen; we are not told,
however, that this constitutes an evil act. She makes no mention of
witchcraft, recounting instead that a woman led her to the Avilian
field "telling her that here one could eat a good meal."[88] The discrepancy between this account and the *inquisitio* of the previous trial
is significant and confirms that the judges must have used heavy pressure.[89]

Even if the inquisitors' interpretive distortions could have been the
final factor in transforming our ritual into evil, they still do not sufficiently explain why the animals should have been condemned irre-
vocably to death.

҉ The answer is found in an affirmation by Pierina de' Bugatis, which
results among other things in validating the mass of considerations
presented in the preceding pages. In fact Pierina says that, once resuscitated, the animals "are never good for labor."[90] Note that the
animals do not die, they are just no longer capable of hard work. This
consideration does not weaken Pierina's faith in the Lady and in her
powers as mistress of men's prosperity. The causes for the occurrence,
however, must have escaped her, and, for even better reason, they
must have done so gradually as the myth passed orally from person
to person, until the original idea of a simple weakness had changed
into that of a death sentence, opening the way for an interpretation
of the malevolent sense of the myth.

We still must note finally that the testimonies given in Modena
probably also lacked the detail of the condemnation to death;
otherwise Spina would not have been silent on the subject.

If now, generalizing from the absolute chronology of the trials,
we set out the testimonies we have been examining according to a
logical-historical order that recapitulates the probable evolution of the

resuscitated oxen motif in the context of witchcraft and its persecution, the following sequence emerges: (1) the oxen resuscitated by "the mistress of the game" (*domina ludi*) are no longer capable of hard work (Milan trial, 1390); (2) the oxen resuscitated by "the mistress of the sabbat" (*domina cursus*) die within three days (Spina, 1520); (3) the oxen are resuscitated by the devil, after which they are condemned to death, and they die within a short time (Trentino trials, 1505); and (4) the oxen are bewitched, resuscitated by the devil, condemned to death, and die within a short time (Canavese trial, 1474).

Analyzing then our fourfold documentation in relation to the dissolution of the *domina ludi* through the history of witchcraft in northern Italy, almost the same sequence emerges: (1) the mythology of the Lady preserves its original characteristics: in Pierina de' Bugatis the awareness of her power to grant prosperity to men is present and alive (Milanese trial, 1390);[91] (2) the *domina cursus* is the author of the animals' resurrection, but her character as mistress of prosperity seems to be somewhat blurred (trial against Zilia, 1519; Spina, 1520), but in this case we could be misled by the gaps in the trial's documentation; (3) "mistress of the good game" (*dona del bon zogo*) has not disappeared, but the devil has taken her place at the center of the sabbat; it is the devil who resuscitates the animals (trials in Trentino, 1505); and (4) the Lady exits definitively from the scene (trial in Canavese, 1474).

We could work within these schemata to write the history of witchcraft in northern Italy in the fifteenth and sixteenth centuries, enlarging our examination to all the elements that emerge from the trials and from the treatises on Italian demonology.

Before concluding, however, it is appropriate to observe that in the Modenese trial of about 1520, the mythology of the Lady of the Game still preserves many of those characteristics that were supposed to constitute her original attributes and that seem instead to have been lost for good in the Canavese and the Trentino. The only possible explanation for this is that the Inquisition influenced popular beliefs much later in this region than elsewhere. We can suppose that this influence received a definite push during the three years when Spina was vicar of the Inquisition at Modena. Between the trial of 1489 (brought to light by Ginzburg), in which the *striacium* is described as "a tranquil nocturnal gathering of individuals, united until dawn to eat 'produce of a field or garden,'"[92] and the trial of 1532 against Domenica Barbarelli da Novi, in which the accused confesses to going "to the sabbat of Diana" (*ad cursum Dianae*) where, by order of the Lady, she profanes the cross and dances with demons[93]—between these two dates were Spina's three years of inquisitorial activity, entirely dedicated to the persecution of the *secta maleficarum*. And also why not assume that the *Quaestio de strigibus* influenced the environment of the Holy Office of Modena? In short, we would have to deal here with a dynamic of the culture of the investigators, which does not limit itself to investigating, and only by consequence with a dynamic of the culture being investigated.[94] This consideration may also explain why, well into the sixteenth century, the matter of the *cursus* might have appeared to be a new fact to Spina and his colleagues.

⚄ The Lord of the Animals had a peculiar fate. Although the decline of the hunting economies pushed him, irresistibly, toward his twilight, he is able to bequeath to the divinities coming after him the most characteristic of his attributes. The belief in the magical resurrection of animals is transmitted, over a period of centuries, from the ancient hunting peoples all the way to the Italian peasants who, still on the threshold of the modern era, placed their hopes for a prosperous life in the benevolence of the Lady of the Game.

What we have been studying is probably not an exceptional case, and the tradition of the myth of the oxen is probably only one of the thousand threads tying together what we call "popular religion" (those many practices and beliefs rooted among the masses of Christian Europe) with the religions and the cultures that flourished in the archaic, or simply, pre-Christian era. Of course a definitive answer on this point can come only from a series of detailed investigations. These, if their outcomes are to be reliable, must take into consideration the data and even to some extent the methods proposed by the various disciplines of history of religions, cultural anthropology, and folklore. As we have already seen at several points in our discussion, these disciplines all offer perspectives indispensable to understanding the meaning of many of the religious practices belonging to the subordinate classes, practices that we must otherwise resign ourselves to regarding, as some have already proposed, as mere eccentricities unworthy of the historian's interest.

We are arguing that these perspectives are indispensable, even if not exhaustive, but we should not insist on seeing in popular culture only a patrimony of traditions lacking the capacity for self-renewal. What Bartolomeo Spina discovered by interrogating the peasants of

Modena was not a fragment, the isolated remains of an ancient vanished mythology but rather, as we have seen, the organic component of a belief surviving in the popular culture and widely diffused from the fourteenth through the sixteenth centuries, throughout northern Italy. Also in this regard, the results of our investigation allow for generalizations because they do, after all, confirm the results already set out in the works of other scholars. They allow for generalizations provided that, naturally, in the study of so-called popular religion, we do not stop at the identification of distant myths that are dependent on a determined religious representation, escaping the analysis of the changes that their meaning undergoes in the course of their historical development, as they gradually move from one cultural and religious context to another. A choice of this kind would preclude, furthermore, the possibility of apprehending the circular relationships that, as we have seen with increasing clarity, have, at different times in European history, established themselves between the culture of the subordinate classes and that of the ruling classes, a relationship exemplified in an extraordinarily significant way by the miracle of Saint Germain.

Notes

I would like to thank my friends Giancorrado Barozzi and Ottavio Franceschini for the suggestions they offered during the course of this research.

1. Archivio di Stato di Modena, *Inquisizione di Modena e di Reggio, Processi*, b. 2, lib. 4, fasc. "Contro Zilia."

2. Ibid.

3. See C. Ginzburg, "Stregoneria e pietà popolare: Note a proposito di un processo modenese del 1519," *Annali della Scuola Normale Superiore di Pisa. Lettere, Storia e Filosofia*, 2d ser., 30 (1961): 269–87, and the note of A. Rotondò in *Rivista Storica Italiana* 74 (1962): 841–42.

4. B. Spina, *Quaestio de strigibus, una cum Tractatus de praeeminentia Sacrae Theologiae, et quadruplici Apologia de Lamiis contra Ponzinibium* (Rome, 1576). I used this edition, not having found any example of the "editio princeps," which, according to what one reads at the foot of the page should be from 1523. The *Quaestio* had a certain currency: it was printed again in 1535, 1581, 1584, and 1669. There is still no specific and scholarly study of this theologian, a minor figure but still of some importance in the religious landscape of the first half of the sixteenth century.

5. See the entry edited by A. Prosperi for the *Dizionario Biografico degli Italiani*, vol. 7 (Rome, 1965), s.v. "Antonio Beccari," pp. 429–30.

6. In total there were eighteen trials between December 1518 and April 1520, all except one for witchcraft.

7. This emerges from a series of references that Spina makes in the *Quaestio* to his activities as inquisitor: "Sed et illa quae superioribus diebus incinerata est, ea quae nunc diximus confirmavit" (p. 54); "prout faciebat illa famosissima striges, quae superioribus diebus Ferrariae combusta est" (p. 90). The circumstance is further con-

firmed by the "ad lectorem," where Spina recounts how he was asked by the legal experts who had participated in an interesting trial that had left them "admirati," to write a work on the witches and how he immediately responded to this invitation ("instantiori solicitudine tumultuarieque perfeci" [p. v]).

8. Spina, *Quaestio*, pp. 3–4.

9. G. Visconti, *Lamiarum sive striarum opusculum* (Milan, 1490), p. v (recto).

10. B. Rategno, "Tractatus de strigibus," in *Tractatus universi iuris* . . . , t. 11, p. 2 (Venice, 1584), fols. 348r–350r; cf. fol. 348v.

11. On this problem, see C. Ginzburg, *Il formaggio e i vermi: Il cosmo di un mugnaio del '500* (Turin, 1976), p. xii [*The Cheese and the Worms: The Cosmos of a Sixteenth-Century Miller* (Baltimore, 1980)], and R. Muchembled, *Culture populaire et culture des élites dans la France moderne (XVe–XVIIIe siècles)* (Paris, 1978), pp. 17–18 [*Popular Culture and Elite Culture in France, 1400–1750* (Baton Rouge, 1985)].

12. Spina, *Quaestio*, pp. 1–7.

13. The oldest texts of this polemic can be found collected in J. Hansen, *Quellen und Untersuchungen zur Geschichte des Hexenwahns und der Hexenverfolgung* (Bonn, 1901).

14. Spina, *Quaestio*, pp., 3–4.

15. Rategno, "Tractatus de strigibus," fol. 348v.

16. Visconti, *Lamarium sive striarum opusculum*, p. v (recto).

17. I have studied the ideological content of this polemic, which involves Spina, Giovan Francesco Pico, the jurists Giovan Francesco Ponzinibio and Andrea Alciato, Pomponazzi, and Silvestro Mazzolino (Prierias). It is not possible to point out here the importance that this polemical episode takes on in the cultural and religious context of Italy of the first half of the sixteenth century.

18. G. F. Ponzinibio, "Subtilis ac utilis tractatus de lamiis," in *Tractatus universi iuris*, etc., t. 11, p. 2, fols. 350r–356r; A. Alciato, *Parergon iuris libri XII*, book 8, chap. 22, in idem, *Opera omnia* (Basel, 1582), vol. 4, col. 499.

19. P. Pomponazzi, *De naturalium effectuum admirandorum causis, seu de incantationibus liber*, in *Pomponatii Opera* (Basel, 1567), pp. 1–327, 103–4. On the *De incantationibus*, consult the recent study of G. Zanier, *Ricerche sulla diffusione e fortuna del "De incantationibus" di Pomponazzi* (Florence, 1975).

20. Pomponazzi, *De naturalium effectuum*, p. 102.

21. The copy I have used, owned by the Biblioteca Apostolica Vaticana, does not carry the typographical notes. The work, however, was published in 1523 (see Hansen, *Quellen*, pp. 324–26). Regarding the *Stryx*, see the important essay of P. Burke, "Witchcraft and Magic in Renaissance Italy: Gianfrancesco Pico and His Stryx," in *The Damned Art: Essays in the Literature of Witchcraft*, ed. S. Anglo (London, 1977), pp. 32–52.

22. Pico, *Stryx sive de ludificatione daemonum* (n.p., 1523), p. E II v.

23. Ibid.

24. Spina, *Quaestio*, p. v; emphasis added.

25. I obtained the notes on Spina's life up to 1518 from the *Archivum Generale Ordinis Praedicatorum* (I consulted, at the Biblioteca del Convento Patriarcale di San Domenico of Bologna, the photocopies of the manuscripts that are held at the Convento di Santa Sabina in Rome), as well as from the *Series cronologica admodum Reverendorum patrum qui Magisterio Studii functi sunt caeterorumque qui in almo Studio Generali Bononiensi Ordinis Praedicatorum cathedras moderati sunt* . . . (ms. II. 21.000 della Biblioteca del Convento Patriarcale di San Domenico di Bologna).

26. B. Spina, "Flagellum in tres libros apologiae eiusdem Peretti de eadem materia," in *Opuscula edita per fratrem Bartholomeum de Spina*, etc. (Venice, 1519), fol. K IV r.

27. Spina's works preceding the *Quaestio* do not contain references to witchcraft; if he had been concerned with the *secta maleficarum* even before his inquisitorial experience, some notice of it would probably have come down to us, considering the diligence with which he collected the fruits of his own education (three volumes of *Opuscula*, the first published in 1519, the other two in 1535) and considering the many lengthy passages in which he recounts his own intellectual biography.

28. In fact he relegates the authoritative papal documents on the *secta maleficarum* to a chapter eloquently titled, "Plurima maleficiorum genera officio inquisitionis atque iudicio subiecta ostenduntur, de quibus tamen non esse principalem huius operis intentionem disserere, manifestatur" (*Quaestio*, p. 7). As for the *Malleus*, E. Danet has observed that Institor "ne nous entretient pas de la grande 'contreliturgie' satanique du sabbat. Tout au plus nous la laisse-t-il supçonner en évoquant les chevauchées fantastiques." See H. Institor and J. Sprenger, *Le marteau des sorcières*, introduction, translation, and notes by E. Danet (Paris, 1973), p. 99.

29. See the discussion of the trials in the Canavese and the Trentino at the end of this chapter.

30. For the identification of the *domina cursus* with the devil, see Spina, *Quaestio*, p. 16; for the demonstration of the reality of the demonic transport and of the sabbat, see pp. 17ff.

31. Ibid., p. 24.

32. Ibid.

33. In V. Ja. Propp, *Edipo alla luce del folklore: Quattro studi di etnografia storico-strutturale*, trans. Clara Strada Janovic (Turin, 1975), pp. 3–40.

34. Ibid., p. 19.

35. Concerning the relationships between witchcraft and the fertility cults, see M. A. Murray, *The Witch-Cult in Western Europe* (Oxford, 1921); A. Runeberg, "Witches, Demons and Fertility Magic," in *Societas Scientiarum Fennica: Commentationes humanarum litterarum*, 14, no. 4 (Helsingfors, 1947); C. Ginzburg, *I benandanti: Ricerche sulla stregoneria e i culti agrari tra Cinquecento e Seicento* (Turin, 1966) [*The Night Battles: Witchcraft and Agrarian Cults in the Sixteenth and Seventeenth Centuries* (Baltimore, 1983)], which, on pp. xii–xv [pp. xix–xx in the English edition] discusses the first two studies cited and others as well. As to the relationship between witchcraft and hunting cultures, rather generic references can be found in J. B. Russell, *Witchcraft in the Middle Ages* (Ithaca, N.Y., 1972), pp. 50, 51, 56, 58.

36. See J. G. Frazer, *Il ramo d'oro: Studio sulla magia e la religione*, trans. L. de Bosis (2d. ed., Turin, 1973), pp. 784ff. [*The Golden Bough: A Study in Magic and Religion* (New York, 1955)], and A. Irving Hallowell, "Bear Ceremonialism in the Northern Hemisphere," *American Anthropologist*, n.s., 28 (1926): 61ff. For the question of the religious genesis of these rites, see V. Lanternari, *La grande festa: Storia del Capodanno nelle civiltà primitive* (Milan, 1959), pp. 291–304, and A. Di Nola, "Cacciatori" (culture dei), in *Enciclopedia delle religioni*, vol. 1 (Florence, 1970), cols. 1417–31.

37. Hallowell, "Bear Ceremonialism," pp. 99, 107, 108–9, 119.

38. This kind of typological analogy has been studied by Runeberg, "Witches," pp. 33–90.

39. See J. Le Goff, *Time, Work, and Culture in the Middle Ages* (Chicago, 1980), pp. 155–56, n. 17. The essays contained in this volume, together with Ginzburg's book on the *benandanti*, constitute the principal point of reference for our exploration, in terms of both theme and methodology.

40. See the critical edition of this work prepared by R. Borius, *Constance de Lyon, Vie de Saint Germain d'Auxerre* (Paris, 1965).

41. See Le Goff, *Time, Work, and Culture*, p. 158.

42. On Heiric, see Borius, *Constance de Lyon*, pp. 48–49.

43. Heiric of Auxerre, "Miracula Germani," in *Acta Sanctorum Julii*, vol. 7 (Antwerp, 1731), pp. 255–85, 272. I take the occasion to recall that hagiography records several other miracles analogous to Saint Germain's preservation of the bones, but these are not significant for our purposes. See C. Grant Loomis, *White Magic: An Introduction to the Folklore of Christian Legend* (Cambridge, Mass., 1948), pp. 84–85.

44. Heiric of Auxerre, "Miracula Germani," p. 272.

45. R. Higden, *Polychronicon*, together with English translation of John Trevisa, ed. J. Rawson Lumby (London, 1874), pp. 276–78.

46. Gildas, a sixth-century author, is considered the most ancient of the British historians. In the work attributed to him, *Gildae sapientis de excidio et conquestu Britanniae*, he reviews the history of the island from the Roman invasions up to his own time.

47. F. Lot, "Nennius et l'Historia Brittonum. Etude critique suivie d'une edition des diverses versions de ce texte," in *Bibliothèque de l'Ecole des Hautes Etudes: Sciences historiques et philologiques*, no. 263 (Paris, 1934), pp. 37, 79–80.

48. Ibid., pp. 112, 123.

49. Ibid., pp. 173–74.

50. Ibid., pp. 85–86.

51. See L. Bielier, "La conversione al cristianesimo dei Celti insulari e le sue ripercussioni nel continente," in *La conversione al cristianesimo nell'Europa dell'Alto Medioevo*, Settimane di studio del Centro italiano di studio sull'Alto Medioevo, vol. 14 (Spoleto, 1967), pp. 559–80.

52. Ibid., p. 569.

53. See Le Goff, *Time, Work, and Culture*, p. 156. On this point, see also C. Ginzburg, "Folklore, magia, religione," in *Storia d'Italia Einaudi*, vol. 1: *I caratteri originali* (Turin, 1972), pp. 603–76, 609.

54. S. Sturluson, *The Prose Edda*, trans. Jean I. Young (Berkeley, 1966), pp. 69–70.

55. I obtained the details on Thor and the religion of the Germans that are given in this paragraph, from the article by C. A. Mastrelli, "La religione degli antichi Germani," in *Storia delle religioni*, ed. G. Castellani, vol. 2 (Turin, 1971), pp. 480–88. On this argument, there is the stimulating study by G. Dumézil, *Gods of the Ancient Northmen* (Berkeley, 1973).

56. Among these, for example, A. Bertholet, *Dizionario delle religioni*, trans. G. Glaesser, 2d. ed. (Rome, 1972), p. 436 [*Wörterbuch der Religionen*, 4th ed. (New York, 1985)]. In light of his theory of the "functional triad," Dumézil sees in Thor a god of war and considers his action in favor of agriculture "a by-product of his atmospheric battle" (p. 14 in the Italian edition; a more lengthy discussion of this point is found on pp. 130–32).

57. R. Pettazzoni, *L'essere supremo nelle religioni primitive*, 3d. ed. (Turin, 1957), pp. 114–26.

58. I am thinking in this regard of the distinction made by M. Bloch between ethnological and historical comparisons.

59. Pettazzoni, *L'essere supremo*, p. 126.

60. E. Schulze, *Gothisches Glossar* (Magdeburg, 1848), s.v. I owe this reference to the courtesy of my friend Alessandro Badiali.

61. Pettazzoni, *L'essere supremo*, p. 119.

62. See V. Pisani, "Le religioni precristiane degli Slavi, dei Balti e dei Celti con cenni sulle altre popolazioni indoeuropee d'Europa," in *Storia delle religioni*, 2: 432–33.

63. A. Seppilli, *Poesia e magia*, 2d. ed. (Turin, 1971), pp. 250ff. See J. Grimm, *Deutsche Rechtsaltertumer*, 2 vols., 4th ed. (Leipzig, 1899), pp. 163, 431.

64. Heiric of Auxerre, "Miracula Germani," pp. 257–58.

65. See Pisani, "Religioni precristiane," pp. 432–33.

66. Vincent of Beauvais, *Speculum historiale* (Douai, 1624), p. 783.

67. Regarding this custom, see Frazer, *Il ramo d'oro*, p. 795; and the same work, pp. 175–274, on the cult of the trees.

68. Vincent of Beauvais, *Speculum historiale*, p. 783.

69. Interesting in this regard is Gregory the Great's attitude: see Ginzburg, "Folklore," p. 604.

70. Le Goff (*Time, Work, and Culture*, p. 157, n. 22) formulates some critical observations in regard to the book of P. Saintyves, *Les saints successeurs des Dieux* (Paris, 1907). He notes that "the antique ancestors of the saints were not gods but demigods and heroes" and that "the Church wanted to make the saints not the successors but the replacements of the heroes, situated in another system of values." This judgment seems to me generally correct, even if the case under examination here demonstrates that the substitution (not the succession, naturally) of a god by a saint occurs too.

71. As Lanternari has documented (*La grande festa*, pp. 302–3), in contemporary Sardinia the Lord of the Animals has assumed the clothes of the devil, which shows, according to this author, "how strong is the terroristic, monsterous, and calamitous component in the Lord of the Animals in contrast to that which is purely devotional and propitiatory."

72. The expression is that of LeGoff, *Time, Work, and Culture*, p. 155.

73. Vincent of Beauvais, *Speculum historiale*, p. 785; Jacopo da Varazze, *Legenda aurea sanctorum* (Venice, 1493), p. 113v [Jacobus de Voragine, *The Golden Legend* (New York, 1969)].

74. One of these is the MS 1798 of the Biblioteca Universitaria di Bologna. It is a codex of the fifteenth century, comprising 266 pages. Our legend takes up pp. 188r–190r.

75. Jacopo da Varazze, *Legenda*, p. 113r.

76. For more precise and detailed information on this belief and its diffusion, see Ginzburg, *The Night Battles*, pp. 40ff. (with full bibliographical notations).

77. Le Goff, *Time, Work, and Culture*, p. 157.

78. V. Ja. Propp, *Edipo*, p. 19.

79. Biblioteca Trivulziana di Milano (henceforth B.T.Mi.), *Archivio Storico Civico, Cimeli*, 147, fol. 54r. The proceedings against Pierina and the contemporary ones against Sibilla were brought to light and discussed by E. Verga, "Intorno a due inediti documenti di stregheria milanese del secolo XIV," *Rendiconti del Regio Istituto lombardo di scienze e lettere*, 2d ser., 32 (1889): 165–88.

80. Supporting this hypothesis is the extraordinary similarity between the action carried out by Thor in the *Edda* and that accomplished by the witches' *domina ludi*. It is possible that Perchta, of whom the *domina ludi* is only one of many personifications, shared with Thor the power of calling animals back to life, just as it seems she shared with Odin the function of guide for the "furious army." On this, however, we do not possess absolute proof.

81. See Spina, *Quaestio*, pp. 3, 77–78.

82. B.T.Mi., *Archivio Storico Civico, Cimeli*, 147, fol. 53r. What emerges from Pierina's confession is a very widespread belief connected to the fates and to the familiar spirits. See K. Thomas, *Religion and the Decline of Magic* (New York, 1971), pp. 611–12.

83. This document, together with other papers of the proceedings, was rediscovered, published, and discussed by P. Vayra, "Le streghe nel Canavese," *Curiosità e*

ricerche di storia subalpina 1 (1874): 82–132, 209–63, 654–721; the passage cited is on p. 234 (emphasis added).

84. Biblioteca Comunale di Trento, MS 617. The very frequent recurrence of the same details in the accounts by the Trentine witches discourages me from citing a specific place. These trials were recovered and partially published by A. Panizza, "I processi contro le streghe nel Trentino," *Archivio Trentino* 7 (1888): 1–100 and 199–247; 8 (1889): 131–46 and 131 bis–142 bis; 9 (1890): 49–106.

85. Biblioteca Communale di Trento, MS 617, fol. 24v.

86. Ibid., fol. 21v.

87. Ibid., fol. 9r.

88. P. Vayra, "Canavese," pp. 697–701.

89. The judges were evidently influenced by the unanimous opinion of the witches that the animals of the rite would be dead within a short time.

90. B.T.Mi., *Archivio Storico Civico, Cimeli*, 147, fol. 53r.

91. It is possible that the society of the Lady was originally seen as a force in direct opposition to evil witchcraft. The Lady discloses to her followers, as Pierina recounts (see fol. 53r), whatever they ask her regarding the evil spells. This prerogative—of knowing the causes of the evil spells—will reappear two centuries later, by the *benandanti* of Friuli (see Ginzburg, *The Night Battles*, pp. 21–22). With these latter, Pierina's group has significant points of contacts; the goal for her nocturnal incursions into the houses, that of granting prosperity to the inhabitants, is analogous to that of the *benandanti* who do battle against the wizards for the sake of the fertility of the fields; in both myths, then, we encounter the element of the relationship with the world of the dead. I take this occasion to point out a case that shows a connection between the *benandanti* and the myth of the resurrection of the oxen. F. Musone, in *Vita degli Sloveni* (Palermo, 1893), p. 13, writes that "the *baladanti* [*sic*] are mysterious men who on Christmas night were impelled by an internal force to tramp over the fields, where they met at a road crossing and stopped to eat together, butchering a heifer or an ox of which they ate the meat and threw the bones in the air until at daybreak they put the bones back together again and covered them with the skin as if the animal had returned to life but would always remain skinny." Unfortunately, I was not able to see the book of Musone and am therefore not in a position to be specific about the source (presumably oral) and the date of this testimony, whose importance for our discussion we can intuit. The passage of Musone is quoted by L. d'Orlandi and N. Cantarutti, "Credenze sopravviventi in Friuli intorno agli esseri mitici," *Ce fastu?* 40 (1964): 39.

92. Ginzburg, *Night Battles*, p. 22.

93. *Ibid.*, pp. 182–83, n. 64.

94. On this point see R. Muchembled, "Sorcellerie, Christianisme et culture populaire," *Annales: Economies, Sociétés, Civilisations* 28 (1973): 264–84.

5 🎋 The Kings of the Dead
on the Battlefield of Agnadello

by Ottavia Niccoli

In January 1518, the chronicler Giuliano Fantaguzzi recounts, a printed booklet circulated in Cesena recounting "the visions and battles of spirits that took place in the area of Bergamo."[1] During the same period, the news that in the environs of Bergamo "there were seen visions and prodigies of a great quantity of armed people on foot and on horseback, one against the other" was reported in the diary of an anonymous French cleric who had been living in Rome for many years.[2] At the same time, Marin Sanudo, too, was collecting in his *Diarii* numerous letters concerning this incident, which appears also to have been recorded in the *Journal d'un bourgeois de Paris*. The printed pamphlets mentioned by the chronicler from Cesena were circulating in Italy in at least two different versions, and they were translated into French and into German; some made it all the way from Rome to Valladolid, where one copy came into the hands of Pietro Martire d'Anghiera, who made it the subject of a letter dated February 23, 1518.[3]

This incident, as we can see, had very wide resonance, and Gian Giacomo Caroldo, the Venetian ducal secretary on a mission to Monsignor de Lautrec, had already offered his own scornful explanation for it when he wrote to his brother on January 12: "Of what has appeared in the Bergamo area, nothing is true. A few simple people have seen the fumes above some manure, and they have, because of great fear, decided that those are men in arms. . . . Thus one should not give credence to such things."[4] And yet it remains to be explained

Ottavia Niccoli, "I re dei morti sul campo di Agnadello," *Quaderni storici*, no. 51 (1982): 929–58.

how those "simple people" could have seen a crowd specifically of specters in battle within the wintertime vapors escaping from a pile of manure. We must, furthermore, place this incident within the larger context of the traditions' circulation through nonhomogeneous cultural strata, of their transformations during these passages, and of the ways in which the traditions come to be transmitted, which are often related to their functions within a given social context.

༈ Prodigious visions were certainly not an exceptional occurrence at the beginning of the modern era. A recent book on Spain during the late Middle Ages and the Renaissance is dedicated to such visions, particularly to those with religious content, and especially those concerned with Christ, with the Virgin, and with the saints.[5] Supernatural apparitions, religious or not, appear to present a field of investigation of significant interest, inasmuch as with visions—as, indeed, with dreams—we find ourselves looking at external, and therefore describable, projections of a wealth of internal images.[6] Visions thus represent a precious opportunity for us to know those images. Even the Italian chronicles of the earliest modern era are rich in materials of this kind. Only a few months before the apparitions discussed in these pages, for example, the survivors of the galley, *Magna*, shipwrecked off Cyprus, once they had the luck to reach Famagosta, "say they have seen more saints . . . in heaven with lighted candles."[7] Nor are we dealing with a phenomenon that ceases with the spread of the Reformation, or one limited exclusively to the sphere of the Catholic confession, as we might be led to suspect from this account, which evokes, by contrast, well-known ironies of Erasmus and Rabelais about the worship bestowed on saints by sailors during storms. Apparitions and dreams frequently return in the pages of Melanchthon,[8] and we need only open the *De Spectris, lemuribus et variis presagitionibus tractatus vere aureus* of the Reformation doctor Louis Lavater, published in Zurich in 1570, to find ourselves faced by an impressive and varied picture of supernatural visions. Within this variety, Lavater lingers in particular on the battles of specters, which are to be understood as evil omens:

> At times of imminent changes of powers, in wars, revolts, and
> other very difficult moments, very often remarkable events, con-
> trary to the natural order, happen in the air, on earth, and among
> the living. . . . Visions of swords, spears and countless weapons fill

the air; armies, rushing toward one another and forced into flight
are heard or seen in the air or on earth, and horrifying cries and
the sounds of weapons resound.[9]

Representing this specific typology—visions of battling armies—there
actually exists, well before the pages of Lavater, a vast array of examples deriving from the classical tradition and starting with Pausan-
ius's page on the battlefield of Marathon.[10] An army of phantasms
accompanied Attila to the battle of the Catalaunian Fields, foreshad-
owing its unlucky outcome.[11] The tenth-century Persian voyager, Ibn
Fadlans, going from Baghdad to the Volga, saw, during the night
between May 11 and 12, 912, two fire-red armies come together in
the air with a muffled roar.[12] Analogous examples occur throughout
the late Middle Ages,[13] and during the sixteenth century aerial battles
had become so common that on several occasions they were foretold
by preachers.[14] Indeed the theme appears in France, particularly during
the second half of the century, as one of the preferred subjects of
broadsides.[15] Again on January 28, 1664, during an eclipse of the sun
observed in the vicinity of Ljubljana, the Friulian Capuchin monk,
Cristoforo da Cividale, looking at the sun, saw in succession "at
approximately the interval of a Miserere":

1. Four men, seen in the sun. 2. Two men on horseback. 3. Four
men on horseback. 4. A cavalry company. 5. An army of cavalry.
6. A church. 7. A giant on horseback. 8. A squadron of infantry.
9. A large corps of cavalry. 10. A very large army of cavalry . . .
and, for a good space of time, a proud and painful combat was to
be seen.[16]

The sense of these prodigies is that they are the sign of future wars;
and the pamphlet recounting them concludes with the augury of
"breaking down the pride of the proud Ottoman and giving glorious
victory to the Christian armies."

It is difficult, naturally, to provide a unified explanation for material that is culturally so heterogeneous even while being reiterative.
But the battles of spirits that were confirmed in the Bergamo region
at the end of 1517 seem to have a greater specificity, and perhaps it
is possible, therefore, to situate them within a more precise model
derived from folklore. These battles are even more interesting because
of the possibility, suggested by the multiple accounts that remain of
the events, of giving them a historical reading, of piecing together,

that is, the progressive construction of the model for the events and its subsequent, rapid disintegration.

᠅ The fullest and most detailed description of the apparitions appears in a little book of four octavo sheets entitled *Littera de le maravigliose battaglie apparse novamente in Bergamasca*, lacking the name of the typographer and the place and date of printing.[17] The pamphlet is in the form of a letter, sent by "Bartholomeo da Villachiara to his most dear Sir Honofrio Bonnuncio of Verona," from the castle of Villachiara, on December 23, 1517. The text moves immediately to the heart of the matter: three or four times a day for the past eight days in Verdello, in the Bergamasque region, formidable battalions of infantrymen, horsemen, and artillery have been seen coming out of a woods; these troops advance, marshaled "with the greatest discipline and most perfect order." Ahead of them proceed three or four princes, led by another sovereign who appears to be chief among them all; they move up to parley with another king, who waits for them in the middle of the road, surrounded by his own barons and at the head of his own troops.

> And then, after a brief discussion, that single king with the very fierce demeanor and armed with little patience could be seen to take his glove from his hand, which is made of iron, and throw it into the air, and suddenly with a stormy look, take off his helmet and turn around to the ranks of his men; and in that instant there could be heard so many sounds of trumpets, drums and castanets and the most terrible boom of artillery, no less, I believe, than the noise made at the infernal forge, and such that it could not be believed except from one who had come through it. And there one could see a great abundance of flags and standards coming to meet each other, and with the greatest pride and energy, they assaulted one another, and, due to the most cruel battle, all ended up being cut into pieces. . . . Then a half hour went by and everything became quiet and nothing else was seen. And whoever had the courage to go closer to that place [saw] an infinite number of pigs, who stood there for a little time and then entered into the aforementioned woods.[18]

The writer adds that he wanted to verify these events in person and so he went to the place with other gentlemen; they ascertained that at the conclusion of the apparitions "nothing else is to be found in that same place except footprints of horses and men, marks of carts and fires, and many trees torn down." The letter ends with expressions of amazement and fear ("truly the thing is so terrible that I would not know how to compare it to anything except to death itself"). The writer would have liked to add much other news, but he refrains, because "this matter is so great that anything else would seem like nothing."

꩜ The main elements of this account seem thus to be the place and the date of the apparitions. Within these main elements one finds four (or five?) kings, one of whom holds sway over the others at the head of an endless army on the march; a single, terrible king at the head of another army; his traits of ferocity and fearsomeness in the act of throwing the iron glove into the air; the battle between the two groups; the tremendous din that accompanies this; the prints that are left; the pigs that are seen to go back into the woods at the end of the apparitions; and, finally, the author of the letter. We will return to this last element further on; for now, it is sufficient to say that we are dealing with a historical personage, that is with the Count Bartolomeo III Martinengo da Villachiara, who belonged to another branch of that Martinengo family whose members, in the following generation, mostly embraced the Reformation and who were therefore forced to emigrate to the Grisons and Geneva.

Let us look first of all at the site of the apparitions. There was an open space in front of a woods from which the armed specters emerged. One witness described this area as "spacious fields, covered with snow, where there were two piles of manure, and not very far away there is a woods."[19] The village of Verdello is a few kilometers from the confluence of the Adda and the Brembo rivers. Agnadello, the theater of the battle that in 1509 had pitted the Venetians against the French cavalry and the Swiss infantry, is not far away, and the name signifies by itself the entire area—to the extent that the first accounts that Sanudo collects about the apparitions of Verdello, dated December 29, refer, with a characteristic lack of precision, to "a certain event that happened over in the direction of Treviglio or rather Cassan, where the clash of arms took place with the French and Swiss."

Regarding the date, as was mentioned, the *Littera de le maravigliose battaglie* carried the indication of December 23, which places the beginning of the apparitions at eight days earlier. Thus we go back to December 16, which, in 1517, was the first of the winter Ember

Days. The four Ember Weeks, and the winter Ember Days in particular, seem to have been the periods of the year when the wild army
chose to appear. There is a myth of Germanic origin connected to the
birth of witchcraft that up to now has been assumed to have hardly
even touched Italy but which seems certainly to be reevoked here.[20]

The saga of the wild army is widespread through a good part of
Europe, extending even into the Scandinavian and Slavic countries;
as mentioned, however, it definitely had its origins in the Germanic
world. In fact, as has been cleverly pointed out, ancient evidence of
the myth can be seen in a passage of Tacitus where he recalls how the
Harii are the most ferocious warriors among the Germans.[21] They
fight, he says, on dark nights with black weapons and with their bodies
dyed in dark colors: "None of the enemy [was] able to bear the strange
and hellish appearance of the wild army."[22] They appear, that is, like
an army of the dead, like specters come back from the tomb, and in
this way they triumph over every enemy through terror. This tradition
must have had its basis partly in the custom, confirmed among the
Germans, of frightening their adversaries with disguises,[23] and partly
in specific beliefs spread through the Germanic world concerning the
dead and their nocturnal wanderings. Already at the time of Tacitus
the band of the dead was led by Wotan, whom the Latin writer equates
to Mercury, thus emphasizing his role as divine psychopomp; the
warriors who have died in battle make up the following of this spectral
leader, and to them are added, with the progressive Christianization
of the myth, all those who have died prematurely, such as suicides
and children dying without baptism. The myth could be accepted
more easily even in educated circles, inasmuch as it coincided, at least
partially, with the traditions present in the Roman religion, according
to which the souls of the dead could periodically arise from the underworld to the surface by way of several openings.[24] They arose
primarily by way of the *mundus*, the ditch that was excavated in every
Latin city at the time of its foundation and that put the upper world
into contact with the lower one at least once every year. Furthermore,
the spirits of those who had suffered a premature or violent death
(particularly the warriors who died in battle) were destined to wander
through the air; those spirits could be fearsome and were often subject
to evocation by the necromancers.

The similarities of the Germanic myth to the Roman one probably
favored its diffusion through areas that were increasingly vast and
differentiated, both culturally and territorially. Thus, in the course of

the thirteenth century, the myth seems to have been well enough rooted in France so that in various literary texts of the period (*Tournoiement Antechrist, Roman de Fauvel, Le jeu de la feuille*) we find rhetorical comparisons between an unusual noise and the din of the "Mesnie Hellequin," as the wild army seems to have been called in France.[25] (Hellequin or Herlechinus is the demon who inherited Wotan's task of guiding the band of the dead.) Around 1250, Etienne de Bourbon formalized in his preaching the version of the myth that by then had become completely Christian and demonic: "Sometimes [the devils] play tricks, transforming themselves into the likeness of soldiers, in pursuit or in sport, who say they are followers of Allequinus or of Arthur."[26]

A document dated 1278 is the first to locate the army of the dead explicitly on the field of their last battle.[27] This element will remain rooted in the myth, thus giving significance to the fact that the apparitions of 1517 are confirmed not far from Agnadello and that witnesses refer to that battle in every case to specify the place where the apparitions occur. In the sixteenth century the temporal placement of the wild army seems finally to be set during Ember Weeks and especially during the winter Ember Week. This is made clear in a well-known text of Johannes Geiler von Keisersberg, composed in 1508, but printed in 1516 and then in 1517, the same year, that is, of the Verdello apparitions: "They usually marched during the Ember Weeks, and preferably during the Ember Week before Christmas; that is the holy time."[28]

Nonetheless, the place and the date of the visions—the fact that they consist of armies encountering one another during the winter Ember Days on the site of an ancient battle—are not the only data helping to define them as a manifestation of the wild army. The army, according to all witnesses, was accompanied by a frightful din.[29] Indeed, we have seen that in thirteenth-century France this din had become such a commonplace, that it came to be associated with any unusual noise, especially with a *charivari*, as in a well-known interpolation of the *Roman de Fauvel*. Shortly before that, in the mid-thirteenth century, we hear of an unusual manifestation of Herlekin's band, where it appears composed of artisans filling the sky with the clangor of their tools. The armies of Verdello also encounter one another in the midst of a "most terrible racket," as noisy as that thought "to be made in the infernal forge, which truly is not to be believed except from those who come out of there." Even the fear-

someness and ferocity of the king who throws his iron glove into the
air (the gesture traditionally marking the beginning of a military action)[30] finds its counterpart in the fearsomeness[31] always attributed to
the person leading the band of the dead, whether the latter presents
himself as Herlechinus or as the "man of the four Ember Seasons";
he is so called ("Kwaternik," "Quatembermann") in such areas as
Trentino, Carnia, Carinthia, Slovenia, and Switzerland, close to the
northern and eastern borders of Italy.[32]

One final and important element of the account remains to be
clarified and that is the presence of the four kings (a number chosen
with some uncertainty) at the head of the second army. The passages
from William of Auvergne that have often been cited in connection
with the wild army contain several details that we have not discussed.
In fact, at the end of the 1230s when William refers to the nocturnal
armies ("which some call Hellequin, others an ancient army") in addition to the bands led by Abundia or Satia, he speaks also of four
kings; the kings, who are called forth by the necromancers and are
therefore kings of the dead, "are said to gather from all four parts of
the world, accompanied by armies without number."[33] Further on,
always in connection with the wild army, he returns to this subject:
the four kings who, at the call of the necromancers, spring forth from
the land followed by their armies, receive their name from the parts
of the world from which they come: "So thus the one called first is
the East, the second the West, the third the king of the South, the
fourth the king of the North."[34] The principal among these is the king
of the Orient. There follows a long discussion, aimed at demonstrating
that the four kings can only be kings of demons and that they must
be demons themselves: William tries to Christianize a myth that both
precedes and is foreign to its Christian equivalents. One trace of this
myth perhaps can be found even in the passage, also well known, of
the *Historia ecclesiastica* of Orderico Vitale, where there is an account
of the priest Gauchelin's meeting with the nocturnal army on January 1, 1091, near Saint-Aubain de Bonneval: among the dead, there
stood out in fact "four horrendous horsemen . . . frighteningly vo-
ciferous," who intervene when Gauchelin tries to take control of a
riderless horse belonging to the band.[35]

This aspect of the myth—the conviction, that is, that the army of
the dead was led by four kings and that it could be evoked by means
of necromancer's art—had not completely disappeared by the sixteenth century. In 1544, several students who wandered over the

Swabian countryside bragged about being able to evoke the wild army on the Saturday nights of the four Ember Weeks and on the three Thursdays of Advent.[36] The necromancer's apparatus necessary to this was also used by them to discover treasures; in particular we find it described and used in the swindle of a peasant of Chombourg. This apparatus included a circle traced on the ground, consecrated salt and water, magical herbs, lighted candles, and burning coals. The Swabian students thus became imitators and followers of Wotan, the god who calls up the dead and knows where their treasures are hidden. Their science perhaps had other sources, in addition to the folklore tradition: for example—this is a hypothesis—the *De occulta philosophia* of Cornelius Agrippa, published eleven years earlier in Cologne.[37] Agrippa referred in his book to techniques for divining treasures and especially to the necromancer's arts, which could more easily be exercised on the "errant shades of those lacking burial, and the spirits, turned back from the Acheron, and the hosts of the underworld, whom untimely death dragged forcibly into Tartarus." In these lines it seems we can distinguish the presence of a double tradition: that of Germanic folklore, and the classical one already referred to. Contaminations of this kind must not have been unusual, and even the work of Agrippa offers several examples. Elsewhere he speaks of the four kings of the subterranean world, attributing their names to rabbinical lore:

> Four very powerful kings, corresponding to the four parts of the world, rule over the evil spirits. Their names are Urieus, king of the Orient, Amaymon, king of the South, Paymon, king of the West, and Egyn, king of the North, whom the wise men of the Jews perhaps more correctly call Samael, Azazel, Azael, and Mahazael, under whom many other captains of legions and chiefs are held subject.

Thus the myth of the four kings of the world, who lead the army of the dead and who are called forth from the earth by the necromancer's powerful arts, is still very much alive in Germany in the sixteenth century, even though it comes combined with classical and oriental mixtures and disguises. Furthermore, fragments of the same mythology also survived in the Po Valley region of Italy. A formula invoking the four kings of the world and addressing them with the names given them by Agrippa appears in fact in a paper from the Inquisition of Modena, not dated, but probably locatable close in time to the apparitions of Verdello.[38] Evidence of this same complex of beliefs could be gathered also in the *Littera de le maravigliose battaglie,* which could therefore take shape as the battle of more armies of the dead, some led by the king of the Four Ember Seasons, others by the four kings of the world with the king of the Orient at their head.

⅌ The version of events emerging from the story that we have described seems to be quite polished. The myth of the wild army, even without being named explicitly, is clearly evoked there with great exactness, precision, and richness of detail. At the extreme opposite, where the story is reduced to bare bones we find the skeptical reading of the events that was recalled at the beginning of this essay, the version furnished by the Venetian ducal secretary in Milan, Gian Giacomo Caroldo: "Some simple persons have seen the fumes up above some manure." But the relevant fact is that we also have the intermediate phases, or, rather, the raw materials that were later sorted out, reelaborated, and corrected to give shape to a mythical event. The first traces of this construction actually appear several years earlier, in spite of their apparently not having any direct sequel. An anonymous minstrel story of 1511, with the title *Memoria delli novi segni e spaventevoli prodigii comparsi in piu loci de Italia et in varie parte del mondo lanno mille cinquecento undese (Account of the Strange Omens and Fearsome Prodigies Which Have Appeared in Many Areas of Italy and in Various Parts of the World in the Year 1511)* includes the following lines:

> There where the conflict of the Venetians took place, many strange signs have appeared:
>
> fires scattered through the air at night have been seen by those who often go to look;
>
> the sound of densely packed squadrons and the sounds of trumpets were heard on the seventh day in May.[39]

The *Memoria delli novi segni* is a kind of miscellany in verse of the signs and prodigies that we often find recorded in other sources as well. Therefore already by May 7, 1511, the prime element of what would become a definite appearance of the wild army had been pointed out: on the battlefield of Agnadello ("the conflict of the Venetians," by antonomasia), will-of-the-wisps had appeared (the souls of the fallen?),[40] and, in particular, there could be heard the thunder of a crowded army accompanied by the blasts of trumpets. No vision was described, however, and, above all, one notes that the date had no relevance, coinciding in that year with the Wednesday following the Sunday of *Mirabilia Domine*, the second after Easter. Furthermore, even for the events of December 1517 the chronological placement during the winter Ember Days, very significant as we have seen, is anything but direct: a letter dated January 4, 1518, to which we will return,[41] says that the visions began to appear "about 25 days ago," therefore approximately since December 10; the *Littera de le maravigliose battaglie*, dated December 23, referred instead to only one week before, thus locating the events in the holy days of the winter Ember Week.

The progressive construction of the myth, or rather the adaptation to it of material coming from the accounts of those present at the visions, emerges even more clearly from direct examination of those accounts. Undoubtedly the most remarkable among these is the long letter, already referred to, that was addressed on January 4, 1518, by Antonio Verdello of Brescia to Paolo Morosini, quondam Marco. Verdello, who declared to his correspondent that he had interrogated "several" people about the visions, discussing them at particular length with three credible witnesses, offered on the one hand a very precise description of the place, on the other no less than six different accounts of the apparitions. These latter were all introduced by formulas such as "some say," "others say," "another person says," which lead us to appreciate with extraordinary immediacy the subjectivity and the fluidity of these phenomena, characteristics that allow them, finally, to be more easily accommodated to the preformed schemata of a preexisting mental image. The inherent interest in this plurality of testimony is increased by the fact that in no case is there mention of the possibility, present in other accounts, that the informant might have had the printed text, perhaps already in circulation, and that he or she might have been referring to that. Here we are still in an exclusively oral phase of culture.

The version reported first seems, in any case, to be rather complex. There already appear in this version, as they will later in the printed text, infantrymen, horsemen, artillerymen, and baggage carriers, all rushing across the snow-covered fields between the woods and a little church rising there dedicated to Saint George. These images, however, appear confused as if by clouds of dust ("because of such running there arose much dust into the air"), and in a short time they dissolved ("having moved a little ways forward, they disappeared and became totally lost"). Furthermore they do not leave any trace on the snow ("not the least trace was to be seen in the snow"), whereas the *Littera de le maravigliose battaglie* described at length the footprints of the infantrymen and the horses left as testimony to the marvel.

The version that follows is in a decidedly minor key, mentioning only the "shades in the likeness of men without heads" who "seem to move and now come together, now to be many in number and now very few." In those shades, however, now many and now few, which come together and then separate, we can perhaps discern the first outlines of the encounter and colloquy between the four kings of the dead and the king of the Four Ember Seasons. Furthermore the detail of the headless shades is not without relevance, since in the wild army the soldiers who have died in battle often appear looking just as death has left them: "One carries his viscera in front of himself, another has his head in his hand," as Geiler von Keisersberg had written a very few years before.[42]

The third version sees the introduction of the pigs, who, in the *Littera de le maravigliose battaglie*, appear at the end of the vision of the fighting ghosts: "a countless quantity of pigs who roared and rose into the air running wildly hither and thither." In the traditional folklore schema of the wild army, the souls can also manifest themselves in the shape of, or accompanied by, animals, usually horses and dogs, but also pigs, particularly in some Swiss cantons.[43] Animals beyond number also appear in the fourth witness's descriptions: this witness saw first "several thousands of black and white sheep who walked on the snow"; then "many many oxen, both white and red"; then "many friars, two at a time, white and black"; finally, under the pressure, we might say, of imagining the crowd surrounding him— he was "taken to see where there were many others in addition"— "he seemed to see an infinite number of armed men, on foot and on horseback, many with a lance at their side; it seemed there were still cavalrymen and many walking and running through those fields with a multitude of carts of straw." With a significant leap in quality, which tells us much about the process of visionary creation, the witness managed thus to conform to the most elaborate level of the first of the versions cited in the letter that we are examining.

The last two witnesses, relegated to the postscript, are almost completely negative: a "man of honor" (therefore one to be listened to—but does the evaluation refer to the morality of the person or to his social rank?) looks for a long time without seeing anything and only at the end thinks he can distinguish two shades, decapitated, advancing across the snow and then disappearing. Others summon up their courage to approach the church; they note nothing out of the ordinary, but still others, following their movements from afar, see them being surrounded by shades. In conclusion, "several . . . experienced such fear that they became ill, and several even died of it."

Clearly these visions, as they appear from this remarkable text, were extraordinarily fluid and pliant and susceptible to being fitted to a specific model. This process of adjustment must have been tumultuously rapid, as we can note from the dates of the testimonials themselves, which accumulate without allowing us to establish any clear order that could be both logical and chronological. The letter that we have examined is from January 4. The *Littera de le maravigliose battaglie* is dated December 23, which does not mean, certainly, that it would have been on sale on that date; but it could perhaps have had an earlier circulation in manuscript form. On December 29 Marin Sanudo makes note of the events in his diary in terms allowing us to suppose that he had the text in view or that in any case he was in possession of a source that was already relatively formalized.[44] Finally, there is a letter dated December 28 from Bergamo and addressed by a Marin Saracho to Antonio Orefici of Vicenza, that apparently represents the final phase of the myth's construction prior to its definitive adjustment.[45] The letter speaks first of the daily apparition of two friars ("there appear every day two friars six miles away from Bergamo"), then of two armed men ("there arose out of that woods two armed men with halberds and they come to the top of the hill"): we are perhaps encountering the successive reelaboration of the two decapitated shades seen by the "man of honor" and referred to in Antonio Verdello's letter. Going back to the letter of Saracco, the two armed men finally are transformed into two kings with the crown that they dispute together, until finally one of them throws his glove into the air and marks the beginning of the battle. We have thus arrived close to our point of departure, that is to the *Littera de le maravigliose battaglie*, and to its identification of the visions with a manifestation of the wild army.

It becomes necessary at this point to ask ourselves about the cultural context surrounding this identification. The apparitions, certainly, must have been seen and believed by persons of very different social levels and cultures, even keeping in mind Caroldo's scornful evaluation of the "simple people" who believe they have seen armed men in the smoke emanating from a pile of manure, and keeping in mind the distance that separates that same Caroldo, Venetian secretary to the French *locum tenens* in Italy, from the "man of honor" who sees only "two shades . . . without heads, strong, dark," and above all from the "simple people" who see infantrymen, horsemen, and baggage wagons. There seems to be, that is, an inverse relationship between elaboration and complexity of the visions on the one side and social level on the other. However, the author of the *Littera de le maravigliose battaglie* and therefore of the interpretations of the apparitions as manifestations of the wild army is explicitly named, and it is to him, therefore, that we must attribute the reelaboration of the visions in their definitive form. It was a case, as I have already said, of a historical personage about whom we have specific information: Bartolomeo Martinengo, the son of the count Vettore quondam Giovan Francesco.[46] The Martinengo family belonged to the nobility of Brescia and was subdivided into numerous branches; the one that interests us here was the Villachiara branch, so named from the castle by that name that still exists, located a short distance from Crema just beyond the Oglio. Bartolomeo, a man of arms, had taken part in the wars of the Holy League, and in particular in the autumn of 1514 he had fought next to Lorenzo Orsini da Cere, captain of the Venetian infantry, in the region between Crema, Bergamo, and Brescia; on November 16, 1516, for his good service in that war, he was made count of Villachiara in the Venetian Collegio by the doge, and he took command of Cremona on behalf of Venice. The letter turns out actually to have been sent from the castle of Villachiara, where Bartolomeo probably was at that time; and it is also probable that it was one of his infantrymen who was responsible for the account of the visions that was at the origin of the text later printed in epistolary form under his name—of which he may or may not have been the real author. In the note in his diary written on December 29, Marin Sanudo informs us that "the count Vetor da Martinengo, or rather 'el Contin' [the nickname then used to refer to Bartolomeo], his son, sent a certain servant of his, who, having gone ahead out of duty, was by these phantasms or spirits or whatever it was, badly beaten."[47] It was probably this same servant that Bartolomeo was referring to in his letter when he said that "a couple of our servants have become sick with fear," assailed by terror of the "phantasms"; and perhaps it was this same anonymous "servant" who finally bequeathed to myth his own personal experience.

⅋ The event, as noted at the outset, had great notoriety, which came from the printed edition whose genesis we have tried to reconstruct. First of all, another Italian edition, though slightly modified, was derived from this one:[48] the names of the letter's writer and its ad-dressee disappeared, several embellishing details and rhetorical am-plifications were added, as well as a very significant ending that placed the events of Verdello within an eschatological framework ("I am more than a little doubtful that it can be said within our time and with justification, *consummatum est*"). This edition's circulation, however, must have been much smaller than that of the first, which certainly served as basis for the translation into French (in at least two different editions)[49] and into German.[50] This latter, aimed at a market that could fully understand such a reference, explicitly framed the visions within the myth of the wild army. The heading of the letter, in addition to the names of the sender and the addressee as in the original Italian, also carried the name "von Dieterichs Bern," added to make the dis-cussion specific. Now Dieterich Bern, who in the Italian tradition is none other than King Theodoric of Verona, had become in the folklore of sixteenth-century Germany one of the leaders of the wild army.[51] Teobald Baltner, who had translated into German the *Littera de le maravigliose battaglie*, had thus recognized in it a formulation of that myth and he had, with great probability, identified the Ostrogoth king in the king of "most fierce aspect and armed with little patience" who starts off the infernal battle, throwing his iron glove into the air.

The fame of the spirit battles of Verdello was thus quite well known, especially through the medium of print, even in France and Germany. It turns out, however, to be possible to reconstruct in some way the path of its advancing fame—which provides a useful example of the possible itinerary of cultural images and their relative channels and speed of dissemination, which were strictly speaking nonoral—in Europe of the early modern period. It will be necessary however to distinguish the itineraries of news spread by way of letters from that spread by way of print. The former in fact move more rapidly, but over distances that are shorter: if the visions began around the middle of December, already by December 28 Marin Saracco was in a position, from Bergamo, to write about it to Vicenza, while on December 29 Marin Sanudo noted it down in his diary. The news, however, must already have reached Venice several days earlier, if Antonio Verdello after having gathered information could respond on January 4 to an earlier letter from Paolo Morosini asking him for details. Even in Milan people knew relatively quickly about the apparitions: Gian Giacomo Caroldo wrote of the matter to his brother on January 12, but apparently he had already known about it for several days.

Thus we have a rapid early movement of news within a rather restricted territorial context and primarily within the borders of one state—in this case, of the Venetian republic. After a slightly longer time, the news arrived in Rome, probably in the form of a manuscript copy of, among others, the letter of Bartolomeo da Villachiara. On January 21, 1518, Leo X read to his cardinals, gathered in Consistory, "several letters about the apparitions of Bergamo."[52] And it was in Rome, in all probability, that the *Littera de le maravigliose battaglie* was printed by the typographer Gabriele da Bologna; as the French diarist whom we have already quoted wrote, "the aforementioned books were printed in Rome and sold publicly . . . to people [who were] well known and in great favor."[53] From Rome, in its most complete form and in the dress most appropriate for wide diffusion, the announcement of the battles of the dead again moved on, this time overcoming even greater distances: it arrived in fact in France, at Paris, where presumably one of the two French editions of the letter was printed, and in Troyes, where Nicolas le Rouge published the other; it arrived in Germany, as we have seen; it arrived in Valladolid, as we discover from a letter of February 23 from Pietro Martire d'Anghiera. In the meantime the pamphlet was spread very quickly within the confines of the pontifical state itself: in Cesena, as was stated at the beginning, the chronicler Giuliano Fantaguzzi indicates in his *Caos* that "the printed books of the visions and battles of the spirits that occurred in Bergamo" are beginning to circulate in the city on January 20 (a date that, taking into account the chronology of the whole picture, leads us to presume that the *Littera* had come out of the presses of Gabriele da Bologna around January 14 or 15).

In a rebound from Rome, the news of the battles of the spirits thus quickly returned to northern Italy. The letter of Bartolomeo da Villachiara—at least in the Roman edition, which was the only one to become well known—was actually put into verse by a Paduan ballad singer; the lines were also inserted in that same minstrel's song of 1511 that we mentioned previously, carrying as it does the first mention of miraculous events on the battlefield of Agnadello. The verses, sixteen quatrains, were of unbearable clumsiness, worse even than those of the orginal ditty, but they faithfully described "the signs that have appeared / again in Geradada / when every road was full / of armed men." The reference to Ghiaradadda confirmed the reference to the battle of Agnadello already present in the title: *Segni e prodigi spaventosi apparsi in Lombardia nel confino de Trevi e Rivolta seccha; quali appareno doi or tre volte al zorno a combattere in ordenanza e con ferissime artelarie viste visibilmente per el magnifico Bartolomeo da Villa Chiara; et molti altri huomini degni di fede*[54] (*Fearsome Signs and Prodigies Appearing in Lombardy within the Boundaries of Trevi and Rivolta Seccha; Which Appear Two or Three Times a Day to Do Battle, Arrayed in Ranks and with Ferocious Artillery, Seen Visibly by the Magnificent Bartolomeo da Villa Chiara; and Many Other Men Worthy of Faith*). Trevi and Rivoltasecca (the actual Treviglio and Rivolta d'Adda) constituted a topographical reference that was quite pertinent for the battle of Agnadello, or of Ghiaradadda as it was called. Thus there is no more talk of Verdello: the permanent alteration of the circumstances of place and of time in which the spectral battles were verified is a convincing confirmation of their final assimilation into a mythical model.

?❧ Thus Rome functioned as an efficient sounding box for the prodigious event on an international scale. One gets the impression that the Roman success of the text of the *Littera de le maravigliose battaglie* was due to a precise circumstance that favored its use for propaganda. When Leo X read it in Consistory before the gathered cardinals, he commented that those prodigious apparitions "are a sign that the Turk will put pressure on Christianity . . . and therefore it was necessary to make valid provision and not to procrastinate."[55] As we already know, the motif of the crusade against the Turk reappears frequently in sixteenth-century Italy, and often in forms that were not at all abstract, sometimes involving collections of charity donations and diplomatic contacts directed toward that goal. This is the situation during these months as well. Already from the first days of November 1517 Leo X considered organizing a league of Christian princes against the Turk; after the successful Egyptian campaign of the preceding spring, Selim I was at the height of his power at that moment. Thus on November 7 a commission of cardinals was formed who convened several times during the course of the month to study the most opportune means of financing the undertaking.[56]

The result was a rather lengthy questionnaire prepared and sent to the Christian princes in order to learn their opinions about the method for organizing the crusade, the necessary military forces, and the most appropriate strategies to use.[57] At the very beginning of January, further notices "about the movements of the Turk" reached the pope from Constantinople by way of Ragusa-Ancona; these provoked more intense preparations.[58] In particular Leo X sent letters to all the sovereigns of Europe, and, when he called the cardinals together on January 21, it was specifically to discuss the responses he had already received.[59] Thus the apparitions of fighting armies could be considered a prefiguration of the next anticipated struggle between the cross and the crescent, and they could also be used, therefore, to prepare the way for requests for new taxes. The projected expedition against the Turks was never made; but during the first months of 1518 the pope "sent ambassadors to all the provinces and all the kings in order to raise money,"[60] he sent letters, and he encouraged ceremonies and penitential processions.[61] In addition to the pontifical requests, money was also being collected corruptly: Franciscan friars circulated through the villages of the Venetian mainland during April and May. To make their requests for donations more effective, they combined propaganda for the crusade with preaching for indulgences for the building of Saint Peter's, thus arousing the protests of the Council of Ten.[62]

The context of the propaganda used to frame the visions of Verdello (in Rome especially) could derive from various elements. The little book "of the visions and combats of the spirits" arrived in Cesena on January 20, as we have said, together with another pamphlet whose title was *Signuri stupende del grando aparato face il Turco per pasare in Cristianità* (*Stupendous Signs of the Great Preparation Being Made by the Turk to Move against Christianity*). Most probably this printed piece, whose title itself is significant, contained a letter, also recorded by Sanudo during this period and by Tommasino Lancellotti in 1523 (with the date changed),[63] in which the terrifying aspect of the Great Turk's fleet in the Levant was described with fantastic colors: the ships have red standards with a black cross in the middle, whereas the galley of the Great Turk is all black—sails, rope, oars, and all; only the standards are gold, with a red cross upside-down in the middle. All the ships are loaded with very large crosses, to be used, obviously, for crucifying captured Christians. The simultaneous circulation of the two pamphlets could simply be a reflection of the themes current in Roman circles; the pamphlets' simultaneous circulation could also have been intentional, since they lent themselves well to preparing souls for a collection of funds. Francesco Guicciardini, then in Reggio Emilia as pontifical governor, received the two notices together and tended to unite them in a common interpretation. He wrote on January 19 to Goro Gheri in Florence: "The omen has disappeared, but it has been confirmed from so many sides that I, for my part, do not think it is a hoax, but rather that it portends great preparations on the part of the Turk; it is possible to believe that now it is as it has been in the past—that great things have been signified beforehand by great omens."[64]

The connection that Guicciardini made between the "preparations of the Turk" (as he calls them in a letter of two days earlier) and "the prodigy" of Verdello was not present in the news that he had received from the regions of the apparitions, and we can assume that he found it in the communications that he had with people in Rome. Already by January 8, he had sent to Gheri a copy of a letter about the visions coming from the man from Brescia;[65] that letter, somewhat different from all those so far examined, made no suggestion of a connection between the prodigy and preparations by the Turks. The letter is known to us because of the account of it given by Giovanni Cambi in his *Istorie*, where he explicitly declares that its source was Guicciardini:

> In a plain near some woods and day pastures, one could see coming to speak together a great king from one side and from the other side another king with six or eight lords, who, after standing thus for a brief time, disappeared; and then there came to dispute and do battle together two great armies, and they stayed an hour fighting together. And this happened several times, but it was more than three days between one time and the next: thus the company made a judgment by combat between the great lords. There in Lombardy, there were several curious individuals who wanted to draw near to the armies in order to see what they were; these persons, as they drew close, through fear and terror immediately fell ill and lay on the brink of death.[66]

This version, which, as we see, is independent of the letter from Bartolomeo di Villachiara, comes directly from Lombardy and is lacking in any anti-Turkish sentiment. We can now look, for comparison, at another version with a different provenance, one that we know from the brief summary made of it by the *bourgeois de Paris* in his diary:

In the stated year 1517 [1518], in January, in Rome and around there, as much in the air as on the ground, in a woods, several armed persons were heard fighting one another, and there seemed to be around six or eight thousand men; and it sounded like artillery, bombs, and armor, ringing one against the other; this battle lasted at least an hour or more, without anything to be seen during that time. Afterward one heard many pigs, in similar number, fighting each other; from this the frightened people believed that these pigs signified the Mohammedan infidel.[67]

Now it seems to me that from these lines we can deduce the following: that the news came from Rome and that the version of the events in the hands of this Parisian was substantially different from those in our possession (the phantasms, in fact, are only heard to fight, "without anything to be seen during that time"). This printed version that has not come down to us emanated, therefore, from Rome, or rather it was the translation into French of a Roman printed version, different from the *Littera de le maravigliose battaglie*, but in any case coming from Rome (and we recall that Leo X read to his group of cardinals "*several* letters about the apparitions of Bergamo"). In that printed piece from Rome, the pigs in the visions came to be interpreted as Mohammedans; but we know well that this interpretation cannot be ascribed to the "frightened people," whose real reactions we know through the details. From the first accounts of the events, there was talk of pigs, but their presence was not emphasized in particular, and they were associated with "many many oxen" and with sheep. Oxen, sheep, and pigs were, obviously, a familiar reality in the countryside around Bergamo during those years. Subsequently, in the mythic tradition of the visions, the oxen and the sheep disappeared, not having, as the pigs did, any role in the wild army. That lost Roman printed version, finally, detaching the visions in a definitive way from their peasant roots, accepted the ecclesiastical tradition that, from the twelfth century on, saw the pigs as the incarnation of sin and vice.[68] This was, thus, an operation that reframed the visions with an anti-Turkish purpose in order to solicit a broader consensus for the anticipated crusade.

Twenty years later, in 1538, the Venetian printer Guadagnino Vavassore published a pamphlet of *Avisi da Constantinopoli di cose stupende et maravigliose . . .* (*News from Constantinople of Stupendous and Marvelous Things . . .*). The pamphlet was in two parts: the second was an account, completely untrue, of the victories of Andrea Doria's army over the Turks; and the first part, which constituted a sort of preparation and prelude to the second, was no less than a literal, or almost literal, version of the *Littera de le maravigliose battaglie*, followed by the explanations that would have been given for those prodigies by the astrologers of the Grand Turk. The last to speak, and the most truthful among those astrologers, was the Sage Odobassi, who thus admonishes the Sultan,

> that king, so greatly honored, who will be seen to come for the encounter in the road, will be that Caesar, emperor of the Christians, a great enemy of ours, who, before turning to deeds, will come to meet you in the middle of the way, and he will ask you if you want to become a Christian, and you will answer him no. And then all at once he will turn to his people, and as a sign that they should enter into battle, he will throw his glove into the air with a look so furious that it will strike fear into your people, and in an instant you will see so many arquebuses and so many cannons fired off that it will not be possible to resist them, and finally your people will be put to flight like pigs, without looking back, and in enormous disorder.[69]

The king of the Four Ember Seasons has thus become Charles V. M. Bataillon, analyzing this and other "Turkish" pamphlets without knowing their antecedents, characterizes them as political-religious, imperialistic propaganda and above all as literature of fantasy and comfort that must have been much appreciated by the Venetians.[70] We are dealing with a reading, in this case correct, that is enriched when we consider the remote context into which the *Avisi* reached. One detail should be emphasized: the *Avisi* reevoked very precisely the folkloric myth of the wild army, but only in order to deny it. Among the various analyses made by the Grand Turk's soothsayers— afterward all rendered meaningless by that of Odobassi—there was in fact the one made by the man "who said that, of old, some armed encounter must already have occurred in that place, and that for that reason there still appear there in that place such apparitions with their damned spirits."[71] The ranks of the dead are no longer composed of souls from Purgatory (as they were during the earlier phase of the myth's Christianization), but of the damned: their demonization, parallel to that of witchcraft, by now is complete.

❧ This occurrence includes numerous themes that are of interest to us here. One seems to be the confirmation of the links, already pos-

tulated, uniting Germanic mythology and folklore to aspects of sixteenth-century Italian cultural and religious life, of the subordinate
classes in particular.[72] We have in fact seen how a myth significant
and known in the Germanic world, like that of the wild army, and
linked, among other things, to the origins of witchcraft, could be
sufficiently known in the Lombard plain to be evoked very precisely
in the face of wondrous events that in their first phases are certainly
rather confused. The possibility of following this evolutionary and
rapid passage from the instability of visionary creation to the tidiness
of its later formulation as a specific myth is probably exceptional and
the result of evidence of unusual precision and richness.

But there is more. We find ourselves confronted by an example of
the transmission of cultural data across different social strata and of
a significantly complex culture. J. C. Schmitt has recently set out a
series of considerations on the importance, for a correct study of so-
called popular culture, of investigating the systems of exchange that
traverse the society being studied, "of studying the dynamic relationship [among different levels of cultures] as revealed by the transformations of the narrative." This allows for a response to the
fundamental question, "what is the function of these traditions in the
social context and in the era in which they are witnessed?"[73]

Let us try to follow these traditions through a described event.
First of all we can confirm another observation by Schmitt, who saw
in the earlier years of the sixteenth century one of the most fertile
periods for cultural exchanges. One can also observe, however, that
certain models of analysis proposed and used by the French scholar
for the thirteenth century now appear to be insufficient in this case.
In analyzing his thirteenth-century examples, Schmitt had used a series
of binary models: religious/lay, literate/illiterate, oral transmission/
written transmission. But in the sixteenth century and in the society
under examination, these models are no longer enough. In the first
place there is the presence of the printing press, which is not simply
one more possible pathway, but which instead renders the whole
analysis more complex. Let us examine the channels of transmission
for this event between December 10 and 15, 1517 (the hypothetical
date for the beginning of the visions) and February 23, 1518 (the date
of the letter of Pietro Martire d'Anghiera da Valladolid). This was
about two months, a remarkably limited period of time. Now in these
two months we find evidence for the following channels of transmission: private conversation (oral), private correspondence (written),

ballad singers (oral), and printed material (written). It seems to me that it would therefore be unjustified to take this plurality back to a binary polarity of written/oral. Furthermore, we see that the oral transmission by the ballad singers has been deduced, paradoxically, from the existence of a press. (We know, in fact that the ballad singers had the texts printed that they had recited and that they then sold them.)[74] In other cases, the pinpointing of lost printed versions, known only through diaries or chronicles (the *Istorie* of Giovanni Cambi, the *Journal d'un bourgeois de Paris*), has allowed us to deduce the existence of letters that before being printed were written by hand, but which somehow did not again reenter the genre of "private correspondence," being separated not only from their sender, but also from their addressee, and having become *copies of letters*, an expression which we have used several times that indicates a wide circulation in manuscript, circulated autonomously, and destined in many cases to end up in print. This, very probably, is the case of the *Littera de le maravigliose battaglie*: at first it was a private letter, which according to the tentative reconstruction put into writing the oral account of the "servant" beaten by the phantasms, then a copy of a letter, and finally a printed version that was used for the purposes of propaganda but taken up contemporaneously by a ballad singer and thus destined to return to oral circulation.

To this already complex picture we must add other unknowns. During the excavations of research we find ourselves, meanwhile, confronted with three clearly distinguished strata or levels: that of visions, that of myth, and that of propaganda. These three levels emerge clearly, it seems to me, from our tentative reconstruction, and they are confirmed in my opinion by a small but useful piece of evidence—the different treatment reserved for the pigs. In the first stratum the pigs flourish as a visionary reality, yet in some way concrete, without symbolic weight; pigs, as we know, during the Middle Ages and the early modern era were familiar animals.[75] For a long time they were raised in the forests (the pigs of the visions take refuge in the forest); in Lombardy in the early sixteenth century they were probably kept in an enclosure. We find a clear allusion to the presence of these or other animals that were bred in the area in those piles of manure in whose vapors Gian Giacomo Caroldo saw the true origin of the whole event. At the second level the pig has become an integral part of the myth: we understand this from the disappearance of the oxen and the sheep, which had accompanied the pig in the visions of the inhabitants of the Bergamo area, but which have no place in the myth. Finally, in the third stratum, the pigs have gained symbolic and propagandistic value: they are the Mohammedan infidel, emblem of vice, a formless mob, destined for flight. In this way one can answer, though only partially of course, the question that, according to Schmitt, must be posed regarding the different functions of the traditions: the image of the pig persists, but its function changes substantially.

And finally, let us try asking how all these variables can be arranged in the different compartments of the social hierarchy—that is to say, whether a given pathway (oral communication, letters, print, etc.) corresponds to a given level (vision, myth, etc.) or to a given social category. The result can be a schema of the following sort:

a. "Simple people"; visionary level; oral communication.
b. "Man of honor"; visionary level; oral communication.
c. Antonio Verdello, Marin Saracco, and so forth (middle social level, urban, literate); visionary level; oral communication, private correspondence.
d. "Servant"; mythical level; oral communication.
e. Bartolomeo da Villachiara; mythical level; epistolary communication.
f. Ballad singers; mythical level; oral communication and print.
g. Francesco Guicciardini; level of propaganda; epistolary communication.
h. Context of the Roman Curia; level of propaganda; oral communication, epistolary communication, print.
i. "People [who were] well known and in great favor"; level of propaganda; print.

To this admittedly summary catalog it would be appropriate to add all the readers of Roman publications, from Pietro Martire d'Anghiera to the *bourgeois de Paris*, but this, it seems to me, would not help to clarify the ideas. What seems to emerge instead is an apparent crossing of class lines on the visionary level and, partially, also on the mythical level (as Schmitt has observed, "folklore is neither exclusively rural nor limited to one particular social class").[76] This has been shown in the preceding pages by looking at the more expansive visions and the greater capacity for elaborating them in more complex forms among the lower classes (the "simple people," the "servant"). The level made up of those who provide or accept a reading of the visions in a propagandistic key seems much more unified, not in the pathways of communication but in its social and cultural *status*: we go from the pope himself, to the "people [who were] well known and in great favor," to Francesco Guicciardini.

Let us now take one last step and let us add to the picture outlined so far one further variant, distinguishing the two large territorial-political areas of the Po Valley region of Italy on the one side and the Papal States on the other. (We will leave aside for the moment the diffusion of the event outside of Italy.) The system with the most unknowns that we have tried to construct seems thus to be resolved. We have an early circulation of the event in the Po Valley, in a social context that is lower-middle, lay, and receptive to folkloric influences. The passage of the tradition into the Roman environment signifies a radical leap in level: from the lay to the ecclestiastical environment, from the subordinate to the ruling classes, from the folkloric to the "high" culture. (We should note that Guicciardini's reference to the "great things," signified "now as in the past . . . by great omens," seems to imply an allusion to classical divination.) The passage into the Roman environment signfies, finally, a movement from the visionary and mythical level, to that of propaganda.[77] I think it is important to emphasize that it was a specific political occurrence—the pressure of Selim I on Italy and the justified fear of a subsequent military campaign by him—that primed this process. The event, that is, seems to exert all its weight even over these problems only apparently dissociated from the thread of political history, which is also important to take into account when studying the transmission of the folkloric traditions. We must remember that, only in its Roman dress, was the account of the battles of the kings of the dead able to achieve an international notoriety, and only in its anti-Turkish and international dress was it able, twenty years later, to permit the identification of Charles V with the king of the Four Ember Seasons, and of the anticipated rout of the Turks with the disorderly flight of a herd of pigs. The renewed circulation within popular settings that the event must have enjoyed during the preceding years, by the route of the ballad singers and also of the printed versions, Roman and otherwise, was not enough to pale the anti-Turkish hues that it had taken on during its passage through the court of Leo X.

Notes

1. *Occhurrentie et nove notate per me Juliano Fantaguzo Cesenate*, transcribed in C. Riva, "La vita in Cesena agli inizi del '500: Dal "Caos" di Giuliano Fantaguzzi," thesis presented at the University of Bologna, academic year, 1969–70, pp. 158–59. See idem, "Giuliano Fantaguzzi e il suo *Caos*," *Studi romagnoli* 22 (1971): 251–74.

2. Biblioteca Apostolica Vaticana, Barb. Lat. 3552, fol. 32v. A later hand added, on fol. 1 n.n. r, the title *Diarium sub Julio 2do ab ano 1509 die 3 Martii usque ad 1540 die 6 octubris gallice*. Cf. L. Madelin, "Le journal d'un habitant françois de Rome au XVIe siècle (1509–1540): Etude sur le manuscrit XLIII—98 de la Bibliothèque Barberini," *Mélanges d'Archéologie et d'Histoire. Ecole française in Rome* 22 (1902): 251–300.

3. *Opus epistolarum Petri Martyris Anglerii* . . . (Amsterdam: apud Fredericum Leonard, 1670), p. 337. The other citations are given later in the chapter.

4. M. Sanudo, *Diarii*, vol. 25 (Venice, 1889), col. 209. A. Carile, *Dizionario Biografico degli Italiani*, vol. 20 (Rome, 1977), s.v. "Gian Giacomo Caroldo," pp. 514–17.

5. W. A. Christian, Jr., *Apparitions in Late Medieval and Renaissance Spain* (Princeton, 1981). On apparitions in the early centuries of the Christian era and in the high Middle Ages, see J. Lindblom, *Geschichte u. Offenbarungen: Vorstellungen von göttlichen Weisungen und übernaturlichen Erscheinungen im ältesten Christentum* (Lund, 1968), and M. Aubrun, "Caractères et portée religieuse et sociale des 'Visiones' en Occident du VIe au XIe siècle," *Cahiers de civilisation médiévale* 23, no. 2 (1980): 109–30.

6. For a historical reading of dreams, see J. Le Goff, "I sogni nella cultura e nella psicologia collettiva dell'Occidente medievale," in *Tempo della Chiesa, tempo del mercante* (Turin, 1977), pp. 279–86 [*Time, Work, and Culture in the Middle Ages* (Chicago, 1980)], and P. Burke, "L'histoire sociale des rêves," *Annales: Economies, Sociétés, Civilisations* 28 (1973): 329–42.

7. M. Sanudo, *Diarii*, vol. 24 (Venice, 1889), col. 25.

8. Above all in the "Historiae quaedam recitatae inter publicas lectiones," in *Corpus Reformatorum*, vol. 20 (Brunswick, 1854), cols. 519–608.

9. L. Lavater, *De Spectris, Lemuribus variisque praesagitionibus tractatus vere aureus* (Leiden: apud Jordanum Luchtmans, 1687), pp. 112–13.

10. *Greciae descriptio*, I, 32, 4.

11. L. Weber, "Die Katalaunische Geisterschlacht," *Archiv für Religionswissenschaft* 33 (1936): 162–66.

12. O. Weinrich, note appended to Weber, *ibid.*, p. 166.

13. A full catalog is in K. Stjerna, *Mossfunden och Valhallastrom* [Fran filologiska föringen i Lund, Sprakliga uppsatser 3, 1906], pp. 148ff., which, among other things, I have not been able to consult (cited in O. Höfler, *Kultische Geheimbunde der Germanen* [Frankfurt am Main, 1934], p. 242). Several examples relevant to the case under discussion will be examined subsequently.

14. M. Sanudo, *Diarii*, vol. 10 (Venice, 1883), cols. 48–49; "Diario di ser Tommaso di Silvestro," ed. L. Fumi, in *Rerum Italicarum Scriptores*, 15, 5, 2 (Bologna, n.d.), p. 482. The two notices refer respectively to 1510 and 1513.

15. J. Seguin, "Notes sur des feuilles d'information relatant des combats apparus dans le ciel (1575–1656)," *Arts et traditions populaires* 7 (1959): 51–62, 256–70. The aerial battles are mentioned in any case in all the treatises on the *mirabilia* of the era: F. Nausea, *Libri mirabilium septem* (Cologne, 1532), fols. 37r–38r; Lycosthenes [Conrad Wolfhart], *Prodigiorum ac ostentorum chronicon* (Basel, 1557), pp. 556, 608, etc.; A. Paré, *Des monstrès et prodiges*, ed. J. Céard (Geneva, 1971), pp. 146–47; P.

Pomponazzi, *De naturalium effectuum admirandorum causis sive de incantationibus* (Basel, 1567), p. 130; U. Aldrovandi, *Monstrorum historia* (Bologna, 1642), pp. 143, 717. The English almanac, *Nuncius coelestis*, compiled in 1682 by H. Coley, also described an aerial battle between ships and armies (B. Capp, *Astrology and the Popular Press: English Almanacs 1500–1800* [London, 1979], p. 24). A "naturalistic" interpretation of the phenomenon sees in it an imaginary description of the aurora borealis: F. Link "On the History of Aurora Borealis," *Vistas in Astronomy* 9 (1967): 297–306, cited in J. M. Massing, "A Sixteenth Century Illustrated Treatise on Comets," *Journal of the Warburg and Courtauld Institutes* 40 (1977): 321.

16. *Prodigii portentosi osservati in vari luoghi da molte persone degne di fede. E da PP. Cappuccini con ogni fedeltà osservati, e posti in scritto* (Parma, Milan, and Genoa: per Gio. Ambrosio de'Vincenti, n.d., ca. 1665), fols. 2v–4r. The same events seem to be reported in a letter from Gorizia of February 2, 1664, preserved in the Archivio di Stato di Bologna, *Senato, Diari,* 1656–71, fols. 45v–46r. I owe this last item to the courtesy of Giovanna Ferrari.

17. The *Index Aureliensis* carries the hypothetical information (Rome: Gabriele da Bologna, 1517). As we will see from the present reconstruction, the place of printing seems to be confirmed by the documentation, while the most probable date seems to be January 14 or 15, 1518.

18. *Littera de le maravigliose battaglie apparse novamente in Bergamasca,* fols. Aiiv–Aiiiv.

19. Antonio Verdello to Paolo Morosini, Brescia, January 4, 1518, in Sanudo, *Diarii,* 25: cols. 187–88. The full description is as follows: "There is in the Bergamasque plain about six miles from the city in the direction of Milan a small ancient church and field called San Giorgio, located about in the middle of the three villages called Verdelo, Osio and Levate. There some people swear that also in the past they have seen and heard strange things more than once. Around this church are spacious fields covered with snow." There is no longer any trace in the area either of the Church of San Giorgio or of the forest.

20. This is the hypothesis that appears in C. Ginzburg, *I benandanti: Stregoneria e culti agrari tra Cinquecento e Seicento,* 2d. ed. (Turin, 1972), esp. pp. 61–103 [*The Night Battles*]. See also by the same author, "Charivari, associazioni giovanili, caccia selvaggia," *Quaderni Storici* 49 (1982): 164–77, which makes reference, on p. 177, to a subsequent, more detailed study that should confirm these perspectives within a larger framework. The general bibliography on the theme of the wild army is quite vast, especially within the compass of German culture. One is referred to the seminal studies indicated in Ginzburg's book and in the comment by V. Branca to G. Boccaccio, *Decameron* (Florence, 1960), day 5, *novella* 2, p. 83.

21. L. Weniger, "Feralis exercitus," *Archiv für Religionswissenschaft* 9 (1906): 201–47, and 10 (1907): 61–81, 229–56.

22. *Germania,* 43

23. G. Müller, "Zum Namen Wolfhetan und seinen Verwandten," *Frühmittelalterliche Studien* 1 (1967): 200–12; idem, "Germanische Tiersymbolik und Namengebung," ibid. 2 (1968): 202–17; C. Lecouteux, "Les Cynocéphales: Etude d'une tradition tératologique de l'antiquité au XII s.," *Cahiers de civilisation médiévale,* 24, no. 2 (1981): 117–28, which makes reference to, among other things (p. 127), the cultural associations of warriors furnished with masks in the shape of wild animals. I owe these references to the courtesy of Vito Fumagalli.

24. Cf. F. Cumont, *Lux perpetua* (Paris, 1949), pp. 58, 82–89, 105, 332.

25. O. Driesen, *Der Ursprung des Arlekin: Ein kulturgeschichtliches Problem* (Berlin, 1904), pp. 34–35, 41, 106. Also to be noted are the indications provided by F. Liebrecht in J. Dunlop, *Geschichte der Prosadichtungen oder Geschichte der Ro-*

mane, *Novellen, Marchen u.s.v.*, with additions by F. Liebrecht (Berlin, 1851), p. 474, n. 170, and p. 546, n. 541a.

26. A. Lecoy de la Marche, *Anecdotes historiques, légendes et apologues tirés du recueil d'Etienne de Bourbon, Dominicain du XIIIe siècle* (Paris, 1877), pp. 321–22.

27. The reference is to Markfeld, the site of a battle won in 1278 by the Emperor Rudolph I of Hapsburg against Ottocar II of Bohemia: "Rodulphus, quum proelio Othocarum regem Bohemiae vicisset, in campo ubi proelium commissum fuerat pernoctarit . . . intempesta nocte lemures exercitum horribili clamore et tumultu turbarint" (Lavater, *De Spectris*, pp. 116–17).

28. A. Stober, *Zur Geschichte des Volks-Aberglaubens im Anfange des XVI. Jahrhunderts: Aus der Joh. Geilers von Kaiserberg Emeis* (Basel, 1856), p. 21.

29. F. Liebrecht, *Des Gervasius von Tilbury Otia imperialia in einer Auswahl neu herausgegeben*, Anhang II A: *La Mesnie furieuse, ou la Chasse sauvage* (Hannover, 1856), pp. 181–82; Driesen, *Der Ursprung des Arlekins*; Höfler, *Kultische Geheimbunde der Germanen*, pp. 8–9, 108–10, 300; L. Lazzerini, "Preistoria degli Zanni: mito e spettacolo nella coscienza popolare," in *Scienze, credenze occulte, livelli di cultura* (Florence, 1982), p. 459. On the two examples immediately following that in the text, see Ginzburg, "Charivari," which sets out the hypothesis "that the 'mesnie Hellequin' constitutes the mythic source of the most ancient phase of the charivari" (p. 169). The youths assumed the identities of the implacable dead of the village in order to express the disapproval felt by their age group, in moments of precarious demographic equilibrium, of marriage between a widower or a widow with a young woman or man.

30. According to Luigi da Porto, before the battle of Agnadello King Louis XII of France sent a herald to Venice who as a "sign of challenge . . . threw a bloody glove at the feet of the doge"; and before the battle of Ravenna of 1512 "monsignor Foix sent to don Raimondo di Cardona the bloody glove of battle" (*Lettere storiche di Luigi da Porto vicentino dall'anno 1509 to 1528*, ed. B. Bressan [Florence, 1857], pp. 35, 302).

31. Liebrecht, *La Mesnie furieuse*, p. 177.

32. W. Liungman, *Traditionswanderungen: Euphrates-Rhein. Studien zur Geschichte des Volksbräuche*, vol. 2 (Helsinki, 1938), pp. 640–41.

33. Guilielmi Alverni [William of Auvergne], *Opera Omnia*, vol. 1 (Paris, 1674), p. 948.

34. Ibid., p. 1037.

35. Ordericus Vitalis, *Historiae Ecclesiasticae libri tredecim*, ed. A. Le Prevost, vol. 3 (Paris, 1845), p. 372.

36. M. Crosius, *Annalium Svevicorum dodecas tertia* (Frankfort: ex officina typographica Nicolai Bassaei, 1596), pp. 653–54.

37. H. C. Agrippa, *De occulta philosophia libri tres* (Cologne: Joan Soter, 1553) (the two quotations that follow are on pp. cccv and cclvi). Regarding the work, see P. Zambelli, "Magic and Radical Reformation in Agrippa of Nettesheim," *Journal of the Warburg and Courtauld Institutes* 39 (1976): 69–104, which tends to emphasize in particular Agrippa's relationships with the Platonic culture and the German Nicodemite circles. The reference to the prerogatives of Wotan, already cited, has been made essentially by G. Dumézil, *Gli dei dei Germani* (Milan, 1974), pp. 56–57 [*Gods of the Ancient Northmen* (Berkeley, 1973)].

38. This is a loose sheet, preserved in the Archivio di Stato di Modena, *Inquisizione*, B.1, and containing love spells. The sheet has been studied by A. Biondi, "La signora delle erbe e la magia della vegetazione," in *Medicina, erbe e magia* (Milan, 1981), pp. 190, 192. Biondi juxtaposes this text to the untried suit brought in 1519 against Panfilo Sasso and Anastasia la Frappona (concerning that, see C. Ginzburg, "Un letterato a una strega al principio del '500: Panfilo Sasso e Anastasia la Frappona,"

in *Studi in memoria di Carlo Ascheri*, special issue of *Differenze* 9 [1970]: 129–37).

39. Fol. 1v nn. The printed piece lacks any typographical notes: it is attributed to the Bolognese printer, Giovanni Antonio Benedetti, in the *Short-Title Catalogue* of the British Museum.

40. The will-of-the-wisps or *ignes fatuii* that appeared on battlefields were a recurring commonplace, so much so that even in the mid-eighteenth century Lenglet Dufresnoy felt the need to specify that they "are only the vapors of decay that are naturally emitted from cadavers, and they easily catch fire." Lenglet Dufresnoy, *Recueil de dissertations anciennes et nouvelles sur les apparitions, les visions et les songes* (Paris, 1751), vol. 2, part 1, p. 247.

41. See n. 19.

42. Stober, *Zur Geschichte des Volks-Aberglaubens*, p. 22.

43. H. Plischke, *Die Sage vom Wilden Heere im deutschen Volke* (Eilemburg, 1914), pp. 30–31.

44. Sanudo, *Diarii*, 25: col. 167.

45. Ibid., cols. 189–90.

46. On the Martinengo family in general, see P. Guerrini, *I Conti di Martinengo* (Brescia, 1930), not a very accurate work. On Bartolomeo, see ibid., pp. 484–89, and C. Pasero, *Francia, Spagna, Impero a Brescia: 1509–1516* (Brescia, 1957), pp. 339–40, 356, to which should be added the many items contained in Sanudo, *Diarii*, vol. 19 (Venice, 1887), cols. 121, 146, 157, 169, 171, 182, 193, 214, 238, 258, 272, 289–92, 366; vol. 20 (Venice, 1887), col. 99; vol. 21 (Venice, 1887), col. 225; vol. 23 (Venice, 1888), col. 213, and passim. On the castle of Villachiara, which Bartolomeo had frescoed in 1533 by the Campi brothers, see A. Peroni, "L'architettura e la scultura nei secoli XV and XVI," in *Storia di Brescia*, vol. 2 (Brescia, 1963), pp. 717–19.

47. Sanudo, *Diarii*, 25: col. 167.

48. *Copia delle stupende et horribile cose che ne boschi di Bergamo sono a questi giorni apparse* (n.p., n.d.).

49. *La terribile et merveilleuse bataille que a este veue novellement en la duche de Millan VIII jours durant au pres de la cite de Bergamo: translate de italian en francoys* (n.p., n.d.) [Paris, 1518?]; *La translacion de italien en francoys de la lettre des merveilleuses et horribles batailles nouvellement apparues au pays de Bergame, translate par maistre Michel du Pont, banquier a Troyes. Lan mil cinq cent et dix sept* [Troyes: Nicolas le Rouge, n.d.]. I know this last pamphlet only through H. Monceau, *Les Le Rouge de Chablis, calligraphes et miniaturistes, graveurs et imprimeurs* (Paris, 1896), pp. 230, 232.

50. *Ein wunderbarlich, grausam und erschrockenlich Geschichte von Streyt woelche ist geschehen und neuwlich gesehen worden In dem land Bargamasca . . .* (n.p., n.d.).

51. Plischke, *Die Sage vom Wilden Heere*, p. 39. •

52. Sanudo, *Diarii*, 25: col. 219.

53. Barb. Lat. 3552, fol. 32v.

54. (N.p., n.d.)

55. Sanudo, *Diarii*, 25: col. 219.

56. Ibid., col. 76.

57. Ibid., cols. 95–106.

58. Ibid., col. 204.

59. Ibid., col. 219.

60. S. Vegio, *Historia rerum in Insubribus gestarum sub Gallorum dominio*, in *Bibliotheca Historica Italica*, vol. 1 (Milan, 1876), p. 31.

61. G. Cambi, "Istorie," in *Delizie degli eruditi toscani*, ed. Ildefonso di San Luigi, vol. 22 (Florence, 1786), pp. 138–41, describes precisely the solemn penitential procession celebrated in Florence on May 10, 1518, according to the ordinances of

Leo X. See also L. Beliardi, *Cronaca della città di Modena (1512–1518)*, ed. A. Biondi and M. Oppi (Modena, 1981), p. 142, for corresponding processions in Modena during the same days.

62. Sanudo, *Diarii*, 25: cols. 390–91.

63. Ibid., cols. 335–36; T. Lancellotti, *Cronaca modenese*, vol. 1 (Parma, 1862), pp. 438–39. Similar and dramatic information about the Turkish fleet also appears in the letter, dated February 18, 1518, Milan, from a Fra Giovanni Antonio to the Minorite Zaccaria da Ravenna in Cremona, which also contains the description of numerous wonders interpreted as signs of the next coming of the Turk into Italy. The letter, included in the chronicle of the Cremonese Domenico Bordigallo, has been been published in F. Novati, "La vita e le opere di Domenico Bordigallo," *Archivio veneto* 19 (1880): 334–35.

64. F. Guicciardini, *Carteggi*, ed. R. Palmarocchi, vol. 2 (Bologna, 1939), p. 240.

65. Ibid., p. 236.

66. Cambi, *Istorie*, p. 131.

67. *Journal d'un bourgeois de Paris*, ed. L. Lalanne (Paris, 1854), p. 62.

68. Lecouteux, *Les Cynocéphales*, p. 124.

69. *Avisi da Constantinopoli di cose stupende, et maravigliose novamente apparse in quelle parti . . . Et unaltro aviso dell'armata del Principe Andrea d'Oria . . .* (Venice: Guadagnino Vavassore [1538]), fol. 3v.

70. M. Bataillon, "Mythe et connaissance de la Turquie en Occident," in *Venezia e l'Oriente fra tardo Medioevo e Rinascimento* (Florence, 1966), pp. 451–70.

71. *Avisi da Constantinopoli*, fol. 2v.

72. Besides Ginzburg, *I benandanti* [*The Night Battles*], see also M. Bertolotti, "Le ossa e la pelle dei buoi: Un mito popolare tra agiografia e stregoneria," *Quaderni storici* 41 (1979): 470–99 [and included in the present volume, titled, "The Ox's Bones and the Ox's Hide: A Popular Myth, Part Hagiography and Part Witchcraft"]. But Alessandro Nesselofsky, introducing the *Novella della figlia del Re di Dacia* (Pisa, 1966), p. xlv, had already set out the hypothesis that a complex of Nordic traditions, among them the myth of the wild army, might have held on in Italy at least until the end of the fifteenth century in the territories already occupied by the Lombards.

73. J.-C. Schmitt, "Les traditions folkloriques dans la culture médiévale: Quelques réflexions de méthode," *Archives de Sciences Sociales des Religions* 52, no. 1 (1981): 5–20 (the quotations following are on pp. 8 and 11).

74. Concerning who is writing, see my "Profezie in piazza: Note sul profetismo popolare nell'Italia del primo Cinquecento," *Quaderni storici* 41 (1979): 508–10.

75. See *Porci e porcari nel Medioevo: Paesaggio, economia, alimentazione*, ed. M. Baruzzi and M. Montanari (Bologna, 1981), esp. pp. 29–30 and 72 for material pertaining to breeding in the woods and in the stable.

76. Schmitt, "Les traditions," p. 7.

77. It would be necessary to confirm the repetition of incidents of this kind, if indeed, as I believe, this process of reshaping cultural data during their passage from Rome has been followed in a constant manner during this historical period.

6 ⅋ Jews, the Local Church, the "Prince" and the People: Two Late Fifteenth-Century Episodes Involving the Destruction of Sacred Images

by Michele Luzzati

In a recent essay, "Artists and Clients in the Late Fifteenth and Early Sixteenth Centuries," Salvatore Settis recounts and illustrates an episode of Jewish "iconoclasm." This episode was famous for having provided the occasion for Andrea Mantegna to create the *Madonna of the Victory* (now in the Louvre) and with it to redeem the "blasphemous" gesture of Daniele da Norsa, a Jew from Mantua.[1]

The event, briefly summarized, is as follows. In 1493 a Jewish banker by the name of Daniele di Leone da Norsa bought a house, just after returning to Mantua from Villafranca Veronese where he had probably been managing the lending of money. On the exterior wall of this house, facing the street, there was a religious painting that the Jew, having already received and paid for authorization from the episcopal vicar, arranged to have removed, in this way carrying out an act of iconoclasm, albeit one approved by the local ecclesiastical authority.

Even though permission had been granted for this act, popular reaction was violent: on May 27, 1495, on the eve of the Feast of the Ascension, as a procession was passing along the street where the Jew lived, "figures of saints accompanied by verses were painted onto [his] house," as if meant to provoke a dangerous kind of attack by the members of the other faith against the Jew and his family.[2]

Two days later, Daniele da Norsa, absent from Mantua at the time of the incident, hastened to send a petition to the "prince," the Marquis Francesco Gonzaga, asking him to guarantee that similar

Michele Luzzati, "Ebrei, chiesa locale, 'principe' e popolo: due episodi di distruzione di immagini sacre alla fine del Quattrocento," *Quaderni storici*, no. 54 (1983): 847–77.

threatening demonstrations would not be repeated: the request was successful, and da Norsa, along with other Jews, obtained a general "safe-conduct."[3] But already by July 31, 1495, Francesco Gonzaga—who had fought at Fornovo against Charles VIII as captain of the anti-French league—wrote from Novara to his brother, the future Cardinal Sigismondo Gonzaga, stating that it was his intention that the sacred picture, apparently a Madonna with Child, be restored at the Jew's expense since it was he who had had it removed. In addition to the request from Daniele da Norsa, the marquis had evidently also received several complaints about the Jew's action, which was considered to be sacrilegious and had now decided to remedy the situation.

From Mantua on August 9, 1495, Sigismondo answered the marquis with a more extensive counterproposal suggested to him by an Augustinian friar: not only should the picture be repainted, but, in place of the Jew's house, a church should be constructed, dedicated to the Virgin, who had protected Gonzaga and had granted him what was then considered to have been a victory at Fornovo.

The project came to fruition: the church was constructed, Mantegna painted the *Madonna of the Victory*, and another, anonymous, artist painted a second panel that portrayed the Jews and made explicit reference to their "temeritas" in daring to erase a sacred image. This latter painting is the so-called *Madonna of the Jews*, preserved in Mantua in the Church of Sant'Andrea.

In a detailed reconstruction of the events of the commission and of the iconographic program of the *Madonna of the Victory*, Settis appropriately insists on the mingling of "public and private piety with themes of personal and dynastic propaganda," on the "channeling of popular emotion," and on the "initiative of the court and the prince," "modeling themselves on the public initiative" [*reverentia del populo*]."[4] In this way we can clearly see the dynamic that allowed a specific work to be realized. It is worth our while, now, to return once more to the starting point for that dynamic.

To "scrape away" a sacred image, particularly in a public place as Daniele da Norsa had done, was and would continue to be one of the most intolerable acts of contempt that a Jew could carry out against the Christian faith and against the Christian community of the faithful.[5] And yet not only did da Norsa conceive of the idea of "scraping" "certain figures of saints" from the wall of his house, as he wrote in his petition of May 29, 1495, but he also found an episcopal vicar disposed to give him the necessary authorization, in spite of the predictable popular reaction.

This event, which at that point did not appear to have any precedent, can be explained by the very particular condition of Italian Jews in the last decades of the fifteenth century: this is suggested when we compare the Jewish "iconoclasm" in Mantua with a little-known but analogous episode in Pisa in 1491–92, involving the banker Isacco di Vitale. The latter, in turn, was probably encouraged by yet another similar instance that had taken place in Umbria in 1471, when, on the initiative of the Jew Samuele di Consiglio da Gubbio, sacred images had been destroyed.[6]

The early stages of the event can be traced through the original draft of a long contract drawn up by a Ser Carlo da Vecchiano, the scribe of the archepiscopal curia of Pisa. This contract, dated November 24, 1491, was one to which the notary was to return, amending it later with a series of corrections and erasures.[7]

According to this original draft, the Jew Isacco di Vitale da Pisa, a member of perhaps the richest and most influential of the Italian Jewish banking families,[8] had presented to the episcopal vicar a request, written in Italian, for authorization to "destroy and take away" a painting representing Saint Christopher, located in a "vile, ugly and lowly area, where people almost never go and which is not used for anything," of the house that he owned in the parish of Santa Margherita in the center of the Mezzo quarter. Isacco was having some work done in this house that would have allowed his family "to live better and more comfortably" and that was being carried out "for the comfort, usefulness and need of himself and his family." The removal of the painting of Saint Christopher was indispensable, in the opinion of the masons, in order to continue with the work, and Isacco, fearful of being accused as a Jew of contempt for the Christian religion, wanted to ask officially for authorization by the archepiscopal Curia. Not only that, but he also committed himself to having an image of the saint painted at his own expense in the Church of Santa Margherita or elsewhere, as compensation for the one he was having destroyed.

Still according to the original draft of the contract, the vicar (the Florentine Roberto Strozzi),[9] upon seeing the petition, sent two canons of the duomo (Antonio Perini da Cascina[10] and Niccolo di Giovanni di Bergno[11]) to make an on-site inspection, charging them to report back on whether things were as Isacco had stated—that is, whether it was really necessary to destroy the image and whether it was in fact better to have a new painting of Saint Christopher placed in the Church of Santa Margherita or elsewhere. The canons carried out their mission and reported that the painting's surroundings were "lowly, vile, and in lowly condition," that the remodeling of the house was in fact underway, and that Isacco, by promising to have another painting made at his own expense, demonstrated that he did not intend to show contempt for the Christian religion. In their opinion permission could be granted to the Jew to destroy the painting and to have another made; the whole thing would honor God, Saint Christopher, and the Christian faith. On the basis of this report and with the appropriate edict, the vicar pronounced favorably on the petition of Isacco di Vitale da Pisa.

However, within a period of time that we cannot specify, the notary had to return to the contract that he had drafted and make numerous changes in it. First of all and, one might say, "miraculously," the painting of Saint Christopher had turned into two paintings: one still in the location described as lowly and vile, and another one on a pilaster "that is in the room on the second floor of the house," a large room that was probably the synagogue.[12] If in the first case the destruction of the painting was necessary and therefore comprehensible, in the second case it is hard not to conclude that Isacco da Pisa had a particular wish to eliminate from his dwelling place, and perhaps from a place sacred to Jews, the embarrassing presence of a Christian saint.

The obstacle was somehow overcome, evidently with the consent of the vicar and of the Curia, but not without considerably agitating the waters.

While the original petition stated only that the work in progress was intended to be a routine restoration, now, after a series of additions to the petition, the urgency of the work was suddenly dramatized: the house was "in great disorder and in need of great repair, because it has been and is almost in ruins," and Isacco had to proceed with the destruction of the figures "perforce, by need and necessity." The "necessity" of eliminating the second image as well does not emerge specifically, but only generally, due to the supposedly grave condition of the house. The third change in the revised petition was the disappearance of the clause stating that the Jew would have a new Saint Christopher painted in the Church of Santa Margherita or elsewhere.

The "corrections" to the petition led to "corrections" in the successive documents as well. First among these was that, in place of the two earlier canons, a new commissioner was named, this one also a canon of the duomo.

Evidently it was only after the first petition, after the "visit" of the two commissioners, and after the authorization to remove "one" picture from Isacco's house, and only at the very moment of proceeding to the removal itself, that it became clear that there were two Saint Christophers rather than one. Probably Isacco was counting on killing the proverbial two birds with one stone, and eliminating two Saint Christophers with a single authorization.

This strategy was not successful, and so Isacco presented a second petition, consistent with the truth, that put back into motion the sequence of the "visit," followed by the "report" of the commissioner, and then the pronouncement by the vicar. The notary, fortunately for us, decided not to rewrite everything, but to reuse, with appropriate corrections, the texts that he had already drafted.

The deletion of the clause about the re-creation of the painting of Saint Christopher indicates that a painting donated by a Jew may have been considered inappropriate publicity for the fact that the same Jew had had sacred images removed with authorization by the archbishop. In any case there was the problem of finding a new justification for the destruction of two paintings, at least one of which did not necessarily have to be removed.

The new visitor, the Canon Bartolomeo da Morrona, proved his goodwill by describing the house as being in need of "the greatest repair" "on account of its decrepitude and antiquity"—conditions not even hinted at in Isacco's first petition—and affirming generally that if the paintings had not been removed, da Pisa would have been able neither to finish the "works" begun nor "to anticipate new ones."

But these reasons were insufficient, at least for one of the two paintings, and here da Morrona suggested to the vicar an apparently unexceptionable formula but one that could upset the church's traditional attitude in regard to Jews: "It is not appropriate that such figures and images should be found and remain in the house of Jews."[13]

On the one hand, the Jews were having to retreat in the face of anything that was connected directly or indirectly to the Christian faith and religion, and on the other hand there was theorizing about the appropriateness of the church's retreating from the field occupied by the Jews: at the least, the church should respect the Jews' "scruples of religious observance" that had been proposed as explanation for Daniele da Norsa's iconoclastic gesture. His scrupulousness was probably connected to the fear of incurring the ire of other Jews, even if it was not strictly tied to a precept of the Jewish faith.[14]

The vicar, at least implicitly accepting the reasoning proposed by his commissioner, decided to permit Isacco to eradicate the two images and to do "whatever seemed [appropriate] to him" in the places from which they would be removed "for the improvement, construction and repair and perfecting of his house."

The apparently peaceful and legal course of the Pisan episode of Jewish "iconoclasm" should not fool us as to the truly revolutionary significance of a request of the kind presented by Isacco da Pisa to the local ecclesiastical authority.

It had not been just for a day, or even for a year that Jews and Saint Christopher had lived together in the house in the parish of Santa Margherita: actually they had been there together for at least a century. In the second half of the fourteenth century, the building was owned by a famous merchant-banker, Parasone Grasso, who, in the last years of his life, was the head of the Opera del Duomo di Pisa to which he left all his goods.[15] And perhaps it is precisely Parasone Grasso who should be credited with the hardly extraordinary idea of having the images of Saint Christopher painted on the walls of the house.[16]

Within five years of the death of Parasone Grasso, in 1395 to be precise, a Jewish moneylending bank was installed in his old dwelling place.[17] At the beginning of the fifteenth century, the Jews continued to reside and to make loans there, having sublet the building from Pisan merchants who had rented it from the Opera del Duomo. But the discrepancy between the rent that the Jews paid for subletting the building and what the merchants paid for renting it quickly convinced the opera to eliminate all intermediaries and to rent the building directly to the Jews beginning in 1408, after the fall of Pisa to Florence.[18] Then the Jewish moneylending activity passed exclusively to Vitale di Matassia da Roma, founding father of the da Pisa dynasty, who installed himself, his family, and the bank, in the house in the parish of Santa Margherita, under terms of a regular rental contract with the Opera del Duomo. This latter group—a lay organization but with a religious purpose—thus found itself hosting not only usurers but also Jewish usurers. Although this situation did not go against civil laws, it certainly collided with canon laws, which is exactly what Colino da San Giusto, a trustee of the opera, began to argue in 1440, when in his effort to evict the Jews, either for scruple or spite, he encountered opposition from the Florentine authorities.[19]

Well aware of the semireligious character of the building in which they were living, the Jews of the da Pisa family certainly must have been thinking from the beginning at least of getting rid of the two images of Saint Christopher. Finally in 1466, with agreement from the city authorities, the da Pisa family succeeded in buying from the Opera del Duomo the "palace" where they had been living by now for more than half a century and which up to the end of the sixteenth century was still known in Pisa as the "house of the Jews."[20]

Even though the the property was owned by the da Pisa family and was completely at their disposal, it would still be another twenty-five years before Isacco di Vitale da Pisa would decide to take the step that probably all his ancestors had vainly hoped to take: to remove the sacred Christian "pictures" from their building that housed, among other things, the synagogue.

We can well imagine, behind the decision to come out into the open with an official request to the archepiscopal Curia, all the soundings, the favors, the recommendations, and the pressures of which a very rich family was capable, a family by now profoundly connected to the life of the city. We can well imagine a privileged relationship, slowly built over the course of a whole century, with the Pisan ruling classes, with the power of the Medici, with the Florentine dignitaries, and with the local clergy itself.

Things had arrived at a point where the da Pisa family might well have assumed that the erasure of the images would not provoke much reaction: in a certain way, the agreement (*committenza*) for the act of "iconoclasm" (given that *committenza*, in a broad sense, is necessary here for the destruction as well as for the creation) was ending up involving not only the da Pisa family and their religious brethren, but also a stratum of inhabitants, lay and ecclesiastical, disposed to believe that "it was not appropriate for such figures and images to be found and to remain in the house of Jews."

We can only believe that it was the example of the Pisan "iconoclasm," well known to all Italian Jews and especially to the bankers because of the very close relations that existed among them, that persuaded Daniele da Norsa of the possibility of imitating Isacco di Vitale.[21]

Where the course of the Pisan "iconoclasm" had been gradual, the course of the Mantuan "iconoclasm" was abrupt. In fact, Daniele da

Norsa did not let even two years elapse between buying the house and destroying the images, and furthermore he did not have the roots in Mantua that the da Pisa enjoyed in their city.[22] It took a hundred years in Pisa to erase the two images of San Christopher *on the inside* of a house but only two years in Mantua to erase one Madonna with Child *on the outside* of a house. The agreement (*committenza*) for the act of "iconoclasm" could certainly not work in favor of da Norsa to the extent that it had for da Pisa.

Not only that but, in his haste, Daniele da Norsa omitted a "procedural" step that his Tuscan coreligionist had been careful to attend to. As we have seen, even after Isacco di Vitale da Pisa had obtained authorization from the archepiscopal vicar on November 24, 1491, he still did not proceed immediately to have the two images removed. Instead, strengthened by the permission he had received from the religious authorities, he also asked permission of the civil authority, specifically of the Florentine Magistracy of the Otto di Guardia, which was specifically responsible for matters concerning Jews. This permission must not have been easily obtained, since several months were still to pass before Isacco was at the point of removing the images. It was not until August 3, 1492, and in the presence of the same archepiscopal notary who had drawn up the earlier contracts, that a mason from Pietrasanta proceeded to the removal of the images, a removal that was scrupulously documented by the notary.[23]

Thus another profound difference emerges here between the procedure followed by Isacco da Pisa and that followed by Daniele da Norsa. It appears that the latter, contenting himself with the bishop's permission, did not ask for any specific permission from the civil authorities (and thereby from the marquis of Mantua), which left him vulnerable when the "citizenry" ("the piazza") of Mantua contested his "iconoclastic" gesture. Whereas Isacco da Pisa had correctly interpreted the "signals" coming to him from all sides (and above all from the exhortations of the Observant Franciscans and the discord, often mediated by the state, that they provoked), Daniele da Norsa had overestimated the influence of episcopal authority on the mass of the faithful. He had left an opening for an alliance between the "prince" and the faithful, which when opportunely orchestrated by several regular priests of a lowly station, easily led to an implicit disavowal of the conduct of the bishop and his representatives.[24]

When the notary, in his record of the removal of the Pisan images wrote that this came about by virtue of the archbishop's *licentia* and the Florentine Otto's *confirmatio* of that *licentia*, he was very clearly aware that the last word went to the state, that is to the "prince," when in matters of religious conduct problems of public order were involved. Isacco da Pisa, even after being assured of ecclesiastical permission, correctly added that of the civil authorities.

Even though Daniele da Norsa could presumably have availed himself of the precedents of Pisa and Gubbio and of the extraordinary justification devised by the Canon Bartolomeo da Morrona to explain the removal of Christian images from Jewish houses, he still ended up leaving himself vulnerable to the reactions of the Christian faithful, as they were urged on by the propaganda of the Observants and other orders. When confronted with a prince set on not loosing the opportunity to strengthen his people's *reverentia* toward him, Daniele was not helped by the tardy, though ingenious, inspiration to declare, in the petition of May 29, 1495, that he had had the figures removed precisely to avoid the possibility of an ill- intentioned person damaging them and causing the blame then to fall upon him.[25]

The "prince" (whether by this we mean a "lord" or a republican government directed more or less covertly by a family or an oligarchical group) seems thus to have set himself up as arbiter between the "people" and the local ecclesiastical hierarchies in matters, not necessarily of faith, but certainly of religious conduct. In the case of Pisa, the central government of Florence had decided to support the decisions by the local ecclesiastical authority, risking possible popular hostility. In the case of Mantua, even though the "prince" guaranteed the security of the Jews, he did not hesitate to oppose local ecclesiastical authority in order to side with popular objections.[26]

In both cases, however, what emerges is the capacity and determination of the lay power to impose autonomously in local situations the choices that it considers more appropriate even in the area of religious conduct. This is particularly true regarding the Jews, whose circumstances seem to depend less on the decisions and official pronouncements of the ecclesiastical authority and more on the will and capacity of the "prince" to address the feelings of the subjects or the citizens. At any rate, it was that same Francesco Gonzaga who, on June 11, 1495, a few days after the episode of the popular protests, granted a broad safe-conduct to Daniele da Norsa and to the Jews of Mantua and who also on July 31 of the same year had sentenced the "iconoclast," on pain of death, to pay for the redoing of the sacred image. On August 19, 1497, a year away from the festivities for the inauguration of the Church of Santa Maria della Vittoria and the painting of Mantegna, he granted to his Jewish subjects (probably with Daniele da Norsa in mind) a new "absolution," broader than the earlier ones and meant to extend "even to the profanations of sacred images, this sacrilege having reached the ears of the marquis but not having been proved!"[27]

But by now, with the political, military, and religious storm beating down on Italy and after the expulsion of the Jews from the Iberian peninsula, sleight-of-hand tricks like those of Gonzaga (or of the Medici, or of the popes themselves) would soon become impossible. The Italian Jews of the Renaissance would have lost every illusion as to any real progress in the process of integration with Christian society, a process that perhaps reached its highest point in the granting of permissions, both civil and ecclesiastical, to destroy sacred images.[28]

Notes

[N.B. Abridgments of some of the extensive notes have been marked with *omissis*. Appendices in the original Italian article have been dropped from the translation.]

1. S. Settis, "Artisti e committenti fra Quattro e Cinquecento," in *Storia d'Italia, Annali*, vol. 4; *Intellettuali e potere* (Turin, 1981), pp. 712–22 ("Mantova 1495–96: La 'reverentia' del popolo").

2. Ibid., p. 713; additionally, P. Norsa, *I Norsa (1350–1950): Contributo alla storia di una famiglia di banchieri* ([reprint] Milan, 1951), pp. 47–53 (*Daniele de Nursia fu Leone e la Madonna della Vittoria a Mantova*), and idem, "Una famiglia di banchieri: La famiglia Norsa (1350–1950). Parte prima: secoli XIV e XV," *Bollettino dell'Archivio Storico del Banco di Napoli* 6 (1953): 30–35, 74–77 ("Daniele de Nursia e la Madonna della Vittoria").

3. Daniele da Norsa's petition (in Archivio di Stato di Mantova [ASMn], Corrispondenza da Mantova, busta 2447, 1495 maggio 29; partially damaged) has been published by A. Portioli, "La Chiesa e la Madonna della Vittoria," *Atti e Memorie dell'Accademia Virgiliana di Mantova* (1884): 60 (Portioli's essay also came out separately with the publication date 1883, in Mantua, and in the *Archivio Storico Lombardo* 10 (1883): 447–73, under the title "La Chiesa e la Madonna della Vittoria di A. Mantegna a Mantova"). The petition can also be read in Norsa, *I Norsa*, p. 87 (but the mounting is paper, not parchment, as Norsa asserts). This petition should be closely compared with the decree of immunity that Marquis Francesco Gonzaga had already signed by June 11, 1495, in favor of the Jews of his state; and the first of the Jews cited is precisely Daniele da Norsa (ASMn, Archivio Gonzaga Libro dei Decreti, n. 24, fol. 246rv; quoted in Norsa, *I Norsa*, p. 49, and in idem, "Una famiglia," pp. 32, 74).

4. Settis, "Artisti," p. 717; cf. pp. 712, 718 [*omissis*].

5. Daniele Norsa was perfectly aware of the gravity of his gesture, so much so that he justified it in the manner that we will describe (see n. 25) [*omissis*, most scholars have seen his act as perfectly natural]; A. Luzio, "La Madonna della Vittoria del Mantegna," *Emporium* 10 (1899): 359, n59; Portioli, "La Chiesa," p. 59; J. Lauts,

ed., *Die "Madonna della Vittoria,"* 2d. ed. (Stuttgart, 1960), pp. 12–14; and Settis, "Artisti," p. 713. There are numerous sources testifying to real or presumed icono-clastic acts by the Jews and the very violent reactions that they provoked; it would be useful to make a specific collection of these sources (see, in any case, *Index Exemplorum: A Handbook of Medieval Religious Tales,* ed. F. C. Tubach [Helsinki, 1969]). [*Omissis.*]

[The known examples of Jewish iconoclasm], although incomplete, are easily unified through the major works on the history of the Jews, and they are sufficient to show the anguished climate in which a Jew had to operate if he were intent on eliminating sacred images even in a period of apparent decline of the traditional devotions (see R. C. Trexler, "Florentine Religious Experience: The Sacred Image," *Studies in the Renaissance* 19 (1972): 7–41, and in particular pp. 25–30 on the significance of the profanation and the "iconoclasm" on the Christian side.)

6. On February 26, 1471, the painter Jacopo "Bedi" "cancelavit, abbolevit et delevit de quodam muro existente in domo" of Samuele di Consiglio, Jew of Gubbio, "immagines gloriosissime Virginis Marie et beatorum sanctorum Antonii abatis de Vienna et Ubaldi, olim episcopi eugubini," with the pact to "reficere similes imagines in fraternitate Alborum, in quodam oratorio noviter construpto in dicta fraternitate," or elsewhere, at the expense, probably, of the Jew (document edited by L. Bonfatti, in M. Gualandi, *Memorie originali riguardanti le belle arti,* 4th series [Bologna, 1843], pp. 51–53, by the Archivio di Stato di Gubbio, Fondo Notarile, Prof. no. 86, ser Antonio di Niccolo, fol. 157r–v; for this reference, I thank Mr. Ettore A. Sannipoli of Gubbio, who explained to me that the "re-created" picture is almost certainly lost) [*omissis*].

The relationships between the families involved in the "iconoclastia" of Gubbio of 1471 and that of Pisa of 1491–92 can be represented in the following way:

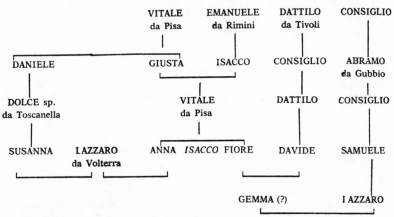

7. The document is published in appendix I of the original.

8. See M. Luzzati, "Prestito ebraico e studenti ebrei all'Università di Pisa (secc. XV–XVIII)," *Bollettino Storico Pisano* 49 (1980): 31, and idem, "Per la storia degli ebrei italiani nel Rinascimento: Matrimonii e apostasia di Clemeza di Vitale dal Pisa," in *Studi sul medioevo cristiano offerti a Raffaello Morghen* (Rome, 1974). pp. 430–33.

9. The archbishop of Pisa at that time was Raffaele Sansoni Riario, nephew of Sixtus IV, born in Savona in 1459, arrested in Florence after the conspiracy of the Pazzi [Lorenzo de' Medici, *Lettere,* vol. 3 (1478–1479), ed. N. Rubinstein (Florence, 1977), pp. 11–13].

He had the diocese of Pisa as his benefice beginning on September 17, 1479, when he had already been cardinal for two years; he was then archbishop of the city until giving it up in 1499 (F. Matthei, *Ecclesiae pisanae historia etc.*, vol. 2 [Lucca, 1722], p. 164; N. Zucchelli, *Cronotassi dei Vescovi e Arcivescovi di Pisa* [Pisa, 1907], pp. 172–75; N. Caturegli, "Le condizioni della chiesa di Pisa nella seconda metà del secolo XV," *Bollettino Storico Pisano* 19 [1950]: 21); Sansoni Riario never made his residence in Pisa. One of his vicars was Roberto di Carlo Strozzi (1451–92), professor of canon law at the Studio of Pisa (see A. F. Verde, *Lo Studio fiorentino: 1473–1503. Ricerche e documenti*, vol. 2 [Florence, 1973], pp. 584–87). On Carlo Strozzi, see P. Litta, *Famiglie celebri italiane*, vol. 5: "Strozzi di Firenze" (Milan, 1839), table 4; G. B. Picotti, *La giovinezza di Leone X* (Milan, 1928) (annotated edition with preface by M. Petrocchi and introduction by C. Violante [Rome, 1981]), pp. 243ff., 246, 278, 280; N. Caturegli, "Le condizioni," pp. 22–23; L. Martines, *Lawyers and Statecraft in Renaissance Florence* (Princeton, 1968), pp. 76, 507; G. P. Marchi, "Lettere pisane del nunzio pontificio Giacomo Gherardi," in *Miscellanea Gilles Gerard Meersseman*, vol. 2 (Padua, 1970), p. 685 ("canonista famoso"). He was canon of the Duomo of Pisa (Caturegli, "Le condizioni," p. 22; Archivio Arcivescovile di Pisa, Visite pastorali, no. 1, fol. 358), and he is generally judged to have been very educated and not without "interessamento pastorale." We find some clue to his sensitivity to works of art in a passage from the minutes of the pastoral visit conducted by him in 1490: "deinde accessit ad plebem Sancti Cassiani [in Valdarno pisano, not far from Cascina], pulcherrimam in eius constructione et hedifitio." For an autograph confirmation of Roberto Strozzi, see *Catalogue of Dated and Datable Manuscripts, c. 700–1600, in the Department of Manuscripts, The British Library*, ed. A. G. Watson, vol. 1 (London, 1979), pp. 64–65.

10. See M. Luzzati, *Una guerra di popolo: Lettere private del tempo dell'assedio di Pisa (1494–1509)* (Pisa, 1973), p. 278. Very little is known about this person who perhaps was ambassador of the republic of Pisa to the emperor Maximilian; he was a canon of the Duomo of Pisa from 1486 (Archivio Arcivescovile di Pisa, Visite Pastorali, no. 1, fol. 241v).

11. The son probably of Giovanni di Bergo, a vintner, of Arrigo (see *Il catasto di Pisa of 1428–29*, ed. B. Casini [Pisa, 1964], n. 139) was rector of the Pisan parish church of San Lorenzo in Chinseca (Archivio di Stato, Florence [hereafter ASFi], NA, R 244 [1461–69], ser Piero Roncioni, fol. 383 r–v, 1467 luglio 27) and canon of the Duomo of Pisa from February 22, 1490 (Archivio Arcivescovile di Pisa, Visite Pastorali, no. 1, fol. 243v).

12. A notarial contract of January 13, 1439 was drafted in Pisa "in schola sive sinaghoga iudeorum posita super secundo solario . . . in domo" of Isacco di Emanuele da Rimini, grandfather of Isacco di Vitale, the author of the petition to the Vicar Roberto Strozzi (ASFi, NA, F 598 [1439], ser Guglielmo Franchi, fols. 86v–87). See M. Luzzati, "L'insediamento ebraico a Pisa," in *Livorno e Pisa: Due città e un territorio nella politica dei Medici* (Pisa, 1980), p. 154. The synagogue of Pisa, the oldest one of which we have records, was still in the house of the da Pisa family in the sixteenth century (see n. 20).

13. Bartolomeo di Benedetto di ser Bartolomeo dei Lambardi di Morrona was probably rather old, but not uneducated. [*Omissis.*]

Advanced age and economic necessity help explain how the Canon Bartolomeo da Morrona might without too much difficulty have agreed to authorize the removal of images by the rich and influential da Pisa family of Jewish bankers. But his statement advising that they proceed to the act of "iconoclasm" ("non decet etc.") seems to reflect a clear conviction, formed in spite of an awareness that many ecclesiastical circles had by now assumed rather rigid attitudes toward Jews. [*Omissis*: in the original

Luzzati summarizes the canon's education and career, showing how the da Morrona were connected to the Franciscans.]

14. Norsa, "Una famiglia," p. 31. Another Pisan example—but now post-Trent—of damage to images on the part of Jews can illuminate the "official" position of the church relative to the sacred images located in the houses of Israelites. In 1613 the Inquisition accused the Jew Raffaello Moreno, originally from Constantinople and living in Pisa for two years (see Luzzati, *L'insediamento*, p. 162): in the house that he had rented, there was discovered, according to the accusation, an "image of the Madonna which the Jews had reportedly defaced." Moreno defended himself saying that when he went to live in the house, he had noted a cloth that covered over part of a wall and he had been told by "some Jews that it was proper to live there, and he need not worry about what the image represented." [*Omissis*. Since he believed that the laws of his faith prohibited him from living in the presence of Christian images, he would have moved had he known what the image was. He noted, in his defense, that he and his family recognized what an offense it would be to deface a Christian image. Moreno was absolved.]

We can see clearly from this trial that a Jew with a sacred image in his house had no other alternatives than either to keep it, perhaps covered over, or else to move to another house. As to Moreno's declaration that the "law" "absolutely prohibits" Jews from living where there are images sacred to another religion, we are dealing with an exaggeration, since the obligation to destroy images does not have absolute value, at least not in the Diaspora (see Y. H. Yerushalmi, *From Spanish Court to Italian Ghetto: Isaac Cardoso, a Study in Seventeenth-Century Marranism and Jewish Apologetics* [New York, 1971], pp. 451–55).

It is clear that, from the point of view of the church, to impose on Jews the presence of sacred images where they already existed in their houses, was part of a catechistical and conversionistic practice that could only legitimize the acceptance of Jews' existence among Christians. The fear of contempt being shown for the images, which seems to inspire the opinion of the Canon da Morrona ("non decet etc."), is the expression of a different attitude, certainly not attributing equal dignity to the two faiths, but at least tending to desist from the "provocation" of the Jews. The church and the faithful were supposed to be involved in a constant "provocation" of Jews, in order to lead them to conversion: to consent to them getting rid of sacred images, even if with the excuse that they might have abused them, meant less commitment to the duty of "beseiging" them to the point of surrender. On this duty the lay authorities, for reasons of convenience or public order, could be flexible, but the church, at least in principle, could not. The exception could perhaps be justified in a situation where some compensation in money or in favors came from the Jewish side, thus counterbalancing the "sacrifice" made by the Christian community, although this could not be supported by any legitimate theoretical reason.

15. On the economic activities of Parasone Grasso, see F. Melis, *Note di storia della banca pisana nel Trecento* (Pisa, 1955), pp. 33–61. The oldest description of his house is found in a book of the possessions of 1367, found in Archivio di Stato di Pisa (ASPi), Opera del Duomo (OD), no. 1319, fol. 1 and no. 1320 (copy of the preceding), fol. 2: "la casa grande de la torre et con li [*sic*] altre case apogiate ad se" was appraised at 1,000 libbre. Parasone Grasso became trustee of the Duomo di Pisa in 1385 (ASPi, OD, no. 440, fol. 1) and died in 1390; the house went through inheritance to the Opera del Duomo, but was to be in usufruct to the nephew of Parasone, Abramo di Ranieri di Lando Grasso, during his natural life (on the father Ranieri, see Melis, *Note*, p. 60). Abramo died August 21, 1400 (ASPi, OD, no. 526, fol. 52).

16. On the apotropaic value of the images of Saint Christopher ("Christophorum

videas, postea tutus eas"), see G. Bardy, "Christophe (Saint)," in *Dictionnaire d'histoire et de geographie ecclesiastiques*, vol. 12 (Paris, 1950), cols. 777–78, and F. Werner, "Christophorus," in *Lexicon der christlichen Ikonographie*, ed. W. Braunfels and V. Herder (Rome, 1973), cols. 496–508. Testimony exists regarding another painting of Saint Christopher in a house of the chapel of San Pietro in Palude (contiguous to the parish of Santa Margherita), a painting probably of "gigantic dimensions": it is mentioned in a contract made by the Merchant Piero di Pone with two craftesmen, a stonemason and a carpenter, on July 17, 1441. [*Omissis.*] ASFi, NA, L 371 (1442), ser Piero Lupi, fol. 111.

17. Daniele di maestro Melli da Bertinoro, already by March 1, 1395, lived and was building up a moneylending bank on behalf of a society of Jews "in domo heredum Parazonis Grassi, posita Pisis in cappella sancte Margherite" (ASFi, NA, B 982, ser Battista Boccianti, fol. 19).

18. Archivio di Stato, Pisa [hereafter ASPi], OD, no. 526, fol. 52 and no. 527, fol. 47v; on November 5, 1402, the house was rented to the merchants Bindo, Jacopo, and Filippo di Gherardo Astai for eighteen florins per year (ASPi, OD, no. 527, fol. 48). On the basis of a notation of August 10, 1403, we gather that the "inhabitant" of the house was a "Consiglio iudeo" (probably Consiglio di Dattilo di maestro Elia da Tivoli) who paid to the Astai thirty-six florins per year (ibid., fol. 48v). For the house in which "the Jews live and practice usury," the Astai paid rent up to June 30, 1407 (ibid., no. 528, fol. 42v, and no. 529, fols. 47v–48). But already by June 17 of that same year 1407, the Opera del Duomo had given the house for rent directly to Vitale di Matassia da Roma, chief heir of the da Pisa, for three years and for twenty-eight florins per year, to begin on October 1, 1408 (ASPi, OD, no. 38, ser Francesco da Ghezzano, fols. 33v–34, and no. 530, fol. 29). In the successive account books of the Opera del Duomo, and through various notarial drafts, the story of this location can be followed, year by year, until 1467.

19. See P. M. Lonardo, "Gli ebrei a Pisa sino alla fine del secolo XV," *Studi storici* 8 (1899): 61–62, 80–82 [*omissis* about further attempts to evict the Jews found in ASPi, Dipl. Primaziale, 1441 aprile 12].

20. M. Luzzatti, "L'insediamento ebraico," pp. 154–55 [*omissis* about the history of the building]. *Der Reisebericht des David Reubeni*, ed. E. Biberfeld (Berlin, 1892), pp. 61, 63, 65–66.

21. Until the fifteenth century there were no direct family relationships between the da Pisa family and the Mantuan branch of the da Norsa family (regarding that, see the following note); but, aside from the close relations, already mentioned, among all the Jewish bankers of north-central Italy (see M. Luzzati, "I legami fra i banchi ebraici toscani ed i banchi veneti e dell'Italia settentrionale nei secoli XV e XVI," in *Atti del Convegno Internazionale "Gli Ebrei a Venezia"* [Venice, June 5–10, 1983]), we can recall that a specific point of contact between the Jewish bankers of Tuscany and the Jewish bankers of Mantua occurred in Verona and at Villafranca Veronese where Daniele da Norsa was a lender (see G. M. Varanini, "Prestatori ebrei a Verona nel Quattrocento," in ibid.). From 1474 at least, the bank of Villafranca was rented to Manuele di Buonaiuto da Camerino, a resident of Florence, and was directed by Leuccio di Consiglio di Leuccio da Viterbo, who lived in Pisa, the son of a collaborator of Vitale di Isacco da Pisa. In 1478, a grandnephew of Manuele da Camerino, Dattalino di Salomone di Vitale, having reached majority, by a contract drawn up in Florence, gave his assent, through the agency of attorneys, to the placement of the bank; and among these attorneys was the father of Daniele da Norsa, Leone di Manuele (Archivio di Stato, Mantua [hereafter ASMn], Notarile Estensioni, 1477 luglio 4, fol. 38; ASFi, NA, P 353 [1478–81], ser Pietro da Vinci, 1478 aprile 9, fols. 18rv, 1478 maggio 4, fols. 39v–40; per Leuccio di Consiglio e per suo padre cfr. ASFi, NA, C 153 [1464–

66], ser Carlo da Vecchiano, Pisa 1465 agosto 2, fols. 115v–116; ibid., D. 127 [1467–68], ser Niccolo Donati, Pisa, 1467 novembre 1, II, c 146v; ibid., Pisa, dicembre 1467, c.n.n.). The passing of the bank of Villafranca Veronese to Daniele da Norsa necessarily involved new contacts with the da Camerino family, who were associated with the da Pisa family in the banks of Florence (V. Cassuto, *Gli Ebrei a Firenze nell'età del Rinascimento* [Florence, 1918], pp. 260–61 and passim). Finally Simone di Vitale da Pisa, the brother of Isacco, at the end of the first decade of the sixteenth century was head of the lending bank of Verona (Archivio di Stato, Bologna, Ufficio del Registro, Copie degli Atti, I, fol. 318, 1510 dicembre 6; Archivio di Stato, Verona, Antico archivio del Comune, Ducali, reg. 16, fol. 14v, 1509 ottobre 23 and 1509 novembre 2).

22. Daniele da Norsa was descended from a certain Abramo "de Norcia," perhaps a brother of the Manuele who began the Ferrarese branch of the family, and who since 1390 had participated in building up a business in Mantua. Norsa, "Una famiglia," p. 3. E. Castelli, "I banchi feneratizi ebraici nel Mantovano (1386–1808)," *Atti e Memorie dell'Accademia Virgiliana di Mantova*, n.s., 31 (1959): 10. A son of Abramo, Manuele, a resident of Rimini, was a member in 1420 of a Mantuan company for making loans on security (Norsa, "Una famiglia," pp. 10, 55–56; Castelli, "I banchi," p. 15) and only in 1428 did he move to Mantua, where he is remembered up until 1444 (Norsa, "Una famiglia," pp. 10, 56; Castelli, "I banchi," p. 16, thinks Manuele was already dead in 1435). The sons, Jacob and Leone, continued to live in Mantua (Norsa, "Una famiglia," pp. 26–30), the latter "the most important banker of his time in Mantua" (ibid., p. 27), who died between 1490 and 1491. Daniele, the son of Leone, was already working with his father in Mantua in 1477 (ibid., pp. 31 and 71); after having been in Villafranca Veronese (as he recounts in the petition of May 29, 1495) and perhaps as early as 1491, Daniele (Norsa, "Una famiglia," p. 31; Castelli, "I banchi," p. 35) came back to Mantua or to the area around it, and, in addition to taking part in moneylending activities in the city, he took over on May 24, 1493, the management of the bank of Borgoforte (Castelli, "I banchi," p. 175). Also after the episode of "iconoclasm," Daniele di Leone da Norsa, together with his sons, continued to practice moneylending in Mantua and in the area, and he died in 1528, probably in his eighties (Norsa, "Una famiglia," p. 34). In spite of their position of prominence in the city (see also V. Colorni, "Prestito ebraico e comunità ebraiche nell'Italia centrale e settentrionale con particolare riguardo alla comunità di Mantova," *Rivista di Storia del Diritto Italiano* 8 [1935]: 406–58, now in idem, *Judaica Minora* [Milan, 1983]), the Norsa family did not enjoy that situation of monopoly in Pisa and of absolute preeminence in the Florentine state that characterized the da Pisa family, whose roots in the Tuscan city were in any case more ancient that those of the Norsa family in Mantua.

23. See appendix II [in the Italian original of this article]. Concerning the competence of the Otto di Guardia regarding all the matters concerning the Jews of the Florentine state, see Cassuto, *Gli Ebrei a Firenze*, pp. 196–97. The register of the deliberations of the Otto, where the *licentia* should have been found that granted to Isacco di Vitale da Pisa permission to erase the religious images from his house, turns out to have been missing since the time when the inventory of the collection was compiled (ASFi, Otto di Guardia, no. 90).

The delay in granting permission could have been due to the death of Lorenzo de' Medici (April 8, 1492), to whom the da Pisa family was particularly connected, but more probably the matter must have inspired much puzzlement in Florence (see n. 26). The mason who carried out the physical destruction of the two paintings was the eighteen-year-old (see Archivio della Parrocchia di San Ranierino in Pisa, Battesimi, C, fol. 45v) Tommaso di Giuliano di Tommaso da Pietrasanta; his father had worked, twenty years earlier, on remodeling the archbishop's palace (Archivio della Mensa Arcivescovile di Pisa, Entrate e Uscite, no. 11, fol. 80); thus, in the choice of both the notary and the mason, Isacco di Vitale da Pisa made it clear that he wanted to move with extreme caution.

24. The *licenza* granted by the vicar of the bishop of Mantua seems not to be traceable, as I was kindly told by Don Giuseppe Pecorari, of the episcopal Curia of Mantua. The episcopal vicar during these years was Bonifacio Pico, as emerges from a series of documents of the Archivio di Stato, Mantua (ASMn) of 1494 and 1495, generously pointed out to me by the director, Adele Bellù. He was a *decretorum doctor* (ASMn, Archivio Gonzaga, F. II.10, Registri Decreti, lib. 20, 29, fol. 280v, 1497 maggio 29) and perhaps originally from Casale, considering that he signs himself *decanus Casalensis*, writing from Casale on September 27 and 29, 1511, to the Marquis Francesco and to Isabelle d'Este (ibid., E.XX.2, busta 745). But of even greater interest than the vicar in the episode of Daniele da Norsa is that of the bishop, Ludovico Gonzaga, uncle of the Marquis Francesco, elected in 1483 and died in 1511. The addressee in 1493 of a letter in favor of the Monti di Pietà and himself a Franciscan (H. Holzapfel, *Die Anfänge der Montes Pietatis* [Munich, 1903], p. 7; A. Ghinato, "I Monti di Pietà istituzione francescana," *Picenum Seraphicum* 9 [1972]: 58; V. Meneghin, *Bernardino da Feltre e i Monti di Pietà* [Vicenza, 1974], pp. 107–12), he did not have a prominent role in the establishment of Monte di Pietà of Mantua (Meneghin, *Bernardo*, pp. 79–119). But even more than his hypothetically favorable attitude toward the Jews, what must have mattered in the "disavowal" of the permission granted by his vicar to da Norsa was the strong tension existing with his nephew, the Marquis Francesco: this is an element that has not been taken into consideration by any of the authors who have been concerned with the case of the da Norsa. Even Bishop Ludovico may have taken part in the conspiracy of 1487 against the marquis. See L. Mazzoldi, *La storia*, vol. 2: *Da Ludovico secondo Marchese a Francesco secondo* (Mantua, 1961), p. 84, and see pp. 208, 440–41. For the "ferocious hatred" between the bishop and the marquis, see U. Rossi, "Commedie classiche in Gazzuolo," *Giornale Storico della Letteratura Italiana* 12 (1888): 304–5. A letter of 1489 from Bishop Ludovico Gonzaga to Bonifacio "de Pichis" (not identified as his vicar) was published by V. Rossi, "Niccolò Lelio Cosmico poeta padovano del secolo XV," *Giornale Storico della Letteratura Italiana* 13 (1889): 151–52. One of the reasons for the conflict between the Marquis Francesco and his uncle, the Bishop Ludovico, lay in the latter's aspirations to a cardinal's hat, a position that was achieved instead by the brother of the marquis, Sigismondo, one of the patrons of the *Madonna della Vittoria*. In this picture of family quarrels, it is truly paradoxical that Sigismondo Gonzaga could have been recently identified as the vicar of Bishop Ludovico Gonzaga (*L'opera completa del Mantegna*, presentation by M. Bellonci, ed. N. Garavaglia, 2d. ed. [Milan, 1979], p. 118). Finally we should note, however, that in Gubbio, where government had not intervened, the advice was given to consult a Dominican theologian (see n. 6).

25. Settis is not correct when he writes, concerning the petition of Daniele da Norsa on May 29, 1495, that "neither here nor elsewhere did he say why he had wanted to remove those figures" (Settis, *Artisti*, p. 713). Da Norsa justified his request to remove the image with the fear that others might damage it and that the blame might then fall onto him. [*Omissis.*]

The excuse was not very strange, then, if we think less of malevolence on the part of the Christians, but rather of the tensions among the Jewish groups themselves and of the "vendette" of the converted Jews. The accusation of having tried to poison the apostate daughter and Christian son-in-law was brought against Vitale da Pisa, in 1484, by a Jew (Luzzati, "Per la storia," p. 438). Raffaello Moreno in 1613 (see n. 14) blamed the damage of the Madonna that he had in his house on some boys "either

Christians or Jews" or else on his "enemies." In 1470, the Jew Falcone da Monza was accused of having profaned a picture representing the Madonna in the house of Salomone da Monza and then of having burned it in the fireplace; but the accusation, brought by a converted Jew "for malevolence and private hatred," turned out to be false. *The Jews in the Duchy of Milan*, ed. S. Simonsohn, vol. 1 (1387–1477) (Jerusalem, 1982), no. 1226. A case of extortion on the part of a Jew, under threat of accusations of crimes "against the Catholic faith," by other Jews took place in Florence in 1435 (G. A. Brucker, *Firenze nel Rinascimento* (Florence, 1980), p. 385 [*Renaissance Florence* (New York, 1969)]. On January 14, 1471, a "new Christian," "Thomas Pacis de Lombardia," presented himself to the episcopal Curia of Lucca to denounce an episode that had occurred in the preceding November in the house of the moneylender Guglielmo di Leone da Fano, whose servant he was. Another "servant," Salomone, was making some waffles (*cialde*) next to the fire when Angelo da Fermo, probably also a dependent of the moneylender, [*omissis*: saw him make the waffles in the sign of the cross, which Angelo understood as a sacrilege]. Archivio Arcivescovile di Lucca, Libri Antichi n. 99/A, fol. 48. Unfortunately we do not know the rest of the episode, which, true or not, is testimony in any case to the Jews' obsession with the potential accusation of "iconoclasm." Note, for example, that the mere cutting into a waffle to allow it to cook better or to give it a more pleasing look becomes, in the record of the accusor's deposition, a *scultura Sanctissime Crucis*. On the *delazione* as an instrument of struggle among the various leading groups of the Jewish community in the late Middle Ages, see M. Kriegel, *Les Juifs à la fin du Moyen Age dans l'Europe méditerranéenne* (Paris, 1979), pp. 133, 140–43.

26. In evaluating the various routes followed by the Pisan Jew and the Mantuan Jew to obtain the authorization to remove the images, we must keep in mind a third element. In addition to the facts that in Pisa the images were on the inside of a house and in Mantua on the outside and that in Pisa Jews had lived in the house for a hundred years and in Mantua only for two years, Mantua was the city of the "prince." It was the capital, while Pisa instead was a subject city. One could deduce from this that the "reverentia del popolo" deserved more attention in Mantua than in Pisa and that the authorization of the "prince" was more necessary in the Lombard city than in the Tuscan one, where the Florentine government would have had difficulty in contradicting a vicar with the name of Strozzi. In reality, I still hold that Daniele da Norsa undervalued the importance of the "prince"-people relationship and that the authorization by the civil powers was perhaps in fact more necessary in Pisa than in Mantua. If Isacco di Vitale da Pisa had not asked for the "license" from the Florentine government, he would have provided the occasion, in the case of popular objections, for an intervention aimed at demonstrating the dominant city's respect for the subject city. The long wait for the granting of the "license" by the Florentine Otto di Guardia demonstrates that the matter was carefully evaluated in Florence, and not without reason, since two years later Pisa rebelled, expelled the Jewish moneylenders, and established the Monte di Pietà (M. Luzzati, "Fra Timoteo da Lucca (1456–1513): appunti di ricerca," in *Miscellanea Augusto Campana* [Padua, 1981], pp. 386–89). Once again Isacco di Vitale da Pisa showed that he had an awareness of the political and religious climate of his city that seems to have been lacking in Norsa. The conflicts between the people, the local authorities, and the central government had already emerged in 1440 (see n. 19) on the occasion of the attempt by the Opera del Duomo to expel the Jewish moneylenders from the house that they owned: since the Opera del Duomo—as Charles VIII showed in November of 1494, choosing it as the site for the negotiations between the Pisans and the Florentines (P. Vaglienti, *Storia dei suoi tempi, 1492–1514*, ed. G. Berti, M. Luzzati, and E. Tongiorgi [Pisa, 1982], pp. 15–16)—was an institution relatively independent of control by Florence and, in the

conditions to which it was subject, more representative of the citizens and the people of Pisa than any other; the position taken by the *podestà* Ludovico Fantoni in favor of the Jews could give credence to the image of the Jewish moneylenders as *longa manus* of the despised dominating city. Around 1471 in Pisa there was an attempted assault on the bank and on the house of Vitale di Isacco, the father of the author of the "iconoclasm" (D. Kaufmann, "La famille de Yehiel de Pise," *Revue des Etudes Juives* 26 [1893]: 84; Cassuto, *Gli Ebrei a Firenze*, pp. 50–51). Indicative of the progressive deterioration of the position of the Jews even in Pisa around the end of the fifteenth century was the fact that on the occasion of the pastoral visit of 1462–63 (see Luzzati, *Filippo de' Medici*) there is no mention of the presence of Jews in the city. In 1494, for example, when asked whether there were any usurers, heretics, prostitutes, concubines, excommunicants, enchanters, and so forth residing in the parish visited, the rector of the Church of Santa Margherita answered "no, except for those Jews who live nearby" and the record of the Church of San Piero in Ischia, similarly, answers "no, except for the Jews who live in his parish." (Archivio Arcivescovile, Pisa, Visite pastorali, no. 1, fols. 424v and 427).

27. This extraordinary statement has not been noted, either by those concerned with the episode of Mantegna's *Madonna della Vittoria* or by da Norsa, who himself quotes and uses the document (see Norsa, *Una famiglia*, p. 76; idem, "Una famiglia di banchieri: La famiglia Norsa (1350–1950). Parte seconda: secolo XVI," *Bollettino dell'Archivio Storico del Banco di Napoli* 13 [1959]: 155). Although without connecting it with the episode of Daniele da Norsa's "iconoclasm," Castelli did point out the phrase (*I banchi feneratizi*, p. 39). The archival collocation is ASMn, Archivio Gonzaga, Libro Decreti, XXVII, c.3.

28. On the depletion of the power and the capacity of the "princes" and the "lords" to safeguard their Jewish subjects, see the observations of L. Cracco Ruggini, "Note sugli Ebrei in Italia dal IV al XVI secolo," *Rivista Storica Italiana* 76 (1964): 954–56.

7 ?&~ The Political System of a Community in Liguria: Cervo in the Late Sixteenth and Early Seventeenth Centuries

by Edoardo Grendi

"It is a common thing that the animosities of our peasants are not without the madness of the blue or the green," noted Andrea Spinola in his extraordinary *Ricordi*.[1] Apparently only the "cities" of the territory duplicated Genoa's tripartite constitutional structure, with its orders of aristocrats, merchants, and craftsmen,[2] but noble clans (*alberghi*) and factions were plentiful in many small country towns (*borghi*),[3] and in the less aristocratic places family alliances were important and had deep historical roots. Cervo, a small place but "inhabited by very unruly people,"[4] presents, instead, a type of fluid political dualism, founded on interfamily relations.[5] The local *podestà* (principal judicial and police officer), nonnoble, uneducated, and badly paid, was easily manipulated by "learned men and clerks who know the Latin of the statutes" and who, in any case, by fraternizing with the principal men of the place, certainly did not remain above or outside of the factions. The key privilege in question was the exercise of justice in its criminal, civil, and agrarian branches,[6] with Porto Maurizio operating as court for crimes of violence and Genoa above all as court of appeal. Thus, the evidence that we have been able to recover comes from the judicial record and from the ensuing petitions to the Senate.[7] This record casts a bright light on the political-territorial structures as well as on the structures of dependence linked to labor and the exchange system. Our hypothesis is that there exists a centrality to the political system that can be understood as a system

Edoardo Grendi, "Il sistema politico di una comunità ligure: Cervo fra Cinquecento e Seicento," *Quaderni storici*, no. 46 (1981): 92–129.

of interpersonal relations offering the local elite (the "principal men") conditional control over the collective resources.[8]

The theme of this essay is the reconstruction of the political system of the community, that is, of the administrative jurisdiction (*podestaria*) of Cervo. The alignments of individuals in the most blatant internal conflicts make clear right away who belongs to the Cervo elite and collectively point to the importance of certain roles and certain internal disputes within the community. But upon which social loyalties are the rivalries of individuals based? Let us immediately exclude the role, still dominant in many Ligurian communities, of patrilineal structures organized as such; instead, we can identify a high incidence of residential solidarity, though not mainly as a principle of collective identity capable of founding significant socioterritorial distinctions. The town assembly and parish embodied a form of leadership that was both parallel to and autonomous from the leadership of the larger community.

The distribution of offices and the distribution of wealth constitute two obvious frames of reference for comparing individual roles. These imply nonetheless the consideration of a social structure that must be understood in the terms of its cultural categories of women, merchants, notaries and doctors of law, priests, ship captains, sailor-farmers, and simple farmers. Membership in the elite was a function of brokerage, a function that poses the problem of resources. The enjoyment of resources postulates consideration of the work calendar and of its outcomes for the producers and the wholesalers in relation to a fundamental constriction of exchange that follows seasonal rhythms.

To what extent did the local merchants both regulate and keep track of the flow of goods? If the exacting of state *gabelles* offered some good opportunities for the merchants, it is primarily the incipient local *gabelles* that seemed to offer particular opportunity for the local monopolists. The political asymmetry organized itself in any case around a complex of roles, without it being possible to distinguish the action of an effective system of patronage at least on the basis of a continuity of the relationships of credit (or of a continuity of the personnel of a ship). The internal rivalries of the *castello* (walled town) represented free and fluid constructions of rival interfamily loyalties, which in the most critical periods expressly involved the elites of the village (*villa*), a latent constitutional opposition that seems to have relied as much on the symbols of residential autonomy as on the controversies over distribution of offices and taxes that the common political unity imposed. These, briefly anticipated, are the contents of this study, which follows an absolute chronological order.

෫ The judicial record shows a whole series of occasional conflicts, in which women were also frequently involved, an echo often of intimate relationships rich with tension but resolved by institutional arbiters.[9] But the judicial evidence also offers us patterns of a greater rivalry, particularly when the political question of the relations between the *castello* and the villages are involved. The patterns were "negative," I would say, because the course of action was determined primarily by opposition. For example, in 1601 while standing before the vicar of Porto, the two factions, Ferrari and Viale, listed the persons whose testimony they considered suspect—that is, their particular enemies. The contention opened with a series of quarrels. It started from a broken promise of marriage by G. B. Viale for his son, Ambrogio, with Violante, daughter of Gaspare Piria, son-in-law of the powerful Gio Antonio Ferrari.[10] Also charged against this same Viale was the accusation of usury at the expense of a certain Siglioli, tenant farmer of the Ferrari, while the *vexata quaestio* arose again concerning irregularities in the appointment to the post of town clerk, which always divided the notaries of the place. Some priests also ended up marshaled on the side of the Viale, nor can one forget the burden of the historical rivalry between the Massone and the Ferrari, the two most aristocratic houses of the *castello*. But it was above all in disputes over the parliament that the sides assumed their greatest cohesiveness: the Viale brothers quondam Francesco sought to organize the vote with the support of the villages, which were complaining about the fiscal partiality of the oligarchy of Cervo, pointing to corrupt voting "with [wooden] balls." The Ferrari, with the connivance of the *podestà*, were accused of having manipulated the nominations by lot, perpetuating their control over the (administrative and judicial council of) *anziani*.[11]

Here are the alignments: *The suspected partisans of the Viale family*: the *podestà*, Gio Antonio Ferrari, with his nephew Gio Giacomo, trained in law, and the sons-in-law, Gaspare Piria (father of the unsuccessful bride) and Gio Francesco Giancardo; Agostino Ferrari and his brothers, the notary Paolo Gerolamo Muratore and his son-in-law, Luca Massone, the "favored" notaries Sebastiano Ordano and Paolo Simoni (also cousins), Gio Antonio Alasio, agent for Muratore,

Pietro Siglioli (the tenant referred to earlier), Antonio Viale, and an Arduino. *The suspected partisans of the Ferrari family*: the brothers G. B. and Giuseppe Viale; the notary Paolo Gerolamo Massone and his son Lorenzo; Giorgio Ferrari and his sons; Stefano and Alessandro Lavello quondam Agostino; Battista Lavello; Pasino Caneto; Gio Antonio Chiesa; Agostino Sicardi; the reverends Agostino Ferrari, Aurelio Salineri and Cornelio Gassarino; the notaries Paolo Gerolamo Muratore and Gio Gassarino; Aurelia Cotta; Agostino and Gio Domenico Carembello; Giuseppe Viale quondam Galino and so on, and, in addition, the Ferrari family said, "all the houses of the Viali and Arimondi," which is to say the most numerous families of the *podestaria*.[12]

A glance at the picture of the Cervo elite, to be set out subsequently, shows us how almost all the principal men of the *castello* were involved. The criminal registers prove how deeply rooted the antagonism was: between 1599 and 1601 we can trace at least a score of disputes that were perfectly consistent with these divisions, the main protagonists being Giuseppe Viale and Francesco Giancardo. They range from violent fights in the sacristy during meetings of the officers of the Confraternity of the Holy Sacrament, to clashes on the streets of the walled town, to subtle attempts to compromise other men's wives.[13] But the alliances had, at least in part, a more substantial historical foundation. In 1576 there were several notable events: a dispute that came before the Senate between Filonia, the wife of Dr. Gio Giacomo Ferrari, and the wives of a Lombardo and Agostino Lavello, relatives of P. G. Massone; the sentence of banishment inflicted on the same Massone the clerk, accused by the Ferrari of having preferentially administered justice; and finally, the accusation of Gio Antonio Ferrari against Angeletto, son of Antonio Massone, for having offended Gio Giacomo and for having shot at Paolo Simone and G. B. Muratore. The unrepentant Angeletto returned to Cervo after the peace was signed by his father and again shot at the same Gio Antonio.[14]

In spite of the law of 1556 that prescribed sortition (*insachetare*) for choosing by rotation from among the notaries of the place for the town clerkship, corruption had continued, to the point where Paolo Simone, the son of Pietro and father of G.B.—three generations of notaries of Cervo who bragged of being "ancient citizens of Cervo"— said that he had assumed the duty from 1556 to 1558, and P. G. Muratore subsequently took it from 1589 to 1593.[15] We are among the allies of the Ferrari, a somewhat brutal alliance considering that G. B. Simoni succeeded in marrying Camilla, the daughter of Gio Agostino Ferrari, only after having used violence and having attempted to kill his father-in-law by poisoning the melons in his garden.[16] The notarial tradition also belonged to the Massone family, a lineage that undoubtedly flourished more in the sixteenth century, although in decline compared to the Ferrari: in 1566 we again find four Ferrari, one Ordano, and two Viale (including Francesco the father of G.B. and Giuseppe, the consul to Bosa for two decades) among the merchants operating in Bosa. Antonio Ferrari, the brother of Gio Antonio quondam Sebastiano, was proposed for the consulate of Cagliari.[17] In 1601 Lorenzo and P. G. Massone were defined by the Ferrari as their "capital enemies since forever." Paolo Gerolamo was banished for four years, and Lorenzo had already undergone thirty trials, a sure indication of strong political pressure, so strong in fact that his brother Luca, the son-in-law of Muratore, had already joined with the Ferrari.[18] It is not by chance that the Massone were by then behind the most powerful Viale brothers quondam Francesco; along with them is a healthy number of the principal men of Cervo as well as several important families from the villages.

We find another historical clash in the lively rivalry during the years 1580–90 between the notaries Pietro Simone and Gio Gassarino, a clue to a more general territorial conflict opposing townspeople (*burgenses*) and peasants (*villani*). The people of the villages, so argued Geremia Gassarino in 1565, make up three-quarters of the population and they "have a great abundance of animals, while the inhabitants of the *castello* are poorer in real estate and if they trade, they do it with the property of others."[19] It is the villages that upheld the decrees of 1547 and 1564 by which the vote of parliament was deemed necessary for all expenditures exceeding five lire, just as they upheld the futile resolution of 1572 excluding the notaries of Cervo from the town clerkship.[20] And the men of the villages were against the unregulated distribution of positions, "such that the offices have always been distributed among about 20 or 25 people, all in agreement about harming the poor and not observing the rules, so that the father chooses his son and one brother another."[21] In 1578, when Gio Gassarino was procurator, they requested elections by secret ballot and no longer by voice, just as they would do in 1601.

The case of Gio Gassarino, notary of Pairole and "persecuted for 20 years," as he wrote in 1592, is a good example. Obtaining the notaryship was a great political and personal achievement, but Gassarino found something to chew on, with teeth that were apparently quite sharp if it is true that he was feared as a person who gave no rest either to his enemies or to his enemies' friends, who all belonged to the parish of San Bartolomeo and whom he was prosecuting for debts or "having them harried by justice in order to instill great fear of it in others."[22] He accused Gio Antonio Ferrari, whose nature, he said, was "to lord it over that place, to consume that community and to oppress all those individuals who wished to oppose themselves to his unbridled desires." Against the brothers of Gio Antonio, he had tried vainly to redirect the accusation of heresy that had brought him before the Inquisition, but he was denounced for having, hand in glove with the *podestà*, caused the record of criminal proceedings to disappear.[23]

This does not remove the fact that his most bitter rivals in the parish were the Arimondi, and in particular Giuseppe and Bartolomeo (also a notary and father of the notary Paolo Gerolamo), codefendant in 1576 with Angeletto Massone, the man who wounded the same Ferrari.[24] It was precisely the Arimondi whom Gassarino, in 1583, accused of a characteristically symbolic offense in his vineyard: burning his scarecrow and substituting for it "a frightful creature on a pair of pitchforks with horns and verses and other riddles written out of envy and to his dishonor," a cursing of great audacity.[25] The dispute in this case concerned control over the offices and moneys of the parish. The quarrel continued into the seventeenth century against Bartolomeo Ordano, a member of the Gassarino family, already old and with nine daughters to marry off: his son Timoteo was wounded by his enemies and one of his daughters ended up pregnant.[26] Thus, these conflicts were without too many nuances that preceded the rising political fortunes of the notary P. G. Arimondo, whose dispute with Gassarino thus became part of the rivalries with the Ferrari to dominate the office of *podestà*. By the end of the century the Ferrari family formed a powerful, though rather isolated, clique, which fatally lost ground to the Viale family's system of alliances. Those alliances also included, as we have seen, Giorgio Ferrari quondam Paolo, whose sons Paolo, Sebastiano, and G.B. we will find again subsequently among the principal men of Cervo. Furthermore both the Viale brothers had married Ferrari women and in particular G. B. Viale had collected the conspicuous inheritance of Gio Francesco Ferrari, strengthening an economic fortune dominant in the first three decades of the new century. Therefore it seems to us worthwhile to examine at least in part the conflicts of the late sixteenth century in the light of the genealogy of the Ferrari family, limiting ourselves, however, to the male offspring of Battista, Bernardo, and Sebastiano. The conflict of 1601 emerged from within Sebastiano's branch of the family and, a fortiori, from within a complex of matrimonial alliances, governed by considerations of social station, that offered few possibilities for validating any principles of exclusion other than those of faction and social rank.

᛭ A densely packed account of powerful people in conflict among themselves presents us with a picture of a region divided in two parts: a jurisdiction of subordinates versus the omnipotent court notaries, a rivalry between the *castello* and the villages, hostilities old and new, conflicts without too many subtleties.[27] In terms of social history, this reveals on the one hand the existence of structures, that is to say a complex of relationships that reveal the collective connections of individuals, their "sense of belonging," and on the other the nature of the personal connections of individuals, that is their system of community roles. In tracing these two themes the method of analysis changes fatefully: from live narration it passes over to an exegesis that is in some way more abstract because it is not directly stated.

The typology of settlement reveals immediately the primacy of the *castello* and town of Cervo at whose borders was the parish church of San Giorgio, later in 1600 becoming N.S. delle Grazie of the Augustinian monks. During the course of the sixteenth century, the villages had carved out of that area the two subordinate parishes of San Bartolomeo and SS. Giacomo and Mauro.[28] The assessment registry (*caratata*) of 1643 enumerates 580 houses (excluding houses of earth, broken-down houses, basements, hovels, and pigeon coops) with 550 owners: a discrepancy in numbers primarily due to the fact that in Cervo some houses were rented out. The names of the hamlets (*villette*), are, according to Giustiniani,[29] those of the area's families. Even where this does not happen, as at S. Maria and at Chiappa, for example, the seventeenth-century documents still show internal divisions among the lineages ("houses of the. . . ," "carob tree of the. . . ,"),[30] a trait that does not characterize Cervo proper, occupied in part by the collateral branches of lineages from other seacoast towns. In effect, with the exception of the Ferrari and the Viale, the lineages of the town all have fewer than 10 households. We later find the Viale

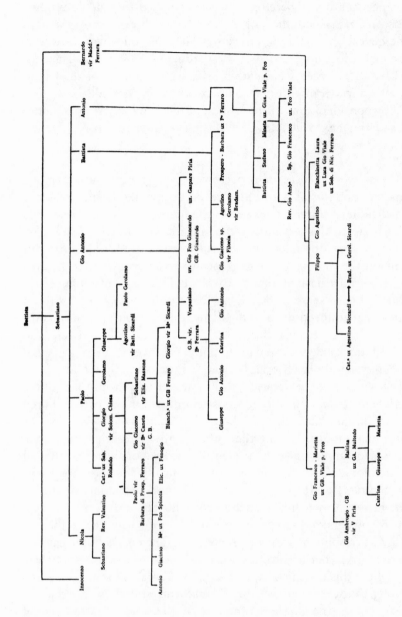

Fig. 1. *Descendants of Battista Ferraro*

family in the villages as well (in about 70 households in all), and the same is true for other surnames that are much less common. Even in the middle of the seventeenth century, Poiolo degli Arimondo and the village of the Albavera family at Pairola suggest the model of the *villages lignagers*.[31] That is also true for the village of the Steri (consisting of 15 households), though no longer for the village of the Freschi (encompassing 14 households).[32]

The reason for the variation in persistence of virilocal matrimonial patterns escapes us. Furthermore, our use of the term *lineage* (*parentela*) is open to discussion and valid only in a metaphorical sense: the assessment records (*caratate*) do not show any communally held property nor do the peace agreements in the area show any familial involvement.[33] The chaplaincies were passed on through descent, and the same principle holds in the case of bequests *pro maritandis puellis*. We can certainly see that the oratory of N.S. del Soccorso of Poiolo worked as a surety for the Arimondo family and that the village of the Albavera family bought grain at its own expense for its poor. But the one and the other activity did not imply a power of lineage as much as administration for the benefit of the residents.[34] Thus it does not seem wrong for us to conclude that the dominant focus of collective identity was, across the board, that of place. Wills offer us precise evidence of this collective identification: the recipients of legacies are the sodalities and chapels of the parish church, the confraternities of flagellants, and the minor oratories that are often assigned legacies for masses, depending on the residence of the author of the will. The result is that if the legacies to the minor oratories in the vicinity of the villages are a simple function of the varying residence, the high percentage of bequests to the sodalities of the church testifies to the breadth of identification with the parish church, which is much clearer than with the oratory of the penitents, which could still have represented an earlier form of political-territorial unity.

The legacies outside of the parish area for the most part are a function of the wealth of the testator. The legacies for masses should clarify the phenomenon further: in the first decades of the century, however, the prayers for the most part were deferred to the charity of the heirs and likewise with funerals, *ut videbitur*, and *juxta graduum suum*. At Cervo we more easily find devotion to the chapel: the church has eight altars, at least three at N.S. delle Grazie and two (and later three) at the oratory of San Carlo. S. Bernardo di Villave

Table 1. *San Giovanbattista, S. Bartolomeo, SS. Giacomo e Mauro*

	San Giovanbattista		S. Bartolomeo		SS. Giacomo and Mauro	
SS. Sacramento		91.4		85.7		81.8
S. Rosario		86.7		81.6		74.5
Nome di Dio		34.4		63.2		45.4
Churches:	San G. B.	37.5	S. Bartolomeo	35.7		
	N. S. Grazie	36.7			S. Mauro	50.9
Flagellant	S. Caterina	64.1	S. Michele	44.9	S. Giacomo	43.6
companies						
Oratories	S. Brigida	43.7	N. S. Rovere	45.9	S. Antonio	41.9
	S. Giuseppe	15.6	S. M. Sossorso	38.8	S. Lucia	23.6
	S. Bernardo	10.6	S. M. Neve	40.8	S. Simone	14.5
	S. Carlo (1624)	17.2	S. Matteo	19.4	S. Biagio	4
			S. Rocco	19.4		
N. S. Carmine	(1648 in S. Carlo)		61.2			14.5
Outside the		21.1		19.4		1.8
parish						
Total wills,		128		98		55
1610–50						

is a small country oratory, so that only San Giuseppe at the center of a hamlet of twelve houses shows the arrangement, more general in the other parishes, of oratories among the villages. The importance of the oratory depends on its church role: only S. Giacomo and N.S. della Rovere were burial sites. We find a permanent chaplain also at S. Maria della Neve (Pairola, the future new parish) and at Poiolo, where the chaplain has the charge to *docere pueros* (as at S. Maria and in the parish churches). Elsewhere there are legacies for a weekly mass. It is the residents, the patrons with full title, who name the chaplain, as elsewhere they name the parish priest. This reveals a primacy of the laity that is reflected clearly in the administration of the goods of the church, a lay authority that, though minimal at the level of the oratory (a pair of custodians), is expressed in a different way at the level of the parish.[35] In every case the assertion of the democratic process in the assembly of the heads of households was not as pointed as in the case of the community parliament. In the parishes the old officials nominated the new, the assembly voted for them, the priest ratified them.

The construction, embellishment, and enrichment of the church naturally represented an important element of the community's prestige: it was reinforced by the dead through their legacies, by the living through their taxing of themselves and their charities, and by the principal families through the building of choirs and chapels. And perhaps this is the reason for the early success of the oligarchy, favored by a statutory formalization that was absent or, at the most, weak.[36] The assembly of the heads of households (*universitas*) continued to gather and meet: it solemnly witnessed the introduction of new sodalities, it provided for regulating the use of water resources or pastures and for deciding on new ornaments for the church as well as for the purchases of grain for the poor. Responsibility still fell to the parish for elementary instruction and health care, for the sale of meat, for the naming of the rural guards and the military officials, and for the payment of the guards. The boundary between lay and ecclesiastical had become quite blurred. In every case the parish or even the oratory was rich compared with the commune. The account books document, for example, that to benefit itself and the oratories the parish regularly sold the coral commonly donated by the fishermen. Donations, legacies, patrimonial incomes, and annuities comprised a fortune much more substantial than the "public" one, which relied purely on the fiscal instrument of the *averia* and *distaglio* taxes.[37]

The commune, that is the parliament and its sixteen officials (*anziani*, appraisors, tax collectors, and health officials), thus represents the level of a territorial solidarity imposed from above, as is shown among other things by the general principle of collective responsibility *in solido* for the debts of the commune, destined to grow to the point of provoking the appropriate Genoese magistracy to take control.[38] In addition to the *averia* tax and the obligations of the tax on olive oil, there were now also *gabelles* on milling and later war expenses (1625–26), as well as ordinary expenses. The register of assessments (*caratata*) certified approximate real wealth and constituted the equalizing basis for a distribution (*distaglio*), which, by taxing each person several more lire according to the value estimated, should have assured that public expenditures were covered.[39] The key issue then was one of dividing the *averia* and the oil tax among individuals, among parishes, or above all among the villages.

On the other side, decisions concerning expenditures were equally crucial. All this posed the problem of the parliament and government. Furthermore, the administration of justice represented the general application of the extraarbitral resolution of local conflicts that the legal class, and especially the numerous notaries in Cervo, had every interest in stimulating. The very poor, naturally, could not sustain the expenses for judicial litigation, much less at Porto or Genoa.[40] Roles of power and prestige and individual opportunities take on substance in the "public" political picture. And yet, the sense of collective identification with the commune undoubtedly remained weak: here in particular the situation of the minority of villages and villagers against the townsmen (*burgenses*) made itself known, although those villagers were certainly not always or exclusively farmers.

?⮝ As we have been saying, the social network of the community was composed of a series of individual connections. The distinction between the sexes is a complicating element in the social structure, but it certainly cannot be the key to an exhaustive interpretation of it. Marriage choices clearly underline the general importance of class structure. Evidence comes from the numerous petitions directed to the bishop of Albenga requesting dispensations allowing marriage between blood-relations. The justifications indicate with numerical precision the range of choice, a choice that was purely theoretical inasmuch as young men of higher or lower status were rejected as a matter of course: typically, in finding a husband for a daughter there was a bias for avoiding, from below, the young men of the villages and, from above, the foreigners who asked larger, usually ruinous, dowries. Thus the choice was almost predetermined. In the petitions the primacy of class considerations was absolutely explicit, and there was neither mention nor implication of an alliance between lineages. The evidence from criminal proceedings confirms this awareness of rank. The issue here involves the relative role of the sexes within the system. Thus, because all witnesses by custom declared their age and property, the women affirmed that they "possess their dowries," a possession that the husband often had to guarantee.[41] It should be said, however, that this was a possession slow to mature: payment of the dowry was spread out over time, from four to thirty-two years and on the average between ten and twenty years. It was valid to make a monetary commitment by pledging to pay a certain annual sum ("dowry payment"). Compensations in land were more common in situations involving the vindication of honor, especially when the protagonists were the brothers of the bride. Hence, we see the hereditary significance of the dowry itself. "Here," affirms a witness in

Table 2. *Dowries and Real Property*

Dowries		Real property	
lire 800	16.1	lire 1,000	19.2
800–1,200	21.2	1,000–2,000	16.2
1,200–1,600	3.8	2,000–4,000	27.2
1,600–2,000	19.3	4,000–6,000	16.9
2,000–2,500	17.9	6,000–10,000	13.5
2,500–3,000	14.7	10,000–15,000	4
3,000–4,000	3.8	over 15,000	3
over 4,000	3.2		

1636, "it is customary to say that it is the sons and not the daughters who inherit, but several times I have seen that, even if there are sons, they still share the inheritance with the daughters."[42]

We have calculated the amount of 156 dowries between 1615 and 1645: they vary between 800 and 5,200 lire. Perhaps it would be useful to make a comparison between the wealth in real property from the estimate or *caratata* of 1643, which had been increased at a rate of 500 percent, and that of 1612. These figures do not mean, naturally, that the estimates were based on fair market value.[43] Even though marrying without a dowry—"in the Moorish manner," as the saying went—was not considered proper, this still does not mean that all girls were endowed. Assuming the contrary, and therefore also assuming the representative character of our dowry sample, and juxtaposing similar percentages, we have a picture that, excluding the poorest levels, points to dowry values corresponding to a third of the real property, which is a significant percentage, except that the principal of the dowry sum, an annual payment, presupposes wealth also in personal property. In any case, "possessing a dowry" was not an empty phrase. Furthermore, if it is true that women could only act legally when assisted by two men (*proximiores*), they enjoyed large marital portions: in cases of widowhood, they were usufructuaries or, in any case, guaranteed a roof and food, something that was guaranteed also to unmarried daughters. Various wills ratify the right of widows to a room in their father's house. This kind of "patrilocalism" is confirmed in the women's practice of making out their wills to the benefit of their natal family. Nevertheless, the women were markedly freer than the men in following their own emotional inclinations in bequeathing household goods, typically valued at the wedding at between 150 and 400 lire or even, in one case, 1,000 lire.

We have a series of indications, therefore, that suggest a relative degree of female autonomy; within this autonomy we must also distinguish the components of female labor, which were expanded by the regular seasonal migration of the men. Salaried labor was divided into the harvesting and pressing of olives; threshing grain; carrying water, sand, lime, and fertilizer; washing clothes. Spinning, the care of the garden and the animals, and going to market are all similarly documented activities. Being the stay-at-home sex par excellence, an extraordinary percentage of women were heads of families, and they appear en masse in the testimonies regarding rural crimes.[44] In the *castello* they had their own sodality of S. Brigida, led by a prioress.

The seasonal migration of men thus qualified the women's roles as workers in the fields, providers, and heirs. A sample for July 1630 indicates that 414 men were absent, 70 percent of whom were under the age of thirty. There were 260 households involved or about half of the total: among those making declarations, 146 were wives or mothers, 57 fathers, 30 brothers and sons or daughters; 140 declared only one absentee, 80 households had two absentees, and 40 reported at least three or four absentees. There were 260 out collecting coral and another 44 in Sardinia (10 on business), 15 in Corsica, and a good 56 in Genoa and at Bisagno (8 hoeing olive groves and 8 hauling night soil), and the rest elsewhere (2 were "selling"). In the entry for August 30, 322 inhabitants of Cervo show up as having just returned from Sardinia, which squares perfectly with other evidence that indicates that for a third of the year (April to August) 65 percent of the men fit to bear arms were absent.[45] It is not by chance that one of the most common declaratory formulas for male work, "I hoe and I go for coral," is no rarer than the declaration that "I conduct my own business, and I leave others to do theirs according to their rank," which bespeaks both personal dignity and also acceptance of the local structure of honor.

Fishing in any case was a stratified activity: in fifty to sixty of the fishing ships of Cervo—each one with 9 men aboard and actually not all from Cervo—the captain and the ship's officer (*popero*) were differentiated from the other sailors. From one year to the next the crew changed: negotiating reenlistment was at the option of the captain and as a result the bond between the merchants and captain remained more solid. The captains "do not touch the oar," gave out the advances (paid with the merchant's money) to the sailors who sign on, made an agreement with the merchant for other loans and for the sale of the coral, managed their chapel of San Teramo (1601), and were always called by their proper title. As the initiators of a fishing trip, which was governed by the regulations of the gangplank, the captains produced the ethic according to which "the safe pay the lost."[46] Therefore, the captains who were often proprietors in joint ownership of the ship, constituted an important social group, both in Cervo proper and in the villages of the lower quarter of San Bartolomeo. A later list, of 1673, enumerated 70 or so captains, 17 of whom turned out to be sons of living captains.[47] The profession thus was often passed on through generations: no longer were endogamic matrimonial transactions a rarity. Increasingly, however, the captain depended on the merchant who "provides the capital": among the 52 off fishing in 1609, only 7 were fishing for themselves.[48]

There were also, however, captains who "fish and have fishing done"—that is, they participated in the investment side of the business. Thus, among the elite of Cervo in 1629, there were 5 such captains. If we correlate them only to the estimates of real wealth, we see that they occupied the median level, a little above the poorest third of property owners. Naturally they usually lived by coral gathering and, in the off season, they became nominal captains who tried to earn further profits from rentals. Probably the ship's officers also deserve to be specially pointed out, though they are difficult to identify. It is doubtful that the list of "people of the sea" went beyond these two categories. Domenico Alassio, captain, expressed it this way: "I am neither a debtor nor a creditor to anyone. . . . I am a sailor and the captain of a ship, I am not a workman or a laborer."[49] The "culture of the sea" clearly shaped a social hierarchy at whose base there was the person who merely hoed in the olive groves and, at the top, the ship captain. This was well expressed by a testimony that was not very charitable concerning some people: "Both are country people, stupid and not used to navigating ships, but used to hoeing the earth by which they continue to subsist day to day."[50]

A certain degree of precision is still possible for the group of artisans dominated naturally by the caulkers (the Massardo family above all), and below them four bootmakers and cobblers, a pair of ironmongers (Steria), and some masons, coopers, and barbers, the last with a strong practical tradition of surgery. For example, Paolo Muratore enumerated his competencies, stating that he had sold oil, coral, and merchandise for thirty years and is "a merchant, master of the ax and a street-stall vendor, experienced in the art of the surgeon; he is a stonecutter and he makes sieves." He finished with his specific cultural competency: "As a man who has done business in Genoa and Onela, he has learned to keep books as a merchant."[51] People normally moved across the boundaries between the trades. The fishing ships in any case were usually bought from the shipyards of Arenzano and Varazze, and the local shipwrights were not specialized in large works anyway. Thus what made the merchant was primarily his relationship with Genoa. "Public merchant" was a common expression. But there is no doubt that the distinctive element was the ability to "keep books." And there is a particular moral in the testimony by people about quondam Giorgio Ferraro that he was known as an honest person, "not accustomed to cut off credit twice." On the other hand it is also true that "he who knows his own business and is alert, does not pay the loan twice over."[52] This repeats the distinction between stupid people and those of "astute mind," but this time in terms of an imbalance severer than that of wealth: the captain himself and sometimes even an *anziano* of a substantial village could end up being illiterate. This would certainly not be true of the owner-merchant who also trafficked in annuities, as is explicitly attested to by the 1629 list of "principal businessmen." At this level of the elite, the discussion can finally become personalized, thus achieving that precision in names that the modernizing tendency to treat subjects by function and professional role leaves somewhat vague and indistinct.

༄ The table (p. 136) of the elite of Cervo is based on those taxed in 1629, that is 38 persons of whom 17 engaged in business. Note that the persons who are rich only in real estate almost all come from the villages. This does not mean, however, that there are not also merchants from the villages, as in S. Maria (the Vione family) and in Poiolo (the Arimondo family). In comparing the 1629 list to the *caratata* of 1612, which in some cases requires a reference to a parent of the 1629 declaree, one notes several significant discrepancies between wealth "of business" and wealth in property: only 16 of the 36 people in possession of real estate holdings greater than 2,000 lire in 1612 are back on the list of 1629. There must have been some omissions: this is the case for example of Agostino Siccardi quondam Gio Maria, a merchant in oil and coral listed at 2,967 lire in 1612 and one of the richest in 1640.[53] Among those taxed in 1629 there also figure two notaries (a Muratore and a Simoni) and five ship captains (the brothers Lavello quondam Agostino, the brothers Rolandi quondam Pantaleo, and Domenico Steria), confirming the link between ownership and mercantile activity, one route of social mobility. On the other hand, there is not a single artisan among the 38. Let us move to the second comparison with the 1629 list: in 1619 the owners of containers for oil declared more than 6,000 barrels available for a production that in a good year could reach about half of that. Our 38 include only half of that ownership and do not include important owners such as the notary Sebastiano Ordano who owned nine vats, Gio Giacomo Ferrari, living in Andora, who owned six of them, Aurelia Cotta who owned five, and so on.[54] In any case there were more than 400 container owners including 44 who owned more than 16 jars; 20 of them are on our list. Finally we can compare the 1629 list with the general tax of 1640,[55] where the heirs of course appear: 13 were taxed more than 1 lira; of these 11 are on our 1629 list, plus Agostino Siccardi, already referred to, and Paolo Bozzobonello, a new arrival.[56] The value of the houses of residence in 1643 reflects a more general discrepancy between the *castello* and the villages. Instead, only 9 of the 38 possessed a title, an inherited dignity that did not correspond any longer with wealth in personal property: among the titled people were 6 Ferrari, 5 Massone, and 4 Viale but also other families of the *castello* and even of the villages.[57] Taken overall, the elite of 1629 end up divided thus: 15 in the *castello*, 12 in the lower quarter of San Bartolomeo, 4 in the upper quarter, plus 7 at Chiappa. Two families of the villages, however, had also bought a residence in the *castello*.

This is the general picture of what we know from our data about wealth.[58] And nevertheless it is helpful to recall another elitist structure, rarely congruent with this one: that of clerks in the broad sense— that is, priests, notaries, and a few doctors of law qualified as *spectabiles*. A list of fiscal information of 1640 includes 19 priests: the Viale and Terrizzano families predominate, with 5 and 4, respectively.[59] A more general investigation into those registered in the notarial records signals as well the importance of the Ferrari and the minor importance of foreigners among the secular priests, outside of the Augustinian monastery, which held little attraction for the people of Cervo. Endowed usually with 2,000 lire, these local priests were in effect *rentiers*, indistinguishable from the context of the social relationships of their family members. The position is very different for the notaries who served as many as eight customers at a time, which explains their

Table 3. *Principal Businessmen*

	1629			1612 Declared value
	Age	Business		parent
G. B. Viale Ferraro qd. Fco	68	m*	80,400	3,180 +
Sebastiano Ferraro qd. Giorgio	54	m	27,500	Gio	3,875
Paolo Ferraro qd. Giorgio	48	m	26,300		
Castigliano Arimondo q. Fco	60	m	30,000	6,528
G. B. Lavello q. Stefano		c & m	21,100	Stef.	555
Gio Agostino Viale q. Pietro		m	25,000	4,860
Giuseppe Viale q. Fco	73		17,300	3,180
Giacomo Viale q. Antonio			17,500	1,600
Andrea Vione q. Gerolamo		m	18,000	1,750
Ambrogio Vione q. Antonio		m	18,800	
Alessandro Lavello q. Agostino		c & m	17,000	250
Sebastiano Muratore q. PG			16,000	Not. PG	2,460
h. Ambrogio Arimondo q. GB			15,800	Batt.	1,440
Sebastiano Simoni q. GB	29	n	16,600	GB	1,625
h. Francesco Mantica			16,000	Frco	3,965
Serafino Arimondo q. Damiano	38		15,600	3,735
Simone Arimondo q. Lorenzo			15,800	Lor.	1,545
Agostino Rolando q. Pantaleo		c & m	15,600	620
Battista Rolando q. Pantaleo		c & m	15,000	560
Nicola Freschi q. Giorgio			15,500	Gio	2,920
Domenico Steria q. Gio		c & m	15,100	1,860
Giacomo Simoni q. Gio		m	15,100	1,720
Domenico Salineri	49		15,000	2,735
Gio Francesco Massone q. Gius.	33		14,600	2,526
Luca Massone q. Bened.		m	14,600	1,487
Giacomo Arimondo q. Lorenzo			13,800	1,380
Ambrogio Arimondo q. Lorenzo			13,800	1,380
Gio Ambrogio Carchero q. Giorgio		m	13,800	Gio	3,365
Gioacchino Calvo q. Gio			13,500	Gio	665
Lorenzo Calvo q. Angelo			13,100	2,103
Luca Rittore			13,600	2,200
h. Biagio Mantica			13,500	1,805
Giacomo Albavera q. Michele			13,600	1,845
Sebastiano Freschi q. Matteo			13,600	3,065
Domenico Vione q. Giorgio			8,000	?
Gerolamo Viale q. Gio Agostino		m	19,300	1,630
Pasino Caneto	71		14,300	1,555
Gerolamo Gassarino q. Nicola			13,600	1,665

*m = merchant; c & m = captain and merchant; n = notary.

constant moving about. These especially included the Massoni and Simoni, who sometimes formed real notarial dynasties, but also the Muratore, Arimondo, Gassarino, and Ordano were important.[60] The political role of the notaries can hardly be overestimated, a role that was more than an auxiliary one in respect to that elite of wealth and

1619 Containers of oil		Title	Tax of 1640 Tax	1643 Parish	Value of house
jars	182	m.	h. 2.16	S. G.B.	
jars	121	m.	1.0.1	S. G.B.	550
		m.	1.8.3	S. G.B.	700
jars	68		2.12.9	Poiolo S. G.B.	365
jars	98		12.12	S. G.B.	600
jars	53	m.	2.9.7	S. Mauro	300
jars	36	m.	h. 1.3.4	S. G.B.	
jars	27	m.	h. 19.6	S. G.B.	
			6.11	S. Maria	335
			7.9	S. Maria	320
			7.10	S. G.B.	150
jars	13		10.4	S. G.B.	300
jars	114		h. 8.9	S. Maria	150
jars	46		h. 1.5.4	S. G.B.	225
				S. Mauro	100
			16.6	Poiolo	100
			h. 14.6	Poiolo	100
jars	34		9.10	S. G.B.	400
jars	38		19.9	S. G.B.	450
jars	25		1.4.6	Freschi	200
			13.6	Steri S. G.B.	529
			h. 1.2.11	S. Mauro	180
				S. Maria	420
jars	60	m.	17.6	S. G.B.	400
jars	27	m.	13	S. G.B.	180
				Poiolo	200
			6	Poiolo	100
			10.6	S. Bart.	100
jars	26		1.15.8	S. Mauro	225
			h. 19.3	S. Mauro	250
			7.8	S. Mauro	
			h. 14.6	S. Mauro	100
			h. 13.11	Pairola	100
			h.	Freschi	175
				S. Maria	125
			h.	S. G.B.	
			12.7	S. G.B.	160
jars	26		h. 1.00.7	Pairola	200

of business who were protagonists in the basic dealings with the external market.

Having thus defined the elite, or the elites, of Cervo, let us now attempt to check these names against the positions of power and prestige—that is, the *anziani* and the priors of the sodalities of the church. Here the statistics tell us little, except to emphasize the fact that during a fifty year span a third of the *anziani* of the *castello* were from the Ferrari family and less than a tenth from the Massone family. The ascendancy of the Ferrari family in the *castello* can be measured by the plurality among the *anziani* of members of the "lineage," a circumstance confirmed also by the priories and invisible subpriories that they held. This is true for the Viale family, too, although they were less frequently among the *anziani*. Outside of the massive presence of these two families in the *castello*, we can point out only a few individuals like Galino Alasio, Paxino Caneto, Agostino Sicardi, the two notaries P. G. Muratore and Sebastiano Ordano, and more likely than not the rival notary Paolo Massone. These are the officeholders at the *castello* between 1596 and 1630.

This illustration covers 56 of 75 prominent *anziani* and 74 of 84 prominent priors: it is clear that there was some continuity of personnel in the priory.[61] For the villages we will merely point out the dominance among the *anziani* of several figures such as the notary P. G. Arimondo, Paolo Gassarino (son of the notary Geremia), Serafino Arimondo, and Nicola Fresco.[62]

The owners of businesses compose an elite who occupied over a third of the *anziano* positions in the period 1596–1650, though ten or so of the notaries occupied a seventh of the positions. It is more difficult to distinguish the captains because of the many doubts about their precise identities. Taking the example of the *castello* as guide, we can discern a hegemony of notables (physicians, notaries, and owners of businesses) in the church sodalities and a situation relatively more mobile in the parliament. Admission to this community assembly was open to men between the ages of seventeen and seventy: once the quorum of 80 was achieved, "those of Cervo would close the door, putting those of the villages in a minority." It is they in fact who urged participation based on taxpayer status and limited to one member for each domestic unit.[63] The commissioner Casella perceived the great confusion and proposed that the community council elect deputies to the parliament, a reform that was carried out only at the end of the century.[64] But it is in the area of public finance that we find the greatest innovations. The institution in 1623 of a specific magistracy for finance laid the groundwork for a closer control of expenditures, which must be submitted for annual review. Immediately afterward the values of the distribution of imposts (*distaglio*) on the register of the *averia* tax doubled and what was exceptional in

Table 4. *Anziani and Priors*

	Anziano	Prior		*Anziano*	Prior
Galino Alasio	4		Luca Massone	1	1
Paxino Caneto	4	1	P.G. Massone notary	2	
Gio A. Chiesa	1	1	Paolo Massone notary	1	2
Ferrari, Gio Ant.	1		Benedetto Massone notary	1	1
G.B. di Gio Ant.	3		P.G. Muratore notary	3	4
Agostino	4		Francesco Muratore	2	
Gerol. di Agostino	4		Sebastiano Ordano notary	3	
Sebastiano q. Nicolò	1	1	Paolo Simoni notary	1	1
Gerolamo q. Paolo		4	Agostino Sicardi	3	2
Giuseppe q. Paolo		5	G.B. Viale Ferraro	5	6
Giorgio q. Paolo	1		Giuseppe Viale qd. Frco	2	4
Sebast. di Giorgio	4	7	Giuseppe Viale qd. Galino		4
Paolo di Giorgio	2	1	sp. Franc. Viale di Luca Gio		7
G.B. di Giorgio		6	sp. Gio Franc. Viale di Nic.	1	3
sp. Gio Giacomo		7	sp. Gio Franc. Viale di Giuseppe		2
Stefano Lavello	2	1			

1625 became normal from 1627 on.[65] This came as the result of absorbing the increased milling *gabelle* and of the growth of the commune's debt. In 1645 the annual interest obligations rose to 2,200 lire, more than the *averia* and the milling tax put together. These obligations came from 1,300 lire required to pay for internal indebtedness of recent growth and 900 lire for the more traditional external debt.[66]

There was no success in instituting new *gabelles* as had happened earlier in almost all the communities of the district. A *gabelle* on the movement of merchandise at 0.5 percent *ad valorem* and on monopolies in grain, in wine, and in other consumable goods was proposed. One early experiment had been tried in 1631 and repeated in 1649, both times meeting with strong resistance. Such *gabelles* institutionalized the principle of control over provision of basic necessities in the most radical terms, something the Abbondanza of Genoa never planned to introduce.[67] In this area Cervo was lagging behind its neighbors: this lag and the effective resistance that defended liberal provisioning, including the consumers' "classic" right to first-purchase of foodstuffs unloaded at the beach,[68] all help explain Cervo's inability to raise more taxes.

☜ The state *gabelles* contracted on the wharf and then approved by parliament were a different matter. The *averia* anticipated only a gain from the collection of debts, an undertaking that was not simple and that necessitated injunctions, seizures, and so on. And yet an occasion for even greater greed was represented by the tax on olive oil. The positions of receiver and cashier were both coveted responsibilities and were purchased with the best offer. The offer of service implied the ability to collect several hundred barrels of oil and to negotiate the loads bound for Genoa with guaranteed profits from the collection of the tax at the Magistracy of Provisions in the capital.[69] In 1648 about 400 of Cervo's heads of household paid the oil tax, and, according to the census of 1619, there were a little over 400 possessors of jars and vats. The full-empty situation is expressed by this graph that illustrates, to scale, the relatively unequal distribution by comparing the number of producers to the quantity of containers in Graph A and the quantity of production to groups of container owners in Graph B. One-tenth of the richest producers produced 20 percent of the total; one tenth of the container owners owned 50 percent of the receiving capacity. This imbalance is a typical expression of the product's commmercialization.[70] Many consignments were tied up due to presale, and often the sales themselves were rushed by the threat that

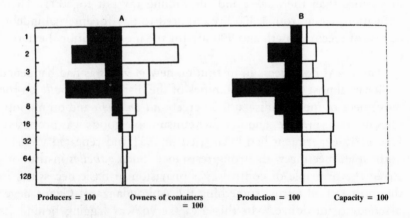

Fig. 2. *Producers/Container Owners*

exports might be suspended: the wholesalers collected the oil, manipulated the Genoese currency, made a profit on commissions, and generally delayed the resale.

The Ligurian custom of forced commercialization positioned olive oil and wine against grain. The Mediterranean trilogy here is unbalanced, so that coral and the sale of labor compensated for an insufficiency of grain as well as of fabrics, iron, cheese, and other things.[71] There is no question, however, that in Cervo, true wealth was olive oil and true poverty belonged to those without their own oil. Oil figured in bequests, in debts, and in payments and constituted a form of "capital," a standard of value measured in 5-barrel units and used to evaluate coralline: this oil was exchanged frequently, and it was these exchanges that led to disputes. Let us examine a series of declarations registered during different periods:

January 1589: 158 people declared 581 barrels;

November 1593: 277 people declared 483 barrels;

November 1607: 101 people declared 646 barrels and 270 declared 628 bushels of olives (equivalent to 63 barrels of oil)—12 people owned three-quarters of the oil;

October 1625: 99 people (a quarter of those taxed) declared 2,500 barrels; 6 people declared 1,615 of these barrels; and 22 declared more than 20 barrels each for 85 percent of the oil;

February 1645: 229 people declared 1,857 barrels of which 540 were bought; 17 declared more than 20 barrels, for a total 672 of which 358 were bought.

It is important to remember that following the annual price cycle, the old oil was worth 15 or 20 percent more than the new, so that in October and November we should be on the verge of a speculative situation: the incidence of home consumption is clearly expressed by those 270 who in November 1607 declared 628 bushels of olives, an item that is not consistently present in the other records. In October 1625 we see the probable reflection of a situation frozen by the war, a "pure case" of the process of concentration that we can see at the beginning of 1645 when, by February 15, one-third of the oil had already been bought.[72]

Economic historians have been concerned primarily with *conjunctures*—that is, the variations in production and price. Certainly the former is a phenomenon of great importance: we can calculate, on the precarious basis of the tax appraisals, that biennial production could vary in ratios from 1:5 to as much as 1:6.[73] However, the correlation with the main market, Genoa, reveals a field of oscillating prices between the amounts of 100 and 160 (annual averages, 1596–1656). Casual notations of prices in Cervo at different times register slightly greater variations of 100 to 180, but perceptibly lesser variations in oil prices than those for grain, which varied between 100 and 300. Thus, the truly critical relationship is between a surplus of oil and the price of grain. But mediation between oil production and the market includes relatively hidden developments that could perhaps be gathered with some precision had we the acts of one of those magistracies on usury that were in operation in western Europe in the second half of the sixteenth century.[74] We know that in 1531 and in 1571 advance sale at a determined price was forbidden. Loans in goods and produce were also formally forbidden then, and notaries were requested to register only loans in money without interest: in effect it does not take much to understand that in every case the transaction involved the immediate supply of cash for future compensation in oil, and it did not really matter that they were trying to regulate the official function of the exchange, since the tax on relative exchange—that is, oil for money—remained crucial. At Diano in 1575 a price was established verbally on March 15, to which the advance sale agreements had to refer, "and it should no longer be in the hands of the creditor to name the day on which he wants the price set, even though according to the form of the documents he could do it."[75] In any event, the cash loans kept maturation dates *ad voluntatem* along with the equally customary dates of S. Martino, S. Michele, and Christmas.

It is extraordinary to see in the notarial record how the notion of a fair price, the price current at the time among merchants, appears to have emerged relatively late, certainly no earlier than 1636, when there was already developing an official legitimization of collecting interest on *lucro cessante*.[76]

The notarial deed, beyond being a partial document compared with the totality of the transactions, is also typically a literary and ideological document. The modernizing approach of historians has led them to posit a realistic evolution of the antiusury laws toward recognizing the reality of mercantile transactions. However, there has not been enough reflection on the fact that the same mercantile model represents a cultural transposition that is external to the reality of those transactions commonly motivated by necessity and by interpersonal relationships. The "current price" among "merchants" implies a reference to transactions in goods that are radically "other" with respect to the normal relationship between producer and wholesaler; furthermore the significance of the current price is not illuminated by any evidence about the "customs" of the area, as it could be for fishing.

By the seventeenth century, capital from coralline was no longer calculated in oil but in lire. The amount advanced to sailors remained remarkably standard even though with time the expenses of the expedition increased and therefore so did the nominal value of the share. Since initially each fishing ship required a capital investment of between 600 and 650 lire, a certain return for the oil was necessary. In effect the fishing calendar depended directly on that of oil, which led to the dissatisfaction with the Genoese prohibitions on export, especially since the sailors had to return home in time for the early September grape harvest.[77] The imbalance in the relationship is evident immediately: the captain mediated between the merchant who "provides the capital" and the crew whom he recruited with lavish advances; he was both monetary speculator and protagonist of the social experience of fishing for coral, which was a collective undertaking fragmented by the participation of various crews of nine sailors each but led by joint captains of the dock who united the fleets of at least two communities. The joint responsibility for losses and gains,[78] guaranteed by a system of division into sixteen parts, gave to the undertaking a typically corporate structure. The enrollment contracts testify to a structure of roles that described the functions of each man, except for the captain. The ship's officer was compensated at seven or eight quarters, and the two balancers, hired on the basis of skill, were compensated at five quarters and a half. Ten quarters went to the captain and eight quarters to the owner of the ship.[79]

The crew altogether could receive between nine and ten shares, and the merchant as provider of the advances could draw two shares or more, since the total number of shares was not rigidly set even if the expedition had been structured in the usual way. In the first half of the century the value of one share was set at 400 lire, which theoretically indicates an expenditure on equipment of 800 lire or more. The division was made naturally on the basis of net expenses and presupposed the sale of the coral. The profit paid off the monetary investment and the net earnings paid for the investment of four months' work. Both of these were highly uncertain and variable, and both were regulated by the same rate per share that, in the first half of the seventeenth century, varied from 30 to 72 lire, with the mode a little below 50, that is, 12 percent of the money invested, a percentage that emerges as well from other evidence.[80] In fact it is difficult not to read into this structure a kind of capitalization of human labor with payment fixed "by the rate." The nature of the undertaking was always very speculative: what appears on the books as a 100 percent loss meant for the sailors shipwreck or slavery, which left them with the related problem of redeeming themselves.

It is the merchants in any case who sold the coral to the Genoese or at Livorno. They "give the accounting." In fact they held all the cards in their hands: they had the coral in their warehouses or under the control of fiduciaries; they kept the loyalty of the captains, who were often joint owners of the ships for which the merchants resupplied the capital from year to year; they controlled sales and the records of accounts; they maintained personal relationships with the external buyers; they chose the time for sale, which could persuade the sailor to sell his own still-uncertain share in advance, just as he had sold his own labor in advance, by signing on. The relevant clause in fact was devised in such a way that the contract had the form of a loan in any month of the year, with the possibility of redemption without necessarily leaving on voyage. Perhaps it is an index of economic structures that only one-fifth of the recorded enlistments occurred before departure and that October, November, and March were months with net enlistments greater than the trimester of December through February, when presumably people lived off of the sale of their own oil. In any case, it is a remarkable confirmation that the composition of the crews varied from year to year without fiduciary relationships taking even minimal hold during that time: the enlistment for fishing every year was an option within the framework of a family economy regulated by variables that had a set chronological and cyclical pattern. For the common sailor the rate of earnings could be equal to two bushels of grain (one or even more expected) plus maintenance for four months and perhaps some benefit if the ship were hired out.

On the other side, the "independent" captains, those who produced their own capital, were a small minority: in 1609 eight fishing ships were tributaries of G. B. Viale Ferraro, six of Giorgio Ferraro, five of the widow of Battista Arimondo, five of Agostino Sicardo, three of G. B. Lavello, and so on. In 1631 the concentration was still greater: G. B. Viale Ferraro had progressed to the point of being patron for fourteen ships, and Giorgio's sons, Sebastiano and Paolo, had nine ships.[81] Since the corallines came back in at the end of August, the mowing and threshing of the grain and barley were business for the women, and there really was some grain even if the *caratata* registries do not do justice to this form of farming.[82] It seems correct, therefore, that our few data on annual consumption should refer to women. Maintenance was to be guaranteed above all to widows. A dozen or so wills allow us to distinguish three levels of consumption: a first standard of consumption anticipates one bushel of grain (and barley) fully paid with a bushel of figs, two scandagli of wine, and five pounds of oil; the second standard consists of two bushels of grain, four scandagli of wine, and half a barrel of oil; the third standard comprises two and a half or three bushels, six scandagli, and one barrel. This formulation, however, typically sounds a single note and expresses the social asymmetries in terms of commodity wealth,[83] but it contributes little in any case toward the goal of quantifying the commodities of Cervo and the grain deficiency in particular.[84]

An investigation into the millers reveals the milling of only fifteen hundred bushels in 1624–25, while two-penny milling was calculated at twenty-five hundred bushels, an estimate based on bulk.[85] It seems interesting that in every case there is evidence of an import of flour. It is a fact that none of the merchants of Cervo except for Gio Agostino Viale della Chiappa called himself a grain merchant, confirming the testimony that at Cervo in the years 1640–50 there were no merchants specializing in grains,[86] which explains the need to replenish supplies at Alassio, Oneglia, and elsewhere, which was likewise the goal of the local shopkeepers. It is that much more significant that several operations involving the buying and selling of grains were recorded by notaries; but, with a few exceptions, we cannot know the reason for a private indebtedness current with the merchants of Oneglia, Diano, and Porto.[87] This leaves the impression that the circuit of oil-grain exchange was not strengthened by the fact of their being the same brokers, which belies the hypothesis of a long and personalized circularity of exchange with monetary solutions only compensatory for debit-credit entry items. In effect the loans appear to have rather casual recipients: the relevant transactions in the notarial records do not document a structuring of the interpersonal relationship. The lack of this solidarity in the circuits of exchange is probably the reason for the delay and the resistance to monopolies of basic necessities, as we found when we discussed the local *gabelles*: tradition counted precisely to the degree that specific mercantile practices were lacking locally.

Before departing and immediately after returning, the men had to work at hoeing around the olive trees and in the vineyards. Alternatively in springtime a ditch was made around the plant (*soppa*) that was filled up again with fertilizer in the autumn.[88] The extremely subdivided ownership of oxen (by the feet or else by the "hooves"), allowed for plowing, also payable by the day.

In 1642 there were 584 properties with vineyards and 554 mixed with olive groves. By contrast, there were 3,383 properties planted exclusively with olives, clearly the reigning plant.[89] In any case there still existed a surplus of wine; ripened in a hurry, the grapes were picked very early and by the end of October the "poor devils" were selling their wine when the first olives were just beginning to be gathered, an operation that was drawn out for months, particularly in the good years. Out of anxiety over a possible freeze, the olive pressing was quickly completed in the hundred and more olive presses (*gombi*) of the *podestaria*.[90]

In effect the agricultural calendar seems to have been harmonized with the fishing calendar, allowing for full utilization of human resources. But this occurred within a period of equilibrium narrowly bound by weather and by the amount of income and expenditures. Time was clearly in the hands of the merchant brokers. There were no communal economic resources, except in the grasses along the streams, and here pasturage legislation hurt the poorest but was certainly upheld by that third of the producers of oil who were capable of pressing a reasonable quantity of oil in a year. For those without olive trees, there was only hoeing, gathering coral, and migrating. But (and it is a typical complaint about olive culture) the numbers of those without oil could rise dramatically from one year to the next.

❦ The elite of Cervo sat, thus, on a precarious throne of community resources. The personal tax of 1629 created a certain discontent among the principal men of the *podestaria*: it struck at all forms of wealth, not just real estate, the ascertaining of which had been the fruit of "sinister informants."[91] Those taxed invariably protested that they had no business except the oil that they gathered directly and the ships that they outfitted. Gio Agostino Viale della Chiappa admitted to having sold wine and oil and to having bought grains, but nonetheless he maintained that he was not a merchant.[92] A few years later, however, the witnesses as well as the interested parties spoke more freely, confirming the profits from their mercantile activities in oil, coral, and grains at around 10 percent, and they even talked of maritime exchanges and of *lucro cessante*.[93]

Reconstructed on the basis of local notarial records, the individual *dossiers* can only be partial because the Sardinian trade and especially the Genoese operations are mostly missing. Let us look at the case of the very rich G. B. Viale Ferraro. His father Francesco, trader in Sardinia, was for a long time consul at Bosa.[94] In 1584 he had divided his goods between G.B. and his brother Giuseppe, both married to Ferraro women: G.B. even assumed a double surname as directed by his father-in-law, Gio Francesco, of whom Marietina was sole heir, inheriting seven outfitted ships, a fortune estimated at 15,000 to 16,000 scudi (that is, 60,000 lire), and the *juspatronatus* of a chapel. The son-in-law certainly did not squander this fortune or that inherited from his father. He appeared often in the annuity registers: a list of 1596 shows forty-four contracts at 7 and 8 percent drawn up starting in 1588, for an accumulation of 16,567 lire,[95] the income from which the daughter and heir Marieta was still collecting in 1640. We know furthermore that he managed to outfit as many as sixteen ships in one year, establishing a real hegemony in coral; that he collected up to 1,000 barrels of oil; and that he had conflicts with his son Gio Ambrogio then living in Genoa. The inventory of his belongings at death is significant: four houses, lands, two mills, one hundred barrels of oil, twenty-four somate of wine, more than fifty scudi of silver and other coins, books of accounts and of debtors (among them Francesco Viale di Genoa, owing almost 6,000 lire), nine chests of coral, a ship of his own and another eight in joint ownership with the captains, and cellars, warehouses, olive-presses, and other items.[96] The lands are the same that in a later document turn out to belong to Marieta, by then the unhappy wife of a Multedo from Alassio, and they were appraised at 19,400 lire and produced an annual income of 785 lire.[97] We can add the houses and other things. In any case his wealth in real estate must have been well balanced by that in personal property, even if this latter cannot be assigned a value.

The key documents in this regard are the books of debtors. Thus Giorgio Ferraro in 1618 divided among his four sons credits amounting to almost 18,000 lire due from 228 debtors, of whom 50 or so owed less than 10 lire, 38 more than 100 lire, but none more than 1,000 lire.[98] The sons Sebastiano and Paolo also dealt in corals and oil, and they certainly did not give up the activity in short-term loans, or at least this is the notarial evidence. Thus for example in 1628 Sebastiano

negotiated thirty short-term loans for a total of 2,125 lire and converted another thirty into advances on corallines (1,612 lire), while
during the same year Paolo negotiated twenty-one loans for 3,386 lire
plus another fifteen on coralline (913 lire) and five annuities for 2,500
lire. The receipts were consistently lower and normally the general
receipts formed the basis for a new loan. Among the debtors there
were many ship captains but, overall, a majority of the people were
from the villages, even though it was not possible to discover specific
evidence of an active patronage system. The dowries from the family
were at their height: a sister of Paolo and Sebastiano had 6,300 lire,
and the same Paolo gave a daughter in marriage to a Spinola of Savona
with a dowry of 5,200 lire plus a trousseau worth 1,000 lire.[99]

In any case the loans, and not just the annuities, often had their
own long history. The loans of Gio Antonio Chiesa who died in 1610
went back as far as 1583.[100] Although more evident at the peaks of
the price curve (as distinct from the credit curve), indebtedness was
general, and the heirs took care to distinguish debts from credits.[101]
Occasionally we can follow some histories of indebtedness: the loss
of the guarantee through appraisal, the ceding of land, perhaps held
back later for rental; in any case the correct methodology for investigation seems to be that of the history of individuals or of families.[102]
In effect, verification by notarial records is only partial, and it is
necessary to consider carefully the civil judicial records: the apparent
"gossip" found in them was an integral part of a transactional complex
that cannot be omitted unless one wants merely to make banal generalizations about what appears obvious.

In the "civil acts" of the commune, debts to foreigners have a
particular prominence, presumably because of the principle of the
commune's own responsibility for the general reputation of the community. Such particular prominence was produced by a series of local
brasseurs, persons specialized in the collection of debts who invariably
acted as tax collectors and agents for foreign traders. Among these
was Galino Alasio who had a modest fortune in real estate but who
above all appeared in typically protean roles. Thus he identified himself time and again as "schoolmaster, merchant, and loan collector,"
"innkeeper and dealer in corals," and others reported that he was "an
astute and sagacious person, accustomed to initiate suits against many
persons as is well known."[103] Thus in the years from 1610 to 1620,
he worked as a horse and cattle trader and as an agent for Camilla,
widow of Gio Antonio Chiesa, in her suit with the Augustianian

Fathers. In 1619 he made an agreement for six years with the Riccardi of Oneglia, fabric merchants, who had had difficulty collecting loans worth 4,354 lire in Cervo. For this activity he received 400 lire in an annual salary.[104] A less brilliant collector than most, he was imprisoned in 1625 by the same Riccardi family, and he freed himself by paying forty-two barrels of oil with the help of his cousin Pasquale Muratore and Tomaso Casamilia, who was incidentally Alasio's confraternity brother with whom he had recently begun building the oratory of San Carlo in the town. Again, in 1648, Alasio worked for the Riccardi as a fiduciary agent. A man like this not only had the contract for collection of *averia* at least five or six times, but he was also an *anziano* for four years and captain of the militia five times.

In other words, the case of Galino Alasio illustrates the important role played by an elite of middlemen, different from that of rich merchants and that of the professional men such as the notaries. In this case political success was joined with a talent for what we might call harassment, not compensated for by the active role of lender. Which is to say that the useful model of a patronage system is based on a presupposed loyalty that does not appear to be the only or even the dominant gage of personal influence. Thus, one of the key tasks of historical reconstruction is a concrete reconstruction of personal roles in the context of the community. Taking up more generally our initial theme of political dualism, we can find a political alteration following the confrontation of 1601: now dominant is a Ferrari clique, led this time, however, by that Giobatta Viale Ferraro and by the sons of that Giorgio Ferraro who in 1600–1601 acted in opposition to the regime. This clique was certainly formed from the "richest men" and the "principal men" of Cervo, but once again the judicial and political records paint in the details of a picture confused with alliances and conflicts.

꙰ The notary Paolo Gerolamo Muratore testified in the first years of the seventeenth century about the predominance of the Viale brothers, both G.B. and Giuseppe, who "have conducted their business in their own way and have promised beatings":[105] "They make," he said, "50,000 scudi and they have [many] relatives and followers." Their influence extended even to Genoa, as Prospero Ferrari learned much to his own distress when he was left in a bad way by a case that unfortunately dragged on. Locally, poor Prospero had to carry on his case with the help of three notaries of Cervo.[106]

The *podestà* was vigilant. Already in 1605 it had come to his attention, *ad aures*, that quite a few persons had gathered in the house of the notary Muratore, among them the notary Sebastiano Ordano, the honorable Gio Giacomo Ferraro, the notary Benedetto Massone with his son Luca and Lorenzo Massone, Prospero Ferraro himself, and a Gio Antonio Alasio to draw up a petition to the Senate concerning the last parliament, and they had already gathered twenty-five signatures. Immediately they were denounced under the law against meetings of secret groups *de conventiculis.*[107] At a distance of almost twenty years another *podestà* of Cervo wrote to the Senate to refute the calumnies that had been made against him as a "renegade and partisan of the duke of Savoy," rumors that had been stirred up by a group composed of the son of the notary Muratore, the same notary Ordano, the Massone family led by the notary Paolo, Paolo Giulio Ferrari, Pasino Caneto, Bartolomeo Calvo, and Ambrogio Siccardi. This group represented an almost perfect continuity with the conventicle of 1605.[108] Furthermore, it is the *anziani* themselves who in 1624 declared to the Senate that "the magistrates who come to this place for the most part know little about justice, and there are some there who can barely write their own names." As a result, they were forced to resort to the learned men and lawyers of the factions.[109] All of this demonstrates the continued preeminence of the men of the law and explains how in 1619 the *anziani* had proposed that the notaries should be excluded from the office of solicitor, a proposal that fomented undying disputes: "The region of Cervo remains peopled for the most part by sailors and stupid people" and, more to the point, by "too many notaries."[110]

But it was precisely the notaries, or some of them, who were among those most capable of a true opposition. In general an opponent of the regime accumulated penal sentences against himself; such a situation reflected his loss in the competition for the honor, as is the case with the militia captain Stefano Lavello. An important episode of 1621 is recorded in the criminal records about the occasion of the visit of a colonel to review the militia and to appoint a local captain. As the candidate of the *anziani*, Paolo Ferrari competed for the post with Stefano Lavello, the candidate of Genoa. The former succeeded, provoking a reaction from the Lavello brothers, from G. B. Massone quondam P.G. and from the captain Tomaso Bianco: "There are some who have made small casks," displayed as a sign of insult.[111] The witnesses against Stefano Lavello recalled his twenty-four criminal trials in court, the inquisitorial investigation against him by the Dominican fathers of Diano, and his being "a man who creates division between one party and another." "The principle of bad government is carried out in this region," it was explained, "because the *anziani* are created by nomination in such a way that one who wants to be an *anziano* has months to lobby with friends and relatives." From the mouth of an Arimondo came the same complaint heard in 1601 from the villages.[112] The colonel from Genoa declared that "even in Genoa he had heard talk about the disunity of this place and that this place was divided into two factions."

On this occasion, however, Lavello had few allies against the powerful Paolo Ferrari. Gio Giacomo Muratore, son of the notary, had been banished for having offended the *anziano*, G. B. Viale Ferraro. In this era, however, it was Paolo Gerolamo Ferrari quondam Gio Antonio who filled the judicial records. The most important among the "principal men" remained outside of the village conflicts: when G. B. Ferraro, the brother of Paolo and Sebastiano, quarreled with the wife of a Pineta, he sued her, "since," he said, "the insult that is made by a lowly person of bad reputation should be punished ex-officio," a principle that we hear word for word even on the lips of a matron from the area.[113]

This does not imply a consistent hesitancy on the part of the principal men to clash with persons of an inferior rank. The most characteristic signs of rank were possession of an agnatic chapel, a pew in church, distinctive dress, and the custom of walking and standing about under the pier. The boundaries of common deference were best transgressed in the secret assault, in throwing stones on roofs, and in spreading excrement on the bench where the principal men and the *podestà* often lingered for conversation. Until 1625, however, there were no blatant episodes that can be taken as a guide to such behavior. The criminal documents are full instead of occasional conflicts, largely involving women, without motives ever really emerging: people testified to the facts alone. In addition, the range of alliances was multiple. In fact, the legal formula proper for freeing oneself from the suspicion of partisanship asked if the accused was "a relative, friend, retainer, servant, creditor, comrade or employee [of someone else]." But could unbiased evidence be given in that context? The accused and interested parties were very reticent in this regard. "We are all from the same village," declared one Rittore della Chiappa, "however, everyone conducts his own affairs; I do not put myself in their way and I leave them all to do what they want."[114] It is as if, once the loyalty of the lineage was dissolved, each person had to fend for himself, or at least this is the image of themselves that they wanted to communicate.[115] It is clear in any case that the predominance of a few imposed a general deference. The fissuring of the community and the reconstitution of the factions made necessary the invasion of the Franco-Savoyards and the sacking of Cervo.

In 1625 the *anziano* G. B. Viale Ferraro was a prior, along with Agostino Siccardi, an Albavera and a Merello. It was a time of war, and in March Sebastiano Ferraro was given the responsibility of contracting a loan in Alassio to buy reserves of grain. Overrun by the troops of Commander Fabri, Cervo was conquered and sacked, resulting in damages of 200,000 lire.[116] Although the head of the *anziani* and Paolo Ferraro had immediately protested the damages inflicted, it seems that in fact a few houses were saved. Giuseppe Viale's testimony typically provides us with a dramatic tableau of a crowd in the church, the squire entering with sword drawn, the worshipers falling on their knees, and the "slight softening" of the invader who imposed a tribute of 3,000 doubloons. G. B. Viale Ferraro rounded up the first installment and took responsibility for finishing the payment by selling seven hundred barrels of oil in Porto Maurizio.[117] During the subsequent years, however, there were also disputes about another loan besides Sebastiano's, one contracted in Alassio by Giuseppe Viale quondam Galino and even more about the behavior of Giacinto Viale as receiver of the oil: both men claimed compensation for provisioning the Savoyards. Here, though, the charge was of having bought immunity for their own houses. But who was in the church on that fatal day? "A good number of the women" were there, obviously, but also present was a group of men, none of whom was there totally by chance: the Viale brothers (G.B. and Giuseppe), the Ferrari brothers (Sebastiano, Paolo, and G.B.), the sons of Giuseppe Viale (Giacinto and Francesco), Battista Martino (who had already twice been an *anziano* with Sebastiano Ferraro), Giuseppe Viale quondam Galino, G. B. Ferraro quondam Antonio, Francesco Giudice, Agostino Lavello (the son-in-law of Sebastiano Ferrari), the captain Michele Viale, Zaccaria Arimondo, a Terrizzano, and another Ferrari.[118]

The commune, and therefore also the villages that had not presented themselves to the *castello*, to the great irritation of the Fabri, should have taken collective responsibility for the expenses incurred to avoid having the countryside put to fire. The Massoni and Muratori (the notaries Benedetto and Paolo Massone and the sons of the notary P. G. Muratore) led the *anziani* in 1626 and 1627. Their services to the republic of Genoa were extensive.[119] The opposition to those in power chose a "constitutionalist" line. Paolo Massone maintained that it was in the competence of the parliament to decide on the merit of the invaders' request and entrusted to the fiscal auditors the examination of the actions of the Viale and Ferraro. It was not by chance that against the *anziani* the Viale and Ferraro families used the parish assembly that they obviously controlled. Furthermore, evidence indicates there was a hostility toward Massone on the part of P. G. Arimondo, the powerful notary of the villages, who was supported by Gio Francesco Massone, agent for Giacinto Viale.[120]

In 1628 and in 1629 the Ferrari once again controlled the council of *anziani* of the *castello*. But the Massone were in good shape to pursue the conflict in Genoa, so much so that in 1631 there was again a rumor that the Ferrari wanted to sack the houses of the Massone. In 1632 a noisy disturbance by the *villani* who refused to go to the *castello* for a military muster, along with the separatist proposals of P. G. Arimondo, illustrates how the habitual hostility of the villages focused on a matter of heavy symbolic significance, this time rekindled by fiscal exactions.[121] It seems in any case that G. B. Viale Ferraro, who had died in the meantime, and his allies, who had also taken refuge in the church, finally won the dispute.[122] In 1634 Pasquale Muratore, the head of the *anziani*, denounced to the auditors the *podestà*, who, together with Paolo Ferraro, was the richest man in the area. Because Muratore was "familiar enough with the *podestà* to be able to lie in wait for him," he had managed to have him imprisoned.[123]

However, it is significant that there emerged a "party of notaries" under the guidance of the Massone and Muratore, a party that relied primarily on the villages and followed a learnedly constitutionalist political line that was a kind of institutional reactualization of the private Massoni-Ferrari conflict. There is no doubt, in fact, that the political dualism was nourished by the rivalries and the contests for positions of honor in the *castello*. That dualism was strategically linked with disputes over the seats in parliament, which remained the place where the villages, even though they were in a minority, stood up to the hegemony of those from the *castello*. The conflicting alliances thus reveal their historical roots or at least how there were poles of hostility

154 *Edoardo Grendi*

around which crystallized more incidental alliances of close family relationships (such as father and son, father-in-law and son-in-law) and clients. On these occasions the political-institutional structure of the community came under discussion. The same incidental quality of the criminal registers also reflects these alliances. This then is the political system of the community reconstructed in a liberally ethnographic vein. We hope in the future to confirm this reconstruction for the first decades of the eighteenth century, during a dramatic period when the olive trees froze in 1709 and forced the reconversion to external activities, that is, from fishing to commerce.

Notes

1. Andrea Spinola, *Ricordi*, vol. 1, manuscript in Biblioteca Berio, Genoa, *Manoscritti*.
2. This was certainly true for Albenga and Savona. The other "cities" were Noli and Ventimiglia.
3. At Rapallo in the middle of the seventeenth century there still existed the parties of the Fregoso and of the Adorno. Factions (*colori*) and clans (*alberghi*) were widespread in towns and cities in the fifteenth century.
4. Archivio di Stato, Genoa (hereafter, ASG), Sala Senarega, *Atti Senato*, filza 1423, Sala Gallo, *Sindacatori*, filza 713.
5. For a typology of the peasant coalitions, see E. R. Wolf, *Peasants* (Englewood Cliffs, N.J., 1966).
6. For criminal justice, the *podestà*; for civil justice, the *podestà* and the *anziani*; for rural justice, the *anziani* alone.
7. The records of the criminal magistracy of Porto Maurizio are missing, although good series exist of the local petty criminal and the civil magistracies (Archivio Comunale, Cervo Ligure, hereafter ACC). Difficulties persist in consulting the Rota Criminale of Genoa.
8. P. Schneider, J. Schneider, and E. Hansen, "Modernization and Development: The Role of Regional Elites and Noncorporate Groups in the European Mediterranean," reprinted in S. W. Schmidt et al., *Friends, Followers and Factions: A Reader in Political Clientelism* (Berkeley, 1977).
9. Arbitration remains a personal choice, that is, it is not presumed in the structure of a lineage (Genoese chapter "de committendis propinquorum quaestionibus in albergario").
10. The resistance of the Viale was judged to be "an unreasonable and intolerable thing, these people being some of those individuals who slander other families, who in most cases stand aloof from great troubles" (ASG, Sala Senarega, *Atti Senato*, filza 1638).
11. ASG, Sala Senarega, *Atti Senato*, filza 1635.
12. The Viale made up seventy or so households, and the Arimondo had forty-eight in 1656. P. G. Massone and the Viale brothers were sons of sisters; Sebastiano Ferrari was the son of a sister of Chiesa and the husband of the daughter of Giuseppe Viale (Archivio di Stato, Imperia [ASI], *Notaio G. B. Simoni 1591–1628*, testimonies).
13. ACC, *Registri Criminali*, ad annos.
14. ASG, Sala Senarega, *Atti Senato*, filze 1424, 1417.

15. ASG, Sala Senarega, *Atti Senato*, filze 1315, 1567.
16. ASG, Sala Senarega, *Atti Senato*, filza 1602.
17. ASG, Sala Senarega, *Atti Senato*, filza 1358.
18. The sons of Muratore later denounced this alliance. ASG, Sala Senarega, *Atti Senato*, filza 1904.
19. ASG, Sala Senarega, *Atti Senato*, filze 1228, 1353.
20. ASG, Sala Senarega, *Atti Senato*, filza 1357.
21. ASG, Sala Senarega, *Atti Senato*, filza 1431.
22. ACC, *Atti Civili*, 1591–92.
23. ASG, Sala Senarega, *Atti Senato*, filze 1502, 1511, 1519, and Sala Gallo, *Sindacatori*, filza 716.
24. Bartolomeo had been sent to Sardinia for five years. ASG, Sala Senarega, *Atti Senato*, filza 1438.
25. ACC, *Atti Civili*, 1596–97 and ASG, Sala Senarega, *Atti Senato*, filza 1538. ACC, *Registri Criminali*, 1583–84. [*Omissis.*]
26. ASG, Sala Senarega, *Atti Senato*, filza 1667.
27. A detailed investigation could be conducted of the language. In every case there is a remarkable recurrence of the accusations of heresy within the structure of the interfamily rivalries.
28. The parishes were constituted respectively in 1505 and 1536. The map was drawn by Sergio Saroni to whom we are very grateful.
29. On the "Descritione" of Giustiniani, see D. Galassi, M. P. Rota, and A. Scrivano, *Popolazione e insediamento in Liguria secondo la testimonianza di A. Giustiniani* (Florence, 1979).
30. ASI, *Notaio Sebastiano Ordano*, 1614–33 (for S. Maria: "case dei Salineri") and *Notaio Sebastiano Simoni*, 1635–42 (for Chiappa: "carrubeo dei Viale" etc.).
31. G. Delille, "L'ordine dei villaggi e l'ordine dei campi: Per uno studio antropologico del paesaggio agrario nel Regno di Napoli (secoli XV–XVIII)," in *Storia d'Italia*, *Annali*, vol. 8 (Turin, 1985), pp. 499–560.
32. In 1656 at the village of Freschi, there were only seven Freschi among the fourteen households, and at Rocca, as many Mantica as Siglioli (plus Rittore and Merello).
33. As happened instead at Sestri Levante even in the preceding era: F. Robin, *Sestri Levante, un bourg de la Ligurie génoise au XV siècle* (Genoa, 1976). In the notarial files there is one sole piece of evidence about a single common property of the Gassarino family, alienated to the oratory of S. Maria della Neve.
34. In the same way, the inhabitants of San Giuseppe and Chiappa reached agreement on the weekly distribution of water.
35. There is some information regarding this in my "Introduzione all'analisi storica delle comunità liguri: Cervo in età moderna," *Miscellanea Storica Ligure* 8, no. 2 (Studi di micro-analisi storica).
36. A reference to the statutes of the parish of San Giovanni Battista is in ASI, *Notaio B. Massone*, 1630–37.
37. See G. Felloni, "Distribuzione territoriale della ricchezza e dei carichi fiscali nella Repubblica di Genova (secc. XVI–XVIII)," a paper delivered at the Ottava Settimana di Studio F. Datini, [Prato], 1976.
38. The magistracy for the control of the affairs of the commune was instituted in 1623. In general such a magistracy worked through commissioners who were sent out into the territory. The principle of responsibility *in solido* led to a chain of acts of revenge. The *anziani* wrote in 1633: "when some creditor seeks to detain men of the community, the detainees acquire grievances against the creditor and they detain others from the same jurisdiction and thus it goes from one to another." (ASG, Sala Senarega, *Atti Senato*, filza 1930).

39. Theoretically, the lire registered were 300, practically however not much more was collected than 250, the sum that appears in the records of the *caratata*. Each one paid the amount registered multiplied by the value of the distribution (*distaglio*).

40. This was given as the frequent reason for a petition. The Sindacatori were conscious of these facts but there were a thousand obstacles in the way of their functioning as an annual court of appeal.

41. In the notarial records the dowry usually amounted to 100 lire.

42. ACC, *Atti Civili*, 1636–38.

43. From 1612 to 1643, the accumulation went from 260,595 lire to 1,245,688 lire. The appraisal was really very approximate and very different from that computed ad hoc by the official appraisers.

44. The census of 1667 lists over a hundred women heads of households out of 537 households.

45. ACC, *Atti Civili*, Miscellanea 1606–55.

46. ASI, *Notaio Antonio Massone*, 1683–93.

47. ACC, *Atti Civili*, 1683–84.

48. ASG, *Carati del Mare*, filza 39.

49. ACC, *Atti Civili*. 1632–33.

50. *Ibid.*

51. ACC, *Atti Civili*, 1641–42.

52. ACC, *Atti Civili*, 1636.

53. ASG, *Finanza Pubblica*, filza 2604, "Nota dei principali di azienda": next to that are the considerably reduced amounts proposed by the *anziani*. The *caratata* of 1612, organized by name, is in ASG, *Magistrato delle Comunità*, reg. 709.

54. ASG, *Antica Finanza*, filza 1034.

55. ASG, *Finanza Pubblica*, filza 2606.

56. Pozzobonello in any case was heir to Domenico Salineri.

57. The list of titled people is in the list of those taxed in 1640.

58. The *caratata* of 1643 in ASG, *Magistrato delle Comunità*, reg. 710.

59. ACC, *Atti Civili*, 1641–42.

60. The *spectabiles* instead are Ferrari and Viale. On the Genoese notariat, see G. Costamagna, *Il notaio a Genova tra prestigio e potere* (Rome, 1970).

61. There seems to be in any case a kind of specialization of roles.

62. Here the sample of priors that could be extracted from the notarial files is too limited. It is significant that on many occasions two *anziani* were assigned in a single year to the parish of San Bartolomeo where the division with Chiappa was nominally binding.

63. ASG, *Sala Senarega, Atti Senato*, filza 1807.

64. More precisely, in 1698.

65. During the years 1612–24 the value of the *distaglio* was 12 lire. In 1625 it was 25 lire (in two taxes), 18 in 1626, 24 in 1627, and 30 in 1630–34.

66. Among the creditors were G. B. Morchio, G. B. Trucco, Gio Ant. Carchero, Biagio Mantica, Giuseppe Rolando, Deo Sicardi, various members of the Simone family and still others. ASG, *Magistrato delle Comunità*, filza 674.

67. The contractors committed themselves to maintaining the stocks and warehouses where they sold at the highest price (which included a profit in commission); it was obligatory to resupply stocks from them and forbidden to import on a private basis except for private consumption; furthermore whoever sold his own wine had to pay the contractor the equivalent of the commission.

68. A right sanctioned by the criminal statutes of Genoa of 1576.

69. The declarations in this regard were common in other Ligurian communities: levying the tax in kind could be cleverly delayed.

70. ASG, *Antica Finanza*, filze 1034 and 1054 bis.

71. The records of the *gabelle* on trifles show these commercial "dependencies."

72. The data collected in Archivio Storico Comunale di Genova, *Abbondanza*, filza 886 for 1589; ASG, *Antica Finanza*, filza 1035, for 1593; ACC *Atti Civili*, 1607–9 for 1607; ACC, *Atti Civili*, 1628–29, for 1625.

73. The oil tax was biennial, according to the common pattern of alternating harvests.

74. At Porto Maurizio in 1564.

75. ASG, *Sala Senarega, Atti Senato*, filza 1431.

76. Mentioned in 1622, ASI, *Notaio G. B. Simone*, 1614–23. The reference was to the "current price on the beach or in nearby places."

77. With the corallines, they were said to set sail with a capital of 60,000 lire (ASG, *Sala Senarega, Atti Senato*, filza 1869).

78. But there is also a testimony to the opposite effect, ACC, *Atti Civili*, 1636.

79. The most common regime was the joint ownership between captain and merchant.

80. ACC, *Atti Civili*, 1636, where they even admitted earnings of 30 percent.

81. Other merchant-owners of fishing ships: Giacinto Viale quondam Giacomo with four ships; p. Agostino Rolando and p. Batt. Rolando with two apiece; Gio Francesco Massone two ships; Agostino Steria nine ships.

82. There was one, for example, who harvested in his fields five scandagli of wine and a barrel and a half of oil; he also got from it three quarts of figs, two rotoli and ten libbre of grain, and three rotoli and nine libbre of barley (ASI, *Notaio Sebastiano Ordano*, 1604–26).

83. It is clear that the excess was easily salable. In every case the most well-off also settled on an annual contribution of money.

84. Paolo Ferraro declared that the land of Cervo yielded enough to live on for only half the year, but it is doubtful that he is referring only to grain. We can observe that in 1789 Cervo held back 2,200 imported bushels for consumption to cover a shortfall.

85. ACC, *Atti Civili*, 1625–26. The notation for milling for 1631 is 3,000 bushels.

86. ASG, *Sala Senarega, Atti Senato*, filza 1934.

87. Lists of debtors primarily are in ACC, *Atti Civili*, passim.

88. A seventeenth-century document speaks of works "to break and crush."

89. ASG, *Magistrato Comunità*, reg. 710.

90. Ibid., for the precise ninety-three presses.

91. ASG, *Sala Senarega, Atti Senato*, filza 1888.

92. ASI, *Notai G.B. Simone*, 1627–54, and *S. Ordano*, 1631.

93. ACC, *Atti Civili*, 1636.

94. I have some doubts, however, in naming Francesco Viale quondam Nicola who was consul for twenty-five years and dead in Bosa in 1594 as father of G.B. and Giuseppe.

95. ASI, *Notaio P. G. Muratore*, 1581–1617.

96. ASI, *Notaio S. Ordano*, 1604–26, act of February 18, 1628.

97. ASI, *Notaio B. Massone*, 1636–48; the appraisal is from 1643.

98. ASI, *Notaio S. Ordano*, 1611–23, act of March 8, 1618.

99. The Spinola family later denounced Paolo Ferraro as someone decidedly too pushy.

100. ASI, *Notaio S. Ordano*, 1611–23, act of September 18, 1618.

101. ASI, *Notaio P. G. Arimondo*, 1620–31, act of March 13, 1630.

102. See the two works by G. Levi, respectively in *Quaderni storici* 11 (1976), and in *Storia d'Italia, Annali*, vol. 1 (Turin, 1978).

103. ACC, *Atti Civili*, 1636 and 1643–44.

104. ASI, *Notaio*.

105. ACC, *Atti Civili*, 1607–8.

106. ASG, Sala Senarega, *Atti Senato*, filza 1758.

107. ACC, *Registri Criminali*, 1605–6.

108. ASG, Sala Senarega, *Atti Senato*, filza 1831.

109. ASG, Sala Senarega, *Atti Senato*, filza 1830.

110. ASG, Sala Senarega, *Atti Senato*, filza 1619.

111. ACC, *Registri Criminali*, 1621–22. There also existed a Sardinian rivalry between Arimondo and Lavello (ASG, Sala Senarega, *Atti Senato*, filze 1734, 1784).

112. Ibid.

113. ACC, *Registri Criminali*, 1620–21 and 1630–31.

114. ACC, *Registri Criminali*, 1644–45.

115. See the observations of Y. Castan, *Honnêteté et relations sociales en Languedoc 1715–80* (Paris, 1974).

116. ASG, Sala Senarega, *Atti Senato*, filza 1886.

117. ACC, *Atti Civili*, 1632–33, for the testimony of G. Viale.

118. ASG, *Magistrato Comunità*, filza 138.

119. For Masone, ASI, *Notaio S. Simone*, 1628–51, and ASG, Sala Senarega, *Atti Senato*, filza 1887; for Paolo Ferraro, ASG, *Atti Senato*, filza 1872.

120. ASG, Sala Senarega, *Atti Senato*, filza 1904, the accusation is of "having given offense."

121. ASG, Sala Senarega, *Atti Senato*, filza 1917.

122. Much less in the case of the acts of revenge of Giuseppe Viale quondam Galino (ASG, Sala Senarega, *Atti Senato*, filza 1938).

123. ASG, Sala Gallo, *Sindacatori*, filza 739.

8 ?§ Unwed Mothers in the Late Nineteenth and Early Twentieth Centuries: Clinical Histories and Life Histories

by Gianna Pomata

In the second half of the nineteenth century, information about the mothers of foundling babies begins to appear in the periodic reports issued by foundling hospitals and maternity shelters. These are, in fact and in name, "clinical histories," recounted in detail by the health directors of those institutions for an audience of physicians. The purpose of the reports was to circulate widely so-called observations on the most interesting cases of childbirth, with the interest being fundamentally clinical and didactic, understandable in an age when hospital births were uncommon and obstetrics provided only very limited opportunities for observation. Besides offering brief references to the mothers' social conditions, these clinical histories give information about the condition of their health at the moment of admission to the shelters, about the probable number of previous deliveries, about the course of the birth, if difficult, and of the confinement, if sickly.

At the end of the nineteenth century, these clinical histories, by now increasingly condensed and apparently more for statistical than clinical use, are supplemented by "personal notes" about the women, intended to fulfill administrative needs: to verify, for example, the conditions for the granting of financial assistance, a matter that could entail having to reconstruct the woman's history, her place of work, and her relations with her lover and her family. This type of note, dictated by the requirements of administrative and social control, will

Gianna Pomata, "Madri illegittime tra Ottocento e Novecento: storie cliniche e storie di vita," *Quaderni storici*, no. 44 (1980): 497–542.

become progressively more detailed, taking shape in the 1920s as personal summaries, or real "life histories," now gathered from a sociological as well as a medical point of view and concerned with the phenomenon of "unwed motherhood."

Both the clinical observations and the personal-information forms, with their close attention to individual cases, tell us a great deal about the experiences and the specific circumstances of the women to whom they refer. At the same time, both clinical histories and forms also tell us much about those who wrote them: they reveal attitudes and behavior on the part of the physicians and administrators of the foundling hospitals and, later, of the social workers as they deal with these same women.

In the appearance and then in the transformation of the materials we are concerned with here, we see a change in the social treatment of unwed mothers. What happens first of all is that the unwed mother ceases to be a forbidden object of knowledge, as she had been, in fact, so long as the foundlings were being received through the turning box (*la ruota*) and the foundling hospital was unable, therefore, to identify the mother. In principle the unwed mother ought to have remained a forbidden object of knowledge even after the *ruota* was eliminated, because, by law, motherhood outside of marriage was supposed to remain wrapped in secrecy: for illegitimate births, the civil code prohibited investigation into either paternity or maternity.[1] But this prohibition existed only in principle, because in actuality during the late nineteenth and early twentieth centuries, this formal prohibition coexisted with widespread practices of identifying and investigating the unwed mother (but not the father), practices attested to precisely by the clinical histories and the information forms on which the present work is based.

This of course was not a matter of contemplative knowledge. In its medical as well as its administrative aspect, the investigation of unwed mothers had practical aims: persuading or compelling the women to take responsibility for their babies, to acknowledge them and suckle them, and to rear them not in the traditional way, but according to the prescriptions of medical science.

What follows is an example of how maternity can be imposed and lived as a social obligation: an attempt, on the one hand, to reconstruct how this obligation came to be justified and imposed and, on the other, to understand the reasoning and the circumstances of the women who either tried to escape it or decided to accept it.

✺ The Investigation of Maternity

In the foundling hospitals of the big cities, the *ruota* was eliminated between 1870 and 1880.[2] This was a decisive step toward the introduction of what, in the juridical and administrative language of the time, came to be called the "investigation of maternity," the introduction, that is, of the practice of identifying and controlling mothers of foundlings. But it was not a purely juridical question: the developments in the "investigation of maternity" are intertwined above all and in very significant ways with developments of late nineteenth-century medicine. The physicians of the foundling hospitals and the maternity homes were the principal promoters of this investigation; the ends used to justify it and the forms it assumed in practice were, as we shall see, chiefly concerned with health.

It is now clear that the unwed mothers who at the end of the nineteenth century gave birth in the foundling hospitals' maternity wards were the first women to go through the experience of hospital delivery. They were the poorest and weakest women, temporarily isolated from their network of social support by their illegitimate pregnancies and forced to resort to the hospice either because they had no other place to give birth or because they wanted to keep the birth secret. A woman gave birth at the hospice or in the hospital, in fact, only as a last resort; even married women had occasional recourse here, but only as a way to have their babies accepted among the foundlings.[3]

The clinical histories vividly describe these women's extreme weakness due to overwork as adults and malnutrition as infants—the result, in the physicians' language, of "preexisting rickets" (*rachitide pregressa*). I reproduce here the beginning of one history, neither the most extreme case nor the most striking:

Under the Number 294, there took refuge in this Hospital on October 5, 1869, a woman of 24 years, a seamstress, unmarried, and pregnant for the first time. Daughter of very poor parents, who abandoned her among the foundlings until she was 18, she had to struggle from the first months of life until the above-mentioned age with the most squalid misery, by reason of which, suffering from a deficient diet, she began very early to be tormented by rickets, so that by age two she was unable to move by herself, and subsequently she could [do] it [only] with great difficulty, supported by large sticks, without which she has been able to walk freely only for the last two years.[4]

I would like the reader to keep in mind this image of an unwed mother: it will be useful further on when we examine medical theses on the nourishment of foundlings to compare this image with the duties assigned by the physicians to women such as this one. Of the 643 women admitted to the maternity hospice of Milan in 1869 and 1870, at least 183 had a sickly confinement. This condition prevailed, wrote the obstetrician at that maternity hospice, because "the women who have sought shelter here are all of the lowest social condition and in addition come for the most part from places in which malaria and pellagra predominate. . . . To this one should also add that the majority of the inmates are unwed pregnant women."[5]

From what we can tell, these women stayed a very brief time in the maternity hospitals where they were "admitted already overwhelmed by birth pains and they wanted to leave as soon as possible, declaring the impossibility of nursing their own child. One can believe," writes the director of a foundling hospital, "that the shelter requested by the mother, usually in a state of emergency, is only the means selected beforehand by which to have the baby more easily accepted into the foundling hospital."[6] The women also tried, if they could, to speed up the delivery time. The obstetrician of the maternity hospice of Milan, Edoardo Porro, wrote that "most of the pregnant women conceal for as long as possible the early labor pains in order to shorten the time that they must remain under surveillance and attendance in the delivery room."[7] This suggests that the women had an aversion to and mistrust of medical observation, which is understandable if we remember that the maternity hospices were set up primarily to provide instruction for obstetric students and midwives; even in the hospitals it was the poorest women who were "made available for teaching purposes."[8] The material for observation—that is, the number of women in labor—was scarce, and therefore it was necessary to make, so to speak, intensive use of them. The women gave birth hastily, as Porro, for one, acknowledges, "in order to avoid the annoyance and the shame of many and repeated explorations, of many questions, of a full diagnostic examination."[9]

As we shall see, in the early twentieth-century repugnance to and diffidence toward medical handling in general were still widespread among women of the lower classes. But here it was a matter of a specific and justified fear of the hospital. In fact, in the 1870s and 1880s, giving birth in a hospital was dangerous: there mortality among women could reach 20 percent. The illness to which such mortality was primarily attributed was referred to as puerperal fever; it had become epidemic and it struck almost exclusively in the maternity hospices, especially the larger ones and those annexed to hospital wards for infectious diseases. There is no reason to think the phenomenon was visible only to the physicians or to those who read the statistics on hospital deaths. It was, so to speak, visible even to the naked eye. Even the common people could see it: as one physician writes, "a panic fear would arise in the unfortunate families forced to send a pregnant woman to the hospital."[10] The fear of the hospital and of medical intervention encountered among the servants and the peasants who gave birth in the maternity hospices was, therefore, not unfounded or irrational: it was probably tied to a certain perception, perhaps confused, perhaps not expressed in terms of cause and effect, of the connection between widespread death among women in labor and birth in hospitals.

Puerperal fever struck those women almost exclusively who gave birth in hospitals and therefore, more than any others, those women whose histories interest us here: the unwed mothers. But associated with this illness is something of importance for women in general, something that concerns the most general connection between physicians and women and that constitutes a premise for the chain of events that I am trying to reconstruct. The policy of identifying and controlling unwed mothers, to instill the social obligation of motherhood in women who before had been allowed to escape from maternal duty, is tied in a decisive way to the attitude of the physicians. For this it is necessary to understand what it meant, concretely and socially, for the physicians of the late nineteenth century to gain jurisdiction and control over birth and maternity. The matter of puerperal fever provides a good observation point on this problem.

In the 1860s and 1870s the specter of puerperal fever brought into question the social prestige of physicians, especially of obstetricians. There was discussion as to whether the illness should be considered contagious and if so how the contagion spread. Upholding the contagious nature of puerperal fever, however, meant admitting that the carriers of the contagion could be these same physicians, in particular the obstetrical students and the aspiring midwives, who, for didactic purposes, had to carry out repeated examinations of the women in labor—examinations that, as we have seen, the women tried to avoid by shortening their delivery time. We must remember that we are dealing with the years immediately preceding the introduction of microbiology, when the theory of contagion was not universally accepted by the medical community and was even rejected as unscientific by the authorities.[11] Hospital practice, therefore, did not yet recognize the principle of asepsis. The idea that puerperal fever was contagious not only harmed the prestige of the obstetrician, attributing to him responsibility for the contagion, but it also put into gravest doubt the institution of the obstetrical clinic, of which the maternity ward of the foundling hospital provided a prime example. It is not surprising, therefore, that this idea met strong resistance in obstetrical circles.[12] The entire medical community, in fact, was seriously divided over this question.

In 1876, for example, the surgeon Ferdinando Palasciano maintained that "to gather women in labor to give birth in a maternity hospice or a delivery room, instead of in their own or someone else's private home, means subjecting them to *conditions* that increase the probability of death sevenfold over those to which they are exposed by the simple process of giving birth at home."[13] Palasciano and other proponents of the contagious theory of puerperal fever believed that the maternity hospices ought to be abolished. Where this was problematic, as in large cities with fluctuating female populations, or when, as in the case of unwed mothers, moral and familial reasons hindered birth at home, the proposal was to send women in labor to board with midwives, at the expense of public charity.[14]

The custom of giving birth at a midwife's house seems to have been very widespread, especially among unwed mothers, since this, even more than hospital birth, allowed the event to be kept secret. Probably only the poorest of these women, those who could not afford to pay the midwife, resorted to the free or almost-free assistance of the hospice or hospital. Even at the beginning of the twentieth century, the maternity wards of the foundling hospitals felt the competition with the midwives. In 1916, a report of the Foundling Hospice of Verona laments that "the Maternity Home (which ought to have formed the seedbed for wet nurses for the Foundling Hospice) showed signs of a hidden and selfish war. It is commonly thought to be almost an annex of the municipal brothels for the pregnant women assigned to them. The unwed mothers of the province are monopolized by some midwives, who in every age never failed to make their evil skills valued even by the authorities, in order to exploit the offense for their own exclusive interests."[15]

The question of puerperal fever, therefore, constituted a major obstacle to the development of obstetrics and to the medical control of births in general. It hindered, for medical reasons and by admission of these very physicians, the spread of hospital delivery, and it damaged the interests of the obstetricians, putting them again in competition with their traditional rivals, the midwives. The medical community succeeded, however, in overcoming this contradiction, and by the end of the century the internal fracture was healed. The side that prevailed was the obstetricians'—the proponents, that is, of hospital delivery. In the 1890s, public medical opinion on the relative advantages of hospital versus home birth was completely overturned: now hospital birth was judged unanimously to be safer.[16]

What had happened? How could the contagion theory of puerperal fever be asserted while still ignoring all the practical consequences that its proponents of fifteen years before had believed inevitable? In the interim there had been a decisive turn in the history of contemporary medicine: the introduction of microbiology and, with it, the discovery of the bacterial transmission of disease. A consequence of this theoretical turn was the introduction in medical practice of antisepsis and asepsis. At this point physicians had available precise and rapidly expanding scientific knowledge about the ancient and mysterious problem of "live contagion" and they also had available the technology to control it. The rituals of disinfection and sterilization, which became widespread in medical practice by the end of the nineteenth century, are the expression of this new capacity for control.

The adoption of antiseptic and aseptic practices in the treatment of women in labor was precisely the medical solution to the problem of puerperal fever and the decisive element, therefore, in overcoming obstacles that, for the same medical reasons, had interfered with the expansion of obstetrical intervention.[17] At the end of the nineteenth century, the obstetrical clinics, rather than being closed or limited, were in full expansion. During these years the first gynecological annexes were introduced near the hospitals or the maternity wards of the foundling hospitals[18]—something that, considering the necessity of excluding every possible source of contagion, was deemed "unpardonable" in the discussions of the 1870s about puerperal fever. Certainly no one thought any more of encouraging deliveries by midwives. The object, on the contrary, was for the obstetrician to reach an ever-growing female population, establishing the so-called Obstetrical Corps (*Guardie Ostetriche*) to bring medical assistance to the homes of poor women in labor. The first Obstetrical Corps was established in Milan in 1887; by 1912 a guide to Italian obstetrical institutes showed eighteen such corps in thirteen of the principal cities.[19]

With this development, then, by the end of the nineteenth century physicians had gained control over births, a control legitimized by the appeal decisive in our society: technical efficiency. But apart from the practical efficiency created by the new aseptic techniques—and after all puerperal fever disappeared only very slowly from the hospitals[20]—it is important to emphasize that this efficiency was also social and symbolic. The new aseptic techniques were used, for example, to guarantee a now unbridgeable distance between the obstetrician and the midwife. Much of the discredit heaped by physicians on midwives at the turn of the century is repeatedly based on the latter's resistance, through ignorance, to the adoption of antisepsis and asepsis.[21] The medical victory over puerperal fever was also a great social victory for obstetricians, allowing them to add enormously to their own power and prestige. Their new and indisputable competence regarding births formed the basis for increasingly direct medical intervention in the entire experience of maternity.

One aspect of this victory deserves to be emphasized here: the fact that it was a victory over contagion. The contagion theory of puerperal fever had gravely threatened the physician's social prestige because it implied that his contact could be unclean and contaminating: his very own hands could transmit the infection. The figure of the physician emerged from the victory over puerperal fever with a new halo of purity. At the turn of the century, his new public image is that of the controller of infection. It was precisely in this guise that the physicians intervened in the matter of unwed mothers. The control, in this case, concerns a disease that was traditionally the focus of profound collective fear: syphilis.[22] There is not a health report from a foundling hospital or a piece of medical writing on foundlings between the end of the nineteenth century and World War I that does not mention, with more or less emphasis, the problem of syphilis transmitted through lactation, the so-called nursing syphilis. In the name of the struggle against syphilis, a campaign was waged for the hygienic control of nursing; this involved taking the medical history of the mothers and of the wet nurses of the foundlings, as well as direct intervention by physicians in the nursing practices of women of the lower classes.

By direct intervention, I mean really practical, not just theoretical, intervention. Syphilis was a disease in which, during the second half of the nineteenth century, the physician could intervene in close co-operation with the policeman, using a coercive power very similar to that of the police. This was true especially for prostitutes. From 1860 to 1888, Italy, like other European countries, had a health regulation for prostitution,[23] promulgated to protect the army from venereal disease; on the basis of this regulation every policeman had the power to report a woman as a prostitute and any physician, on the basis of this report, could then subject her under coercion to a health inspection and, if she was found syphilitic, send her to the syphilis hospital. These were also the years, we might recall parenthetically, when Casimiro Sperino, a Turinese physician and the author of that regulation, was able to conduct on prostitutes the experiments with innoculation against syphilis that one of his French colleagues had conducted on monkeys; he could, in all tranquillity, then communicate his results to the medical public.[24]

Let us now return to the unwed mothers. The tie between the maternity shelter and the foundling hospital was traditionally this: the unwed mothers who had given birth at the maternity shelter were invited or often forced after delivery to go on to the foundling hospital as wet nurses. This occurred especially in the foundling hospitals of the big cities, where the large number of foundlings meant that a long period of time elapsed between the acceptance of the baby and its placement with a foster family. The function of the maternity shelter, besides serving as a teaching clinic for obstetrics as we have seen, was also to provide the foundling hospital with inexpensive wet nurses, women very vulnerable to extortion.

Offering to serve as a wet nurse was an occasional occupation for poor women, a way to derive money from the temporary physical condition of maternity. A woman whose baby was stillborn or died soon after birth—not infrequent events, especially among the lower classes—could profit by her physical state, offering her milk on a market that was generally very lively. Nursing is a female sexual product, tied to the biological condition of women. Like the market in another female sexual product, prostitution, the market for wet nurses was structured by a network of brokers who procured the wet nurses, especially for private individuals, charging them for the service.[25] Women offered themselves to the foundling hospital when they were not successful in finding a more profitable position, but they kept in contact with the brokers and left the hospital as soon as a better offer presented itself.[26] Only the least thriving wet nurses, then, the weakest or sickest, offered themselves to the foundling hospital, which paid much less than private individuals,[27] and which required that the women settle themselves at the hospital and accept its isolation and discipline. For these reasons the foundling hospitals always had a scarcity of resident wet nurses, especially in the summer months when the women could find work in the fields.[28]

In running the foundling hospitals, it was normal to recruit wet nurses from the maternity annex. The recruiting happened in this way: in order to leave the hospital after giving birth, the woman had to pay a tax as partial reimbursement for the assistance received, even though in theory that assistance should have been free. Whoever could not pay the tax had to work off her debt with the specific duty of wet-nursing for several months, the number varying from hospital to hospital.[29] Furthermore a woman was forbidden to nurse her own child, for fear that she would favor it over the two or three others entrusted to her. Thus the woman entered the foundling hospital not as a mother, but as a wet nurse—that is, as a person kept for mercenary service and at the lowest possible cost. One way to save money was precisely to exploit her by giving her, as a rule, more than one baby to nurse. In the Milan foundling hospital, for example, in 1899 there were seventy-four babies for thirty-two wet nurses (the maximum reported, in July) and twenty-nine babies for twenty-three wet nurses (the minimum, in October).[30] This practice seems to have been the norm in foundling hospitals during the nineteenth century and at the beginning of the twentieth.[31] Naturally, by force of circumstance, nursing had to be "mixed," that is, partly natural and partly artificial, and necessarily promiscuous. But it was precisely on promiscuity— attributed, however, to the habits of the women— that medical criticism of the so-called mercenary nursing would be focused.

In 1887 the Piedmontese section of the Italian Society of Hygiene brought to the attention of the minister of the interior various examples of epidemics of syphilis in families in the villages of Cuneo where they used wet nurses for the unweaned babies in the foundling hospitals.[32] The foundlings, stricken with hereditary syphilis, had presumably infected the wet nurses, who, in turn, infected their own babies and husbands. The outcome is a circular from the Directorship of Public Health referred to generally as "Nicotera's Circular," declaring that the infants were to be accepted at the foundling hospitals only upon presentation of a medical certificate stating whether or not the mother had syphilis.[33] This, I believe, is the first official document reversing the prohibition against inquiries into the maternity of foundlings.

By the late 1890s, the director of health often asked the Prefectures for information about cases of nursing syphilis—information culled from bulletins where the reports of infectious diseases were collected. The prefects responded by sending reports of the inquiries conducted by provincial physicians; from these reports emerges a vivid picture of the treatment of wet nurses in the foundling hospitals, of nursing practices in and out of the institutions, of the attitude of physicians toward these practices, and of the reactions of women to the work of the physicians.[34]

In 1900 the foundling hospital of Mantua was at the center of two of these epidemics and the related inquests. On March 16, Maria S., an unwed mother, entered that foundling hospital carrying with her a baby that had been born on January 27. She had a small sore on her lip, but neither she nor the physician at the foundling hospital made anything of it; around the end of November the doctor noticed on her thorax a rash similar to syphilitic roseola; it was shortly confirmed as such. "The nature of her illness," writes the provincial doctor, "was kept secret from S., and still is; she was sent as a dry nurse to the so-called bread babies, thus saving the greater wages reserved for wet nurses, and without her knowledge she was given mercury injections, which she believed were prescribed to free her from the pain of supposedly rheumatic bones." Between March 16 and November 10, before being assigned the post of "dry nurse," this woman had given her milk to eighteen babies at the foundling hospital. One baby nursed by her infected the wet nurse to whom she then was entrusted after leaving the foundling hospital; two other resident wet nurses, both unwed mothers, became infected.[35]

At the center of these widening networks of contagion there was usually an unwed syphilitic mother; in order to identify her, the physician asked the women of the foundling hospital about their sexual activity. Promiscuous sexual activity, in fact, was sufficient reason to anticipate the disease, even in the absence of clinical evidence. In October 1901, an external wet nurse brought a sick baby back to the foundling hospital at Mantua. To ascertain the origin of the infection, the provincial doctor questioned the baby's mother, who still lived at the foundling hospital as an internal wet nurse, and another wet nurse, also an unwed mother, who in her turn had nursed the sick baby before she was consigned to the wet-nurse outside the hospice.

> The wet nurse Rosa F., 24 years old, reports having been pregnant three times and having relations only with her lover, who pretty much lived with her and was known not only to her family but throughout the region. . . . It is worth noting that after the first birth, F.'s lover fell sick with a disease, which she can not be specific about but which lasted some time. Now, from information that I have been able to obtain, it appears that this man most certainly never had syphilis.

As for the mother of the foundling, Isolina B., "she tells of having relations with only one man . . . about whom there is no information to be had. B. had one miscarriage at 40 days without any cause. In the meantime her lover left for military service, and when he returned he again had relations with B., who then found herself pregnant with the baby who afterward became the foundling." While this second inquest was being conducted, another external wet nurse presented herself, asking to be examined. "With all the symptoms of secondary syphilis," the provincial doctor continues, "she did not know at the time I examined her that she was infected with syphilis, blaming her pains on the humidity of the house in which she lived. She had cut off all her hair, thinking thus to minimize the terrible headaches that tormented her." This wet nurse had infected her husband. In the disease report on the foundling entrusted to her—who was later returned sick to the hospital, where she died—there were unhealthy symptoms that, again citing the provincial doctor, "ought to have made the medical director suspicious." Instead, there was not even an autopsy at the death of the baby.

These histories tell us a lot about the physicians' behavior toward the women and it is worthwhile to focus our attention on some particular instances: the physicians' attitude toward promiscuous nursing; the inquiry into the sexual behavior of mothers (at a time when the civil code protected the "secrecy of unwed motherhood"); and that the nature of the disease was being systematically hidden from women.

First, let us look at promiscuous nursing. The case of Mantua confirms for us what we already knew about nursing conditions in the foundling hospitals: they made promiscuity inevitable. But the physicians blamed promiscuous nursing above all on women: "As to the manner of transmission of the infection," the provincial doctor writes again, "it is to be seen in the common women's custom of switching the sick nurslings from one breast to the other when they do not want to take hold. Sometimes in fact it happens that a baby who will not take milk from one wet nurse will take hold on another. Questioned by me about this, the nun at the foundling hospital responded that sometimes this does occur."

In a situation where a woman could nurse eighteen babies in eight months, never coming under any but the most desultory and inaccurate medical examination, and where she could at times continue to nurse when she was already suspected of having syphilis, it was clearly not necessary to invoke the promiscuous nursing habits of common women in order to explain the possibility of contagion. Yet even in other cases, the inquiries of the provincial doctors are in agreement in singling out nursing promiscuity, as practiced by women of the lower class, as the determining factor in syphilis epidemics, a factor that conveniently obscures possible medical responsibility.[36] The spread of contagion is thus seen as the fault of women. In 1905, the foundling hospital of Bologna, for example, refused to pay for the care of a wet nurse who contracted syphilis from a foundling because the woman admitted to having occasionally suckled the child of an acquaintance.[37] From the administrators' point of view, nursing syphilis was considered an occupational hazard for which the institution could not be held responsible.[38] The attitude of the physicians, imputing the contagion to the promiscuous habits of nursing women, evidently validated this thesis.

The physicians gave constant emphasis in their reports to the promiscuous habits of the women. In reality what emerges from these reports is the sense of a strong nursling exchange network for the sake of kinship, for friendship, for money, or simply for mutual help. A system of natural nursing cannot avoid being in some way promiscuous: sickness or work can make the woman temporarily unable to nurse and force her therefore to have recourse to a substitute. Besides the practice of communal nursing among family and neighbors, the physicians also severely criticized another practice, or rather, another image, one that almost has the outlines of a popular occupation: that of the woman who offered to suck the nipples of the mothers who must empty their breasts because they have ulcerations on the nipples or because they have too much milk. In 1901 the Prefecture of Turin reported fourteen cases of syphilis in the village of Mathi due to

the unfortunate custom whereby women free themselves from the nuisance of excessive production of milk through the offices of other women who lend themselves for such service. One woman of Mathi who, being syphilitic, appears also to practice secret prostitution, sucked the breasts of two women who had recently delivered; they spread the infection to their nurslings, to other babies, to their husbands, etc. This office is studying the means to stamp out the bad habit that gave rise to the epidemic.[39]

But why suspect this woman of prostitution just because she was syphilitic? A physician ought to know very well that the "sucker," as she was called in another report, could easily have contracted syphilis from an infected mother. This suspicion reveals how the physicians really perceived women of the lower class: promiscuous nursing, as these women practiced it, was seen as something analogous to promiscuous sexual practice. Between "promiscuous" and "mercenary" the connection was close and, in a highly commercialized society, very significant. An implicit analogy between the paid wet nurse and the prostitute was probably at work, more or less tacitly, in the physicians' minds, as well as in those of middle-class men and women in general.[40] In those years the woman who was publicly subjected to medical inspection and systematically suspected of syphilis was, precisely, the prostitute. And perhaps the wet nurses themselves were aware of this degrading association: thus perhaps we can explain a fact that recurs constantly in these reports—the women's deep repugnance for medical examination and, above all, for examination of their genitalia.[41] This repugnance could also become active resistance. In the report already cited at length, the provincial doctor of Mantua observed, "it would be advisable to examine frequently the mucous membrane of the genitals and the anus of wet nurses, but such a practice would result in all of them leaving the foundling hospital."

It is true that, for the physicians, the analogy between the wet nurse and the prostitute had a definite basis in fact: the wet nurse, like the prostitute, could be a vehicle for infection. But it is equally true that women were not the only vehicles of infection. No physician, however, thought to identify and place under health control the men who frequented the bordellos. So far as I know, during these years the only indication of serious medical attention to male syphilis, from

the point of view of intervention and control, concerns the possibility
of the transmission of infection through circumcision.[42] But this was
a matter of protective, not punitive attention as was that directed
against the prostitute and, to some extent, the wet nurse.

So, why were only women subjected to such control? Why were
only certain categories of women affected? What explains the bias in
the medical control of syphilitic infection? The idea of contagion is
at the heart of the matter here. If we consider this idea as being subject
to a purely scientific system, its application in this case will remain
inexplicable. In fact, from a scientific point of view, limiting the control to women made no sense. But perhaps, in point of fact, it is
wrong to assume that the idea of contagion was a purely scientific
one, even though the years we are dealing with are precisely those
when the scientific theory of the transmission of disease by bacteria
was being affirmed. Besides, the changes that occurred during the
nineteenth century in the theory of contagion—as one historian of
medicine has reconstructed them[43]—seem inextricably interwoven
with their social applications and were conditioned, as we have seen
as well in the case of puerperal fever, by the social interests being
promoted or harmed. It cannot surprise us then to find the notion of
contagion interwoven, in this case, with very profoundly influential
social interests, such as those concerning the relations between the
sexes. There is no idea more extraordinarily encrusted with anthropological sedimentations and implications than the idea of contagion,
rooted as it is in our culture all the way back to its original biblical
formulation.

In our case, there seems to be a connection between the control
of contagion and the commercialization of sexual services. Medical
control guarantees the circulation of "clean" goods, either in the case
of the services of the prostitute or those of the wet nurse. Because
they are female and not male sexual services being sold, we have a
preliminary explanation for the fact that the control of contagion was
aimed in only one direction. But our explanation is only preliminary.
The question in fact remains: why in this case is the commercialization
associated with the ideas of contamination and danger? Commercialization necessarily implies promiscuity, which then leads us back to
the dangerous nature of female sexual promiscuity, and in the present
case this is what we must explain.

Anthropology suggests that we examine, for one thing, the meaning of the types of contact considered dangerous as vehicles of con-

tagion and, above all, to try to see the symbolic as well as the technical effectiveness inherent in the rites for controlling contagion.[44] In general, the symbolic effectiveness of these rites seems to consist in confirming indirectly the lines of demarcation of the society's moral order. Whoever transmits the infection has transgressed, has crossed some line of demarcation of this order. The sanction for such a person is not directly moral: it is expressed instead by presenting the individual as publicly dangerous and therefore as subject to control. This form of sanction seems typical of situations in which it is not possible to apply a moral sanction directly, inasmuch as it would conflict with other social needs.

Let us return to our case: the type of contact considered dangerous here is that with a sexually promiscuous woman, the prostitute or the wet nurse, especially the wet nurse who hired herself out. The moral norm that they violated is manifestly one of the fundamental norms of our society, the prohibition of women from using their sexual capacities promiscuously. We live, however, in a commercial society, where it is not possible to impede directly women from offering on the market their sexual services; it is not possible especially because the commercialization of these services is useful to other interests. Thus there are two social needs in conflict, and the medical control of contagion intervenes to mediate between them: this control on the one hand facilitates the commercialization of female sexuality (because it minimizes, symbolically and technically, the dangers of female sexual promiscuity for whoever takes advantage of them as services) and on the other hand reaffirms the norm forbidding promiscuity for women by presenting them as guilty of contagion. This explains, it seems to me, why the control of syphilitic contagion addressed itself only to prostitutes and wet nurses; it explains why the diagnosis of syphilis assumed the character of an inquest into women's sexual behavior rather than of a clinical diagnosis; and it explains finally the implicitly punitive nature of this control.

The symbolic and latently moral aspect of medical intervention in this case also explains, in part, why the women were neither informed of the nature of their disease nor educated to recognize, in themselves or in their babies, its first symptoms. The instructions for wet nurses contained in the regulations for the foundling hospitals do not indicate the responsibility of the health personnel to advise women of the risk of contracting syphilis. The prescriptions addressed to outside wet nurses contain only the prohibition against promiscuous nursing without justifying it by the possibility of contagion.[45] Certainly this silence can also be explained by considerations of immediate economic utility, considerations that, in a capitalistic society, typically distort the practice of occupational medicine: they did not wish, for example, to alarm women and thus prompt a reduction in the offers to wet nurse, which in turn would have had the disagreeable consequence for the administrators of the foundling hospitals of forcing them to raise the wages for wet-nursing;[46] they wished also to avoid paying for treatment or compensation for a syphilitic wet nurse.[47] But above all, by keeping the women in the dark, it was easier to present them as irresponsible and thereby ensure that the blame for the contagion fell upon them in every case.

All this perhaps helps to explain the insistence of physicians and administrators at the end of the nineteenth century on the danger of syphilis from wet-nursing. This insistence is particularly strong in the 1890s and is explicitly motivated by fear of a renewed and widespread outbreak of syphilis in the wake of the abolition, in 1888, of the rules of health inspection of prostitutes.[48] In the new Health Regulation of 1901, the health inspection of wet nurses was concerned above all with syphilis: every wet nurse had to be provided with a certificate attesting to her freedom from the disease.[49] And also when, in 1918, Italy passed its "Roussel Law" (legge Roussel), the "new regulation for the hygienic protection of wet-nursing," it was formulated entirely in terms of social prevention of syphilis.

But from the medical point of view, the control of wet nurses did not get to the root of the problem. Nursing syphilis was in reality a consequence of hereditary syphilis: the original carrier of infection was the mother and, above all, the unwed mother. In order to limit effectively the spread of syphilis through nursing, it was necessary to know which foundlings were born of syphilitic mothers. For this reason, many foundling hospitals, beginning at the end of the nineteenth century, required for acceptance of foundlings a certificate declaring that the mother was free of syphilis. This rule was extended by law with the Health Regulation of 1901, which as the first set of norms developed from the "investigation of maternity" were the most neutral and technical. This procedure, in which great latitude was left for simple "suspicion" of the disease based on the woman's habits of sexual promiscuity, is formalized in many foundling hospitals into true and proper "norms for the investigation of the mother."[50]

The necessity for investigating the mother was supported by a

complex theoretical framework: the theory that syphilis was hereditary. The nineteenth-century literature on syphilis boasted of having
discovered the so-called laws of hereditary syphilis (*leggi dell'eredità
luetica*), but in reality there was no genetic foundation available for a
scientific theory of pathological heredity.[51] And actually in nineteenth-
century medicine, the term *heredity* was still more a metaphor than
an actual theory, but a metaphor rich in useful social implications.
Presenting the disease as the repercussion of the preceding generation's
evil habits, it authorized associating a heavy moral burden with it and
attributing responsibility to individual or collective guilt.[52] In the case
of syphilis, the concept of inheritability was adopted in a particularly
metaphorical sense: by "hereditary syphilis" was not so much meant,
as we would expect, syphilis transmitted from the mother to the fetus
through the placenta or through direct contact after birth (this came
to be called "congenital syphilis" and was considered rare[53]), as much
as a vaguely defined constitutional propensity. Syphilis was thought
to be inherited, that is, in the form of a "constitutional weakness,"
an expression that recurred often—more often really than any other
at the end of the nineteenth century—in the foundlings' death certificates.[54] Even if the baby was not clinically syphilitic, the syphilitic
heredity manifested itself in him, according to the physicians at the
end of the nineteenth century, in a general "unfitness to live." How
much greater, then, was the responsibility of the mother, whose sexual
promiscuity had provoked both the disease itself and the birth of an
enfeebled baby? How much greater, then, was the justification for
singling her out, for making her at least nurse this baby, given that,
to avoid contagion, syphilitic infants could be nursed only by syphilitic women, and artificial nursing meant almost certain death for
foundlings.

   "Constitutional weakness," naturally, could mean many things.
It could mean, for example, a death certificate hurriedly and inac-
curately drawn up.[55] More generally it could represent an easy explanation for the high mortality rate among the foundlings, an
explanation that, by shifting responsibility to the mothers, kept the
focus off the organization of the institutions and the treatment of the
babies within them. With hereditary syphilis so vaguely defined, it
could be said without much fear of contradiction that the mortality
and morbidity among the foundlings, so much higher than among
legitimate births, were due to the "special state of gestation and prin-

cipally to the abnormality of conception since those unhappy mothers had so often been contaminated by the syphilis virus."[56]

Here we are well into the age of microbiology. The phrase I have just cited that speaks generically of the "syphilitic virus" is from 1904; in 1905 Schaudinn and Hoffmann, parasitologist and physician respectively, identified the syphilis microorganism, the "pale spirochete." From the diagnostic point of view, even more important than this discovery was the development in 1906 of a method for diagnosing syphilis, known as the "Wassermann test." Syphilis was among the first diseases whose diagnosis, already by the first decade of the twentieth century, was no longer based on clinical observation but rather primarily on laboratory analysis.

The foundling hospitals immediately became places to put the Wassermann test to work: once again there was interest, clinical and experimental in this case, in exploiting "the abundant supply of cases" offered by the hospitals;[57] and there was to be, up until the 1920s, constant pressure from the director of health for institutions to adopt the new diagnostic method and to apply it to mothers and babies.[58]

We should note here that there was a curious consequence of the extensive application of the Wassermann test in the foundling hospitals: through it one could not help but discover, as was already suspected, that the frequency of hereditary syphilis actually diagnosable in the foundling hospitals was much lower than had been maintained up to that moment.[59] That the actual spread of the disease had been greatly overestimated among the foundlings jumps out at anyone reading the health reports of the foundling hospitals. In Milan, for example, it was calculated that, for the period from 1889 to 1898, an average of 8.9 percent of the babies died of hereditary syphilis. When we see how this figure was calculated, however, we find that babies only "suspected" of the disease were also included; that these babies were put in isolation wards (with syphilitics!); that they were nursed artificially; and that, as a certain consequence of artificial nursing, nearly all of them died.[60] In any case, even the most inflated figures cannot justify, by themselves, the almost exclusive attention, relative to other diseases, given to syphilis among the foundlings. Probably here too, as was said of syphilis among prostitutes at the time of the abolition of the Cavour Regulation, it is a matter of saying that "compared with diseases very widespread and more dangerous, against which the state did not take any kind of compulsory measures, the importance of syphilis has been exaggerated."[61]

Clearly there are social structures of avoidance, so to speak, as well as structures of attention, silently at work in a manner with which we are familiar, and these structures of avoidance also play a role in scientific knowledge. The discrepancy between the data on the frequency of hereditary syphilis verified by means of the Wassermann test and those expected (and believed to have been found) on the basis of the medical theory of hereditary syphilis did not mean, at least not immediately, the rejection of that theory, or even any lessening of the emphasis on the social aspects of the disease.[62] Even in 1917, at the first national meeting of the directors of foundling hospitals, attended mostly by physicians, there was talk of the "enormous spread of nursing syphilis."[63] And yet these same physicians were the authors of scientific articles on the use of the Wassermann test in foundling hospitals, which resulted in figures regarding the presence of the disease that were in no way "enormous." How can we explain this contradiction? Or better, how is it that something that now appears an obvious contradiction was not perceived as such? I spoke earlier of the structures of avoidance and of attention in the infrastructure of knowledge. The attention of the physicians in the foundling hospitals was centered, in those years, on the "investigation of maternity." It is understandable then that they focused on syphilis, a disease in which the mother-child relationship is central: from the diagnostic point of view it was because gathering the medical history of the syphilitic mother allowed the calculation of the probability of infection in the fetus and from the therapeutic point of view because the syphilitic baby, nursed by a mother undergoing mercury treatment, felt the effects indirectly, it was said, of that treatment.

The light always falls only here and there, and some things are necessarily left in the shade: another disease, tuberculosis, is almost completely ignored in the medical literature concerning foundlings and unwed motherhood in the late nineteenth and early twentieth centuries, while it shows up, much more than syphilis, in the statistics of cause of death.[64] This is not a coincidence. Tuberculosis involved, for example, the opportunity to interrupt pregnancy, at a time when for many physicians induced abortion was almost a crime.[65] Tuberculosis above all, in contrast to syphilis, involved the necessity of separating the baby from the mother, because in this case it could not be presumed that the infection had come by way of the placenta but only by contact after birth. Tuberculosis then entered with difficulty into a mental landscape dominated by the principle of the "necessity not to separate the nursling from its own mother."[66] Its absence from this landscape confirms for us indirectly the force that this principle had. In a mental landscape the omissions reveal as much as the admissions do.

In 1902 the Prefecture of Terra di Lavoro pointed out to the Ministry of the Interior the "dissonance" between article 186 of the new Health Regulation, which stated that no foundling could be accepted without a certificate declaring its mother to be free of syphilis, and article 376 of the Civil Code, which guaranteed secrecy to unwed mothers. The Extraordinary Royal Commissioner of Aversa was opposed to the application of the rule from the Health Regulation, finding it precisely in contradiction to that of the Civil Code.[67] It is a sign that the introduction of the certificate of immunity from syphilis for mothers of foundlings was recognized for what it was—namely, the beginning of investigations into maternity. But already, by the beginning of the twentieth century, opposition to the investigation of maternity was extremely rare. The secrecy surrounding motherhood outside of marriage had been completely replaced, in fact, by administrative and health inquiries concerning mothers of foundlings. Receding into a now remote past in terms of social attitudes if not of years were institutions like "San Rocco delle Celate," the Roman hospital where, so it is reported at least, unmarried pregnant women entered at night, with faces veiled, and remained for the entire time of birth and confinement in an isolated alcove where no one was allowed to see them except the midwife and the physician, who were forbidden to question them about their identity.[68]

By this point the necessity for maternal nursing of foundlings is already an undisputed principle. I would like to recall that in the middle of the nineteenth century the unwed mother, who stayed at the foundling hospital as a wet nurse, was forbidden to nurse her own child. Now, on the contrary, they tried to entrust the foundlings who would be nursed at home to their own mothers through the granting of subsidies. In a word, women are paid for being mothers. At Rome, for example, the administration of the foundling hospital decided in 1897 to grant nursing subsidies to mothers who acknowledged their babies and took them with them; the provision is praised in a provincial inspection of the foundling hospital as an example of "social affirmation of motherhood"; similar provisions are made at the end of the nineteenth century in many other foundling hospitals.[69]

Purely economic or administrative reasons also led the hospices to seek to identify the mothers of foundlings: the desire not to assume the burden of babies born in other provinces, for example, and above all the calculation that the mother–wet nurses cost less than real wet nurses. The foundling hospitals, in an effort to entice the mothers to acknowledge their babies, gave them a subsidy a little higher, though of briefer duration, than the usual wet nurse's wages. The foundlings entrusted to their own mothers were discharged, then, much sooner than the others from the balance sheet of the foundling hospital.[70]

Just as the certificate of immunity from syphilis, as we have seen, involved an inquiry into the woman's past, so the nursing subsidy afforded a control over the mother's life. They tried to withhold subsidies, in fact, not only from women who had had more illegitimate children—those who persisted in their sin—but especially from those who lived in concubinage.[71] For their part, the women tried to use the subsidy to their own ends: for example, to develop a small dowry. In fact the women often asked the hospice for a lower total amount to be paid all at one time rather than as a monthly subsidy. Or else they delayed the civil marriage until after the birth of the first child, as a way of having the nursing subsidy for a little while and perhaps, later, the marriage reward that the hospice gave for the legitimization of a foundling.[72] The hospice responded to these little tricks by requiring yet another certificate: that of marriageability, signed by the parish priest. It had become very difficult to be an unwed mother under the conditions prescribed by the foundling hospital because so many certificates were required: of freedom from syphilis, of residence in the province, of marriageability, of poverty.

It was during World War I that a particular coincidence of circumstances, primarily the huge increase in foundling mortality and the difficulty in finding wet nurses, started reforms in many foundling hospitals. The acceptance of the foundlings became strictly conditional upon the mothers' being identified and upon their remaining at least temporarily in the foundling hospital to nurse their own offspring and other babies. Given the difficulty in detaining women in the hospice during wartime when they could easily find work outside, some foundling hospitals opened workshops on the premises. The work, however, was given only to those mothers who had acknowledged their babies and who did not avoid the "sacred duty of motherhood," nursing.[73]

Justified during the war as emergency measures, after the war the new regulations for accepting foundlings became established rules. In

1917 in Milan and Rome, it was decided to admit only infants of four months and older, so that at least for those first months the mothers were forced to assume the burden. "The mother of the illegitimate baby," they said on this occasion, "must know henceforward that she will no longer be permitted to abandon the baby to fate, but will be required in some way to provide for its assistance, at least for the first months."[74] In foundling hospitals where the reforms were not being carried out—in small cities and in the South, for example—the health inspections served to apply pressure to do so.[75] Finally, in 1923, the investigation into maternity was introduced as law: it is the law at last to sanction "confidential inquiries to identify the mother of the foundling, in order to ascertain, where possible, the health of the mother, to provide maternal nursing for the foundling, and to encourage the mother herself to acknowledge the child."[76] But what I have reconstructed up to this point proves well, I think, how a series of measures somewhere between persuasion and coercion can be effectively directed to a weak social class without the need for recourse to legalities, and in fact even hovering at the borders of illegality.

The introduction at the beginning of the twentieth century of the investigation into maternity gave society the solution to the foundling problem. If we see, in this solution, an element of social control, we cannot avoid also noting here—as we already have in the case of the control of infectious syphilis—an evident asymmetry between men and women: why did the responsibility for the illegitimate child have to fall solely on the mother? In the late nineteenth and early twentieth centuries, there was also a lot of talk about the "investigation into paternity," but only the investigation into maternity was undertaken in fact.[77] Once again, if we look for the motives for this choice, we find the health argument. The foundling problem was seen primarily as a part of the problem of infant mortality.

In the period we are considering foundling mortality, especially in the first year of life, was very serious and actually remained so, in some foundling hospitals, until World War II. It normally hovered around 30 percent, and in time of war, reached 80 percent.[78] From the medical point of view, especially for a physician who was director of a foundling hospital, one explanation and one justification of this phenomenon were inescapable. We have seen how, at the end of the nineteenth century, the theory of hereditary syphilis might contribute to this explanation. At the beginning of the twentieth century, however, this explanation, based on the thesis of the foundlings' "constitutional weakness," could not hold up with the establishment of a precise method of diagnosis for the disease. And actually, during the first decades of the twentieth century, the attention of physicians turned toward another hypothesis: the incidence of gastrointestinal diseases. In the nosological tables of the causes of foundling deaths and in the debates among physicians, gastrointestinal diseases move to the forefront.

The changes over time in the death statistics can tell us many things if we try to see the diagnosis of cause of death not as a proof but as an opinion. The death certificate, in our society the last word to be said about us, is not a neutral fact but an opinion that expresses something very human and very fragile. It is an attempt at explanation. In the present case, the changing statistics on the causes of death among foundlings tell us, on the one hand, that the doctors were trying to explain that mortality through a hypothesis in some way more close-fitting with the "facts" observed under the new medical theory; but they also tell us that the structure of concern underlying these attempts at explanation was still the same: even gastrointestinal disease, like hereditary syphilis, was still seen as the responsibility of the mothers. If the babies died of gastrointestinal disease, it was because their mothers abandoned them or refused to nurse them, thus forcing the hospices to resort to mixed or artificial nursing.[79]

Given the logic of technical efficiency, the physicians' reasoning was unexceptionable: if the high mortality among foundlings depended on lack of maternal nursing, clearly it was necessary to force the mothers to nurse. The identification and control of the mothers—in other words, the investigation into maternity—was therefore justified. But let us try, once again, to bring to the surface the social and symbolic aspect hidden behind this technical logic. A fundamental symbolic function of indirect social control, as of control based on medical rules, seems to be the elimination of ambiguity.[80] This control also serves to express a reaction of condemnation to something or someone who confounds and threatens deeply rooted social classifications—something or someone who represents, in terms of these classifications, an anomaly. The professional wet nurse, subjected to control as a vehicle of syphilitic infection, is also a socially ambiguous figure, assuming a kind of middle role between two sharply distinct and even opposed social categories: the mother and the prostitute. Equally ambiguous, equally poised on the border between these two figures is the unwed mother: often, of course, the same woman played both roles, being at once unwed mother and mercenary wet nurse. But the unwed mother is a doubly threatening anomaly, not only because, like the mercenary wet nurse, she joins motherhood with promiscuity but even more because she commits an act that truly shatters a "law of nature": she abandons her child. As a promiscuous figure, she is seen as dangerous, and, as a vehicle of infection, she is controlled. But as an anomalous figure in respect to the law of nature, she deserves to be literally eliminated. Such a figure cannot, ought not, exist. A mother cannot be permitted to escape from the duties of motherhood, because otherwise these duties would appear for what they are, not a biological but a social norm.

This perhaps is the social significance of the "investigation into maternity" and it explains the preeminent role that medical control has in these developments. In a society such as ours, where technical-scientific progress is fused with profound social discrimination and irrationality, medical discourse has a strategic role because it allows the justification of discrimination, presenting it as biological necessity or as technical exigency. The peculiarity of medical discourse, which renders it an instrument particularly adaptable to this end, is its capacity to operate simultaneously on the levels of description and prescription. Its structures of avoidance seem tied to the need to reconcile these two levels.

There is one final avoidance that is worth pointing out here. In the medical discussion of maternal nursing of foundlings, the state of health of the unwed mothers, their actual physical capacity to nurse, is never referred to. Nevertheless in the clinical histories of the late nineteenth century, the chronic weakness and malnutrition of these women emerge unequivocally, conditions that by the beginning of the twentieth century could not have totally vanished.[81] What the physicians described in rich detail in the cases of women in labor, they ignored when it came time to prescribe the women's duties as mothers. In this discrepancy between description and prescription we see the social character of a norm that goes well beyond the biological. Paradoxically, the clinical histories narrated by the physicians—like the life histories that we will now examine—speak to us not so much of the biological aspect of motherhood, but rather of its biographical, that is to say historical and social, aspects.

?⬧ The Identification of the Mothers

What are the results of the policy of identifying unwed mothers and inducing them to motherhood? Maternal acknowledgment of foundlings increased in varying degrees wherever the policy of subsidy was practiced.[82] In part, at least, the phenomenon of acknowledgment is easily understandable: there was not only the attraction of the nursing subsidy, there was also, and perhaps even more important, the fact that, once the women were forced to be identified and had been subjected to various pressures from midwives, municipal physicians, and state officials, they must have had difficulty resisting. In Rome during the postwar period, acts of acknowledgment in maternity wards of the hospitals had become so summary and bureaucratic that sometimes women acknowledged their babies unwittingly. This emerges clearly, for example, in the information form of one of the women helped by the Roman organization for Maternal Assistance (*Assistenza Materna*):

> Nineteen-year-old peasant girl, from a little town in the Roman countryside, of little intelligence. Parents old and unable to support her. To our question about acknowledgment she answered that she could not do it because of her very wretched condition and the opposition of her parents. But when we asked the secretary of the Maternity Ward for suitable explanations, he showed us in the books he had at hand that the acknowledgment had occurred the day before in front of witnesses. The girl had not even realized it.[83]

This information form provides an example of the material about unwed mothers gathered in the postwar period. The identification of the woman is motivated by more than an interest in health or in auditing the effects of the administrative subsidy program. What they want to give is no longer just "health assistance" but "complete assistance, that is, social assistance." What is called for, therefore, is a comprehensive look at women's lives, which then permits a general understanding of the "phenomenon" of "illegitimate motherhood."[84]

Persuading mothers to acknowledge their babies was seen at this point as a task requiring female competence. In effect, Maternal Assistance was created in 1917 for just this purpose by a group of Roman ladies belonging to the Woman's Association (*Associazione per la donna*). In that same year the association had called a meeting on the investigation into paternity, and evidently the experience, for women hostile on principle to the "double standard," must have been somewhat frustrating. There was in fact a great deal of talk about the investigation into paternity, but nothing was ever done about it. Maternal Assistance was created specifically as a result of the reform of the Rome foundling hospital, which has already been discussed: according to the women of the association, the reform aggravated the conditions for unwed mothers, forcing them to keep their babies for the first four months without any assistance and then granting them a paltry subsidy. The association women therefore took on the duty of going, first in person and later employing "female visitors," to visit the various maternity wards of the city in order to find unmarried mothers; to assist them by giving them work ("dignified and remunerative, which does not divert them from their activity of wet-nursing"); to request, for the less experienced, the documents necessary to obtain a subsidy from the foundling hospital; to convince them to acknowledge their babies; and to invite them to go to a pediatrician.[85] This female philanthropic activity, clearly, does not call into question at all the principles of maternal acknowledgment or, even more, of maternal nursing. In reality, this activity was strictly governed not only by medical ideas but also by the individual obstetricians and pediatricians of the maternity wards.[86]

An intermingling of medical and sociological interests is implied even in the layout itself of the forms where information about the women was collected. Unwed motherhood is seen as a phenomenon of "social pathology." Side by side with the "history narrated by the young woman," as one part of the form is titled, is the information that the female visitor has collected about her and about her familial and social situation, just as, in a certain way, the clinical history of a disease juxtaposes subjective symptoms and objective signs. There is, moreover, the desire to use the histories for classification in order to construct a typology of unwed mothers.

For various reasons, however, I will not attempt to classify the material offered on these forms, not only because of the scantiness and randomness of the sample (or, more accurately, the fragment) that I have at my disposal, but also because it would not represent the deepest meaning that reading the forms has communicated to me.[87] I must confess at the outset that I have read them precisely as histories, as stories narrated one after the other by voices nearly indistinguishable, because—in spite of the fact that the histories are varied and contain diverse events and outcomes—the individuality of these women is compressed by the structure of the interrogation and by the drafting of the forms; it remains, therefore, inevitably remote. The forms are designed to give voice not to the women but rather to the phenomenon of "unwed motherhood," in order to compose and at the same time to impose a "type." And in fact, read one after the other, the forms give a desolating sense of uniformity and grayness, a sense of circumstances springing up like a trap, long since set in place around the individual, the sense of a casual event transforming itself little by little, and always more painfully, into destiny.

In truth I have never read anything so sad; these forms certainly do not bring together the women's experience as they would have been able to recount it, but they do speak, however, with extreme temperance and also with eloquence of how hard life's experience had been for these women.[88] It is material as lacking in fixed outlines as it is lacking in color; in which there crop up recurring episodes and typical roles, but reappearing always in different circumstances and with irregular or uncertain outcomes. A typology for all of this would seem a betrayal; I will try, therefore, simply to describe it.

The common ground of the histories is poverty, especially in those years immediately after the war. A very real misery, made of precarious daily survival, of forced promiscuity: for example, a single bed for four or five persons, and sometimes many more, even among persons who were not related.[89] There are many histories, especially in the years right after the war, in which unwed motherhood is a direct consequence of destitution, because only it is standing in the way of marriage; but more often the destitution itself is a consequence of illegitimate pregnancy:

> She is a 24-year-old woman, orphan from age 15, who lived fairly well as an itinerant greengrocer: seduced by one of her fellow workers, she became pregnant and was then abandoned. In the fifth month of pregnancy she became ill with nephritis: she was sick at home for three months, exhausting her savings, then selling her little handcart and pawning her scales. In the eighth month of pregnancy, she was forced to enter the hospital of San Giovanni, where she gave birth and acknowledged her child. She came to us with her baby one month after giving birth, in a desperate condition, because she was without a penny, without a home since while she was in the hospital her rooms were rented out, and without the possibility of work because she had lost the tools of her trade and

with the baby in her arms she could not practice her wandering trade.[90]

A frequent condition of conception is rape:

> She relates that one evening three men returning from a fair arrived at the inn. They asked for a room, and the landlady instructed the girl to accompany them. Up in the room the three men attacked her and took advantage of her. The girl was left pregnant and had a child without even knowing which of the men was the father. She acknowledged the child, put it out to nurse, and set herself up as a wet nurse.[91]

But usually, when the pregnancy is the result of a rape, the woman resolutely refuses to acknowledge the baby, as in the case of a twenty-seven-year-old woman of unknown parentage, a country woman, widowed with one child:

> She tells of having been raped with brute force while she was alone in a field "picking chicory" by an individual whom she could not identify precisely. From this single encounter a child was born whom she refused to acknowledge because she says she "has enough" with a five-year-old legitimate child to take care of. An attempt was made to force her to acknowledge it, showing her the danger of the child's repeating her own unhappy infancy, but the woman, in an indifferent monotone kept answering with doltish obstinacy, "I've got a kid in the country," and it was impossible to get her to say more.[92]

Other cases in which women refuse to acknowledge their children involve occurrences of rape by the father-in-law, by the brother-in-law, by a "person already previously hated," by the "sweetheart" with a group of friends (another case of gang rape).

There are two cases of incest with the father, in one case after the woman had already had two illegitimate children by other men. It seems that a previous illegitimate pregnancy or, even more, a publicly known rape, can put the woman in some fashion at the disposal of the men of her village or of her own family. One example is the history of Annita, also the daughter of unknown parents, from whose infancy we learn, among other things, much about the condition of foundlings given to wet nurses by the foundling hospitals:

> The girl was abandoned as a newborn at the foundling hospital of Rome, which had entrusted her to one of the notorious "godmoth-

ers" [*madrine*], who had consigned her to a woman (in the district of Frosinone), who for speculation took three or four foundlings at a time whom she reared nearly without milk, giving them a little of everything to eat. . . . At age five our Annita did not yet talk, at eight she was entrusted to a neighbor who employed her as a maid in her inn. At 14 she was raped by one of the customers of the inn, a man 40 years old, married, who by threats forced her to remain silent. . . . Once the thing was well known, the girl became prey to all the inn's customers, until her employers realized the need to send her away.[93]

If there is a recurring figure in these histories, especially in those set in the late 1930s, it is the figure of the girl who comes to Rome from the country in order to find work, especially as a domestic, who wants to create a family, and who, for that reason, is sexually vulnerable. The broken promise of marriage recurs again and again in these histories. But accident and fortune also have a role here, because at times it was only unforeseen circumstances (the sickness or death of the man) that blocked the marriage.[94] There seems, however, to be a real act of choice on the part of the women, who pass through various experiences of unwed motherhood or of cohabitation with various men, always hoping to create a stable family by meeting someone (and sometimes succeeding) who will marry them and give a name to their illegitimate children. Those are the women, not few in number, referred to on the forms as "recidivist" or "bearers of multiple illegitimate children" (*pluripare illegitime*) whose experiences of misfortune are similar to this case history from the early postwar period:

> At age 21, she was left a widow with two children, in the greatest destitution, from which she raised herself by going to live with another man. By this man another child was born, whom the mother acknowledged. Then abandoned, she resorted to Maternal Assistance, which placed the oldest child in an asylum for abandoned children and arranged for the woman to work, securing a position for her as a cleaner of streetcars. But after three years, when all the women were fired, she fell once again into even greater destitution. Discouraged by the agonizing situation, she joined together with another man, by whom she had a fourth child whom she acknowledged. Left abandoned for a second time, she returned with her three-month-old baby to ask for assistance.[95]

This history shows clearly how unwed motherhood is interwoven with the working life of the women and with their efforts to survive. In general, a state of particular vulnerability for the woman—when she arrives in the city to look for work, after an illness, on leaving the hospital or sanitorium, or when she finds herself without money—seems a precondition to what on the forms is called "seduction."

Unwed motherhood can be simply a transitory episode in a woman's life, preceded or followed by marriage. These women, in general, keep their legitimate and illegitimate children with them. Whether the encounter or cohabitation with a man leads to marriage depends, in the great majority of cases, on the attitude of the man; only once in a while does the woman say that she has chosen to leave the man, for example, "because he was a person of bad habits, he got drunk." Pregnancy (and the implicit or explicit request for support that it carries with it) necessarily creates a situation in which the man has power over the woman. When the man's reaction is not simply to disappear or to abandon the woman, which is usual when the man and woman are of different social classes,[96] a situation of negotiation is created and the man responds by making excuses: "He wants all the furniture in the house, according to custom," explains a 22-year-old Roman shoemaker, unemployed, who has acknowledged the baby and keeps the baby with her "in misery;" "he is a policeman [*carabiniere*] who promises to fix the situation if he makes sergeant"; "he promises to marry me when he has a better position"; "first he wants a steady job."[97] Confronted by the men's excuses, women seem to assume an attitude of resignation and self-justification.

When faced with the financial responsibilities of an illegitimate child, the attitudes of the fathers and of the mothers turn out to be profoundly different. The men absolutely deny paternity when it would lead to a reduction in the income they are used to; they postpone everything until times get better, or they ask for some material advantage in exchange for the burden that they are assuming. The women seem to accept the responsibility of maintaining the baby even when, as practically always happens in these histories, it uses up almost all of their earnings. Besides, in the early postwar years, the subsidy was suspended for some mothers who exchanged the goods that they were supposed to use for themselves at the refectory for bread for the whole family.[98]

To have a baby wet-nursed could cost, according to the sheets of 1936–37, up to 120 or 130 lire, equal to the salary of a domestic, which most of these women were. It is important to consider that usually these mothers could not keep their children with them. After the period of nursing (if they were able to nurse), the mothers gave the children to the wet nurse or, if relations with the family were still good, they sent them to relatives in the country. Many histories indicate a strong attachment to the children, especially among the older unwed mothers, who seem to take refuge in the relationship with the child after several failures at creating a real family.[99] These histories give meaning to the statistics on the frequency of maternal acknowledgment of illegitimate children, a frequency that cannot only be the consequence of the policy of persuasion (or imposition) of motherhood used by the foundling hospitals. There has been a meeting, in some way, between these policies and a line of action of the women.

We must remember, however, that we are dealing with a specific group of women. Our histories examine mothers, all or nearly all of whom acknowledged their own children, for the simple reason that in general only those who have acknowedged their children have a right to assistance. This holds in particular for the forms from the end of the 1930s, because from 1927 on a law was in force that made assistance obligatory for mothers who acknowledged their children.[100] The assistance, and therefore the information forms, are limited to the mothers who acknowledged their children, and therefore this material can tell us nothing concerning the others. But we know that there were others, of course. Notwithstanding the increase in maternal acknowledgment, illegitimate children of unknown parentage did not disappear in the period between the two wars. In 1941 the Opera Nazionale Maternità ed Infanzia (ONMI) aided 172,000 illegitimate children acknowledged by their mothers and 60,000 children of unknown parents.[101]

Many conditions typical of unwed motherhood at the turn of the century still existed at the end of the 1930s: the foundling hospitals always accepted the mothers who refused to acknowledge their children on the condition that, in exchange for asylum, they agreed to nurse their own and one additional baby. On a form from 1937 we read that a mother was forced to leave the foundling hospital where she had found temporary refuge, because she did not have enough milk for two. Nursing was always an occasional expedient for poor women from the country, as our forms indirectly attest in reporting that nearly every mother who was not able to have her baby with her because of her work put it out to nurse in the country. It was also an occupation in which brokers and respectable employment agencies speculated, boasting that they could offer "persons already selected and guaranteed."[102] The contradiction remains between the propaganda for maternal nursing, buttressed by the systematically ignored laws that required nursing rooms at factories on the one hand and, on the other, the mothers' daily reality of work that made it difficult or impossible for them to nurse.

But there was something new. For example the figure of the female visitor, a subaltern who with a meagre and popular knowledge of medicine had a power of definition and judgment over other women.[103] The forms compiled by the visitors are thus histories of women, gathered by women, but guided by a medical perspective. They often contain judgments ("amoral, psychically deficient"; "mentally deficient, amoral, cynical, potential criminal") in which medical jargon is adopted to express distance and hostility. The distance between the unwed mother and the female visitor is well represented, it seems to me, by the disdainful comment written by one of the visitors on the information form of a woman who was having her second illegitimate child: "As anyone can see, she did not hesitate to have a second child. She was so certain of being helped, that she did not worry about whether they were illegitimate." In actuality, the paltry and uncertain nature of the subsidies makes a judgment like this not only unjust but also, clearly, unfounded.

There was also, though I do not know whether this was old or new, the sense of stigmatized identity that perhaps became conscious under the scrutiny and questioning by the female visitor: the identity of an unwed mother or of a daughter of unknown parents destined to retrace the footprints of her own mother, as in the form quoted here, in which the only color in the uniform grayness of these histories is the red snow, a sign of misfortune. And where the mother who does not acknowledge her child appears, like a negative phantasm, the figure that is missing in this whole study, she appears as a mother whose daughter will not forgive her for abandoning her:

> Around the third day after her birth the baby girl was left at the foundling hospital. From here she was entrusted to a wet nurse who raised her, treating her very badly and appropriating to herself the gifts that the little one received from compassionate people. She remained with the wet nurse until she was six, a period in which

the whole countryside became aware of the bad treatment accorded her; the babe was entrusted to an institute for children of unknown parents. Here because the society was all uniform, the little girl grew up without much awareness of her inferior social status. A hunchbacked woman, 45 years old, also the daughter of unknown parents, took care of her. . . . At the first question about her mamma, the hunchback answered: "your mamma will come when the red snow falls" and then "when the week comes with three Thursdays." The girl waited anxiously for these events to take place, and only when she was about ten years old did she under-stand that these were nothing but pitiful lies. . . . Though there were indications as to where her mother could have been found, she did not want to look for her, frightened by the example of some companions who, having found their parents, had had to leave them once again, being immediately subjected by them to hu-miliation and mistreatment. . . .

She has a lively disposition but is a little touchy and always thinks that all of her misfortunes derive from her inferior state, be-cause she is the daughter of unknown parents.[104]

We also learn that this girl entered domestic service and that she had to leave her job because she was pregnant. Then the history ceases.

In early twentieth-century medicine, the clinical approach to di-agnosis was progressively devalued in favor of a diagnostic method based predominantly on laboratory analysis. Compared with labo-ratory analysis, the clinical approach, based on the collection of "his-tories" with detailed narrations of the course of the individual disease, has always appeared more unsatisfactory, something merely empirical and impressionistic. The clinical history, meanwhile, was reduced to the schematized card left for the subordinate health staff to compile.[105] Something similar, though perhaps a little later, happened in the social sciences. In the 1930s the social sciences made use of "life histories," and then, after the war, this practice disappeared. The social sciences of these years were invariably founded on collective categories: an-thropology had "culture," sociology the "social system," with its interweaving of roles that always referred back to the collective mean-ing of social action—that is, to its functional relevance with respect to maintaining the system or to throwing it into crisis. Even historical materialism privileged collective categories, like those of class or struc-ture. Even the critical theory of society analyzed the authoritarian personality through "types" and "syndromes," rather than individual concrete histories.

For Adorno, constructing sociological types made sense because "the world in which we live is typed and 'produces' different 'types' of persons. Only by identifying traits in modern humans, and not by denying their existence, can the pernicious tendency toward all-pervasive classification and subsumption be challenged."[106] But if the duty of criticism is precisely to show how the typification of the individual is first of all a social construct, then the individual histories acquire a cognitive relevance. In them we can certainly see the standardization of an individual, his or her adaptation, more or less coerced, to a norm; but we see it therefore as a history, as the result of a sum of choices, of pressures, and of circumstances. One of these circumstances is certainly the biological condition. But it is always in the context of a biographical experience that we meet a human biological phenomenon such as maternity, for example. Social forces appear decisive in the biographical context. In respect to the biological aspect of maternity, the life histories speak rather of how far it is from being "natural" and of which social pressures must intervene to construct it.

Our culture sets up two different approaches to the problem of life: biography and biology. When we try to understand the events of our history, perhaps we ought to try to have them both present. In the case of women, however, the biological conditioning has been recorded, analyzed, and underlined so often, so appropriately and so inappropriately as well, that a reminder of the biographical aspect, to the experience of concrete individuals, seems long overdue. And perhaps in this case, forms of knowledge and expression based on the capacity to observe and describe individual histories are especially useful, as in, for example, the nineteenth-century clinical histories, useful for their descriptive richness and for the very qualities of empiricism and impressionism that have lost them their scientific value.

Empiricism and impressionism do not seem to me, however, to be very serious failings in the social sciences. Even if they are failings, they can be justified. They permit, after all, a faithfulness to everyday experience and prescientific knowledge; they allow an adherence to everyday language and therefore they are comprehensible to everyone; they admit as evidence what more refined knowledge sometimes hides, that is, the point of view from which we are observing and the practical interests that drive us to know.

For in none of the things that I have tried to reconstruct in this work—the physicians' construction of a social image of maternity based on the exclusive responsibility of the mother for her baby; the attempt to control such female sexual capacities as nursing by forbidding women to nurse promiscuously precisely while promoting the commercialization of nursing; the keeping of many women in a state of powerless ignorance about the threats to their health—does it seem to me there is a definitive interpretation.

In a popular novel of the 1930s, there is a woman, neither married nor a mother and named, paradoxically, Concezione.[107] At the novel's beginning, Concezione has just left the hospital after surgery for a breast tumor. The nurse at the hospital told her that the blame for the disease is hers, because she has never given birth or nursed. This is an example of how fears were passed from woman to woman and how they were accepted all the more readily because of their source. This became possible because of a social structuring of scientific knowledge that produced at the bottom, where the women usually are, a kind of knowledge that shows up as a waste product, as dogma or illusion or fear, rather than as an enrichment of the capacity to judge. Such a structure of knowledge can hide the collective responsibility for the evil that we suffer by presenting it to us as individual guilt. These fears and feelings of guilt correspond objectively to a social discrimination. We know this, but even today the fears and guilt continue to have power over us, both mothers and nonmothers alike.

Notes

I must thank first of all Mr. Giorgio Modigliani and Professor Claudio Modigliani, who put at my disposal, most generously and courteously, the material from Maternal Assistance collected by Mrs. Modigliani. I thank Mr. Fiorini and Dr. Falcitelli, of ONMI, Professors Gatti and Ossicini and Mrs. Jolanda Torraca, for having helped me in the research—unfortunately fruitless—into the information forms of the Maternal Assistance and Profesor Roberto Bachi, for having sent me the proofs of part of his book on unwed motherhood. Thanks to Joan and Piero Boitani and to Fabio Petri, who offered me hospitality in Rome, thus allowing me to carry my research forward; to Gianfranco Contini and Angela Ferraro, who clarified for me various matters of medical competence, correcting several errors, and who are of course in no way responsible for those that remain; to Raffaella Lamberti and Elvira Valleri, who read the typescript with great patience and attention, giving me important suggestions; to Roberto Dionigi, who helped me to reflect on several theoretical knots suggested by my material, and who invited me to confront them explicitly. Most affectionate thanks to Pina Lalli, Cristina Savio, and Mauro Casaleggio, who stayed close to me and helped me in more ways than I can say, through all the moments of perplexity and discouragement that came while I was writing this article.

1. See articles 180 (on the prohibition of investigations into paternity) and 376 (on the prohibition of investigations into maternity). According to article 190, only the son was given the right to investigate his maternity. There exists a vast juridical literature on the "investigation into maternity"; for a bibliography, see R. Bachi and O. Flaschel Modigliani, *Maternità illegittima* (Rome, 1934), vol. 1: *Le fonti*, pp. 110ff. Many of the proposed laws giving assistance to foundlings considered the investigation into maternity; these followed one after the other in almost every legislative session, without success, however, until World War I (on these projects, see Bachi and Modigliani, *Maternità*, 94ff.). In fact, until 1923, there was no national law regarding assistance to foundlings; the local and provincial laws of 1865 were limited to assigning responsibility for them to the provinces and the townships.

2. E. Raseri, "I fanciulli illegittimi e gli esposti in Italia," *Archivio di statistica* (1881): 16–17.

3. Although the abolition of the *ruota* was motivated, among other things, by the desire to stop the abandonment of legitimate children, the foundling hospitals continued to accept them, even at the end of the nineteenth century, in cases of extreme destitution of the parents and for "proven inability of the mother to nurse." In Milan, for example, in 1889, out of the 506 pregnant women accepted into the maternity ward of the foundling hospital, 230 were married and of the 1,770 foundlings, 540 were legitimate children: see Ospizio Provinciale Esposti e Partorienti di Milano, *Relazione generale*, by Director E. Grassi (Milan, 1891), pp. 9, 15 (hereafter referred to as Grassi, *Relazione*, with the corresponding date).

4. E. Porro, *Il biennio 1869–70 alla Maternità di Milano: Rendiconto clinico* (Milan, 1872), pp. 242–43. On Porro see the biographical notes in A. Hirsch (Hrsg.), *Biographisches Lexicon hervorragender Aerzte* (Munich, 1886), 4: 611. Clinical accounts corresponding to that of Porro frequently mention cases of rickets among unwed mothers: see, for example, E. Falaschi, *Prospetto storico-statistico dell'Ospizio di maternità nello Spedale di S. Maria della Scala nell'anno 1873* (Siena, 1874); E. Grassi, *Resoconto del primo anno della Clinica ostetrica di Firenze* (Florence, 1880).

5. Porro, *Maternità di Milano*, p. 9. Of the women whose clinical histories Porro sets out, 21 are peasants, 14 seamstresses, 5 "servants," 3 maids, 2 dressmakers, 2 "dayworkers," 1 an embroiderer, 1 a nurse, 1 a "match worker," 1 a housekeeper. From a list of occupations of the women accepted at the Maternity Hospital of Bologna between 1895 and 1901, one can determine that out of a total of 909 women, 329 were "servants," 240 peasants, 227 workers, 105 "house attendants," 5 street sellers, 3 prostitutes; see L. Bordè, *Rendiconto clinico-statistico dell'Asilo di Maternità* (Bologna, 1904), p. 12.

6. Grassi, *Relazione* (1891), p. 32.

7. Porro, *Maternità di Milano*, p. 53. Other clinical accounts refer to "precipitous deliveries," in which the women seem to give birth in the customary manner of delivery at home, that is standing or sitting in a chair; for example: "precipitous delivery without pains, with shudders as in defecation. She gives birth almost on her feet," "precipitous delivery: she gives birth on a stool without assistance" (Bordè, *Rendiconto*, pp. 38–43).

8. In establishing the Maternity Hospital of Bologna in 1860, it was stated: "In this Hospice there will also have to be a place appropriate for accepting dozens of women students of obstetrics from the whole province, thus forming a practical school for mothers" (cited in U. Rubbi and C. Zucchini, "L'Ospizio esposti e l'Asilo di maternità," in *Sette secoli di vita ospedaliera in Bologna* [Bologna, 1960], pp. 409–10).

Regarding the fact that the poor pregnant women accepted into the public hospitals were "made available for teaching," see the reports on the local schools of obstetrics made by the prefectures to the health director at the end of the nineteenth century: Archivio Centrale dello Stato, *Min. Int., Direz. Gener. Sanità* (hereafter ACS, *Sanità*), 1882–1915, b. 418, fasc. marked *febbre puerperale*.

9. Porro, *Maternità di Milano*, pp. 52–53.

These women may well have experienced the same thing that happened at the Hôtel-Dieu in the first half of the last century, according to the testimony of an observer: "Look in the wards of the Hôtel-Dieu: the throng that crowds around the figure of the surgeon, that throws itself upon the wretch who has a fracture. Everyone wants to effect the cure. The patient does not resist: he dies from the pain. He does not even have time to answer the fifth student, who questions him to find out if he has an illness that might hinder the mending of the broken bones" (cited in M. Wiriot, *L'inseignement clinique dans les hôpitaux de Paris entre 1794 et 1848, d'après documents de l'époque* [Paris, 1970], p. 120).

10. L. M. Bossi, *Come i maggiori centri di popolazione possano meglio provvedere all'assistenza chirurgica gratuita a domicilio delle partorienti povere* (Milan, 1901), p. 7.

11. E. M. Ackerknecht, "Anticontagionism between 1821 and 1867," *Bulletin of the History of Medicine* 22 (1948): 562–93. In Italy, for example, see E. Zavagli, *Riflessioni critiche sul contagionismo* (Fano, 1856).

12. The Viennese obstetrician Semmelweis experienced this fierce opposition from his own colleagues, when, in an article of 1861, he maintained the responsibility of the physicians and of the hospital in the genesis and the spread of the puerperal fever. Regarding Semmelweis, see A. Hegar, *Semmelweis, sein Leben und seine Lehre* (Tübingen, 1882); regarding his theories on puerperal fever, see R. Dohrn, *Geschichte der Geburtshülfe der Neuzeit* (Tübingen, 1903-04), 2: 1–197; in Italy, for example, see A. Guzzoni degli Ancarani, "Pro Semmelweis," *Gazzetta degli ospitali* (1886): nos. 83–85. "One of the roots of the hostility to a contagionist point of view lay in the threat it implied for the physician's status, especially in relation to female patients," writes Charles Rosenberg in regard to the resistance by American obstetricians toward the contagionist theory of puerperal fever (*No Other Gods: On Science and American Social Thought* [Baltimore, 1976], pp. 14 and 213, n. 23).

13. F. Palasciano, *Difesa del voto della Giunta municipale di Napoli contro lo stabilimento di una Maternità nel brefotrofio dell'Annunziata* (Naples, 1877), p. 4 (article by Palasciano). On Palasciano, see *Biographisches Lexicon*, 4: 466–67.

14. *Relazione, discussioni e votazione* of the fourth session of the International Medical Congress on Maternity, Brussells 1975 (I quote from the excerpt reproduced in Palasciano, *Difesa*, pp. 40–94, esp. pp. 57–59).

15. Archivio Centrale dello Stato, *Min. int., Direz. Gener. Amministrazione civile* (hereafter ACS, *Opere Pie*), Serie 10, b. 32.

16. C. Merletti, *Per l'istituzione di una sezione chirurgico-ostetrica nell'Istituto di maternità di Ferrara* (Bologna, 1903), p. 7, which cites "the favorable opinion of all the learned of Italy on this position, maintained for five years or so by Dr. Landucci of the Maternity Hospital of Bergamo, who must also supervise at the same time the surgical section for female diseases." Regarding Cesare Merletti, see *Biographisches Lexicon*, (1962), 2: 1027.

17. L. Acconci, *Dell'asepsi e antisepsi nei parti* (Rome, 1896). On Luigi Acconci, see *Biographisches Lexicon*, 1: 6. By antisepsis was meant vaginal irrigation with disinfectant substances, at first practiced routinely as a prophylactic measure against puerperal fever. Cases of poisoning by antiseptics, however, contraindicated this practice, which then became limited to deliveries involving instrumental or surgical intervention (for example, L. M. Bossi, "Provocazione artificiale del parto e sinfisiotomia,"

Annali di ostetricia e ginecologia [July 1894]; on Bossi, see *Biographisches Lexicon*, 1: 153). Asepsis, however, was adopted as a general rule, that is the sterilization of instruments and objects, including the surgeon's hands, that were to come in contact with the woman giving birth.

18. O. Viana, *Per l'istituzione di un piccolo reparto ginecologico nella Maternità di Verona* (Verona, 1912); P. Sfameni, *Brefotrofio e scuola ostetrica dell'Università di Perugia: resoconto statistico-sanitario del biennio 1906–07* (Perugia, 1908). On Viana and Sfameni, see *Biographisches Lexicon*, 1: 1618, 1446.

19. T. Rossi Doria, *Assistenza materna* (Milan, 1914), pp. 262–63; see also A. Guzzoni degli Ancarani, *L'Italia ostetrica* (Siena, 1911), pp. 523–44.

During the 1890s the clinical movement—that is, the number of women assisted by the Obstetrical Corps—surpassed, in a city like Genoa, that of the two maternity wards (see L. M. Bossi, *Il terzo lustro della Guardia Ostetrica Permanente di Genova* [Biella, 1907], p. 8). This tells us, among other things, how uncommon hospital delivery still was. Only rarely were there more than 300 births in one year in a maternity hospital. In Bologna, for example, in the two years 1908–10, 432 women gave birth in the maternity hospital (see L. Bordè, *Significati e intenti moderni degli Asili di Maternità* [Bologna, 1911]).

20. There were 9,046 cases of puerperal fever reported in 1888, 6,013 in 1890, 3,866 in 1892, 2,479 in 1898. This rapid decline then ceases and in 1923 we still have 2,110 cases. In relative numbers, out of 10,000 inhabitants, the incidence went from 3.03 in 1888 to 0.48 in 1923. Mortality from puerperal fever, out of 10,000 deliveries, went from 20.1 in 1887–89 to 10.2 in 1923, a less noticeable decrease, which indicates that the greatest medical control over the disease consisted mostly of prophylaxis, rather than of therapy. For these data, see L. De Berardinis, "Statistica sanitaria," in *Trattato italiano di igiene*, vol. 18: *Demografia* (Turin, 1930), pp. 313, 513.

It is necessary to consider, however, the physicians' probable reticence about reporting puerperal fever as cause of death, once the disease was considered contagious and therefore possibly implying blame, once, that is, the Health Regulation of 1888 had made the reporting obligatory for all infectious diseases. The physicians admitted that the disease had spread to a degree "greater than what appears in the statistics" (L. M. Bossi, "Sulla infezione puerperale a domicilio e sull'urgenza di modificare il vigente regolamento ostetrico," *Annali di ostetricia* 7 [1898]), but above all they blamed the midwives for not reporting the cases of puerperal fever that had been proved among their clientele (for example, S. Levi, *Sull'andamento del servizio ostetrico in Padova* [Bologna, 1898]).

21. See the proposals to modify the Regulation of Midwives in 1890 in ACS, *Sanità*, 1882–1915, b. 418. These proposals aimed at restricting further the powers of the midwife in respect to those of the obstetrician. The Regulation of 1890 is reproduced, for example, in the *Prontuario dell'ufficiale sanitario in Italia* (Turin, 1891), 2: 78–83.

It would be interesting to juxtapose these criticisms with the instructions that the midwives received. The principles of microbiology could be imparted in this way: "Proceeding from the fact that microbes can be seen perfectly by means of the microscopy, the concept of their existence is very logical and all must be persuaded of their existence even without seeing them" (L. Bordè, *Sulle cause della febbre puerperale: conferenza tenuta alla società delle levatrici* [Bologna, 1896], p. 5).

22. On the image of syphilis in the nineteenth and early twentieth centuries from Ibsen and Mann to *Mein Kampf*, see the references in S. Sontag, *Malattia come metafora* (Turin, 1979), pp. 33, 49, 51, 65 [the Italian translation of *Illness as Metaphor* (New York, 1978)].

23. This is the Regulation of February 15, 1860, known as the Cavour Regulation.

On the norms for control of prostitutes by health and police authorities in Germany during the same period, see R. J. Evans, "Prostitution, State and Society in Imperial Germany," *Past and Present* 70 (February 1976): 106–29; in England, F. B. Smith, "Ethics and Disease in Later Nineteenth Century: The Contagious Diseases Acts," *Historical Studies* 15 (1971).

24. S. Sperino, *La sifilizzazione studiata qual mezzo preservativo delle malattie veneree* (Turin, 1853); see also P. Gamberini, *La sifilizzazione praticata nello Spedale di S. Orsola* (Milan, 1852).

25. The intermediary's fee for wet-nursing was regulated by articles 69 and 72 of the Law of Public Safety, on the basis of which one could not practice "the profession of intermediary for the placement of wet nurses without being previously enrolled in the appropriate registry at the headquarters of Public Safety." But abuses must have been frequent: a circular from the Health Inspectorship ("Vigilanza sull'allattamento mercenario," *Gazz. uff.* December 29, 1902, no. 303) asked the prefects to respect this ruling.

26. Ospizio per l'infanzia abbandonata del circondario di Genova, *Resoconto morale per l'anno 1913* (Genoa, 1914), p. 26. The hospices reacted by paying the salaries of the wet nurses only at the end of each semester, in order to force them to stay in the hospice at least for that period: see, for example, Civico Spedale di Mantova, *Istruzioni sui vari servizi interni dello Spedale civile e dell'Ospizio degli Esposti* (Mantua, 1900), p. 38.

27. In Turin right after the war, for example, the wages paid to wet nurses by private families varied between 60 and 100 lire; the foundling hospital paid them 25 lire (Ospizio Provinciale Esposti di Torino, *Relazione morale e bilancio preventivo 1919*, in ACS, *Opere Pie*, Serie 10, b. 32.)

In Messina in 1911 an inspection report on the foundling unit annexed to the civil hospital stated that "the women who have recently given birth in the obstetrical division pass with difficulty to the foundling hospital, preferring instead to find placement with private families" (ACS, *Sanità*, 1910–20, b. 600).

28. Grassi, *Relazione* (1897), pp. 19, 22.

29. Grassi, *Relazione* (1891), p. 11, and *Relazione* (1901), p. 65; Rubbi and Zucchini, "Ospizio," p. 410.

30. Grassi, *Relazione* (1901), p. 65.

31. Attached to the form for collecting the semestral statistics on the foundling hospitals, there was a questionnaire containing, among other things, a question on the relative numbers of wet nurses and children in the institutions. Here are some of the answers: in Cuneo in 1908 there was 1 wet nurse for every 4 children in the winter and 1 for every 6 in the summer. In Ferrara in 1918 it goes from a minimum of 2.8 nurslings for 1 nurse to a maximum of 3.7 (ACS, *Opere Pie*, Serie 10, b. 32). In the Messina foundling hospital in 1911, at the time of survey there were 31 children and 11 wet nurses. In Lecce in 1919 a report by the departmental medical inspector refers to 11 children entrusted to 2 wet nurses (ACS, *Sanità*, 1910–20, b. 600).

32. *Giornale della Regia Società italiana di igiene* 9 (1887): 96, 869.

33. "Disposizioni dirette a impedire la diffusione della sifilide col baliatico affidato da Istituti di infanzia abbandonata," November 5, 1887; the circular is on pp. 101–2 of the *Prontuario dell'ufficiale sanitario*. The circular established, among other things, that an infected wet nurse had to be cared for in a hospital or in the syphilis asylum at the expense of the foundling hospital.

34. This material is found in ACS, *Sanità*, 1882–1915, b. 1076, fasc. marked "sifilide da baliatico."

On the health administration in Italy during those years, see the few references in E. Ragionieri, "La storia politica e sociale," in *Storia d'Italia* (Turin, 1976), pp. 1762–63.

35. Reports of the provincial physician of Mantua, under the dates January 9, 1901, and February 6, 1902, in ACS, *Sanità*, 1882–1915, b. 1076.

36. See the report by the prefect of Chieti (1909) on an epidemic verified in a village of the province: "It was not possible to ascertain the origin of the contagion because in the commune there is a thriving practice of exchanging nursing among families"; or of the prefect of Como (1905): "As often happens in the small rural villages, nursing women easily also give milk sometimes to the children of their neighbors." Similar comments occur in the reports of the prefects of Bergamo (1906), Milan (1901), Cuneo (1900), Reggio Calabria (1908) (ACS, *Sanità*, 1882–1915, b. 1076).

37. Pref. di Bologna (1905) (ibid.).

38. On this point the Nicotera circular was systematically ignored. The provincial administrations on which many foundling hospitals depended were openly opposed to its application: see Unione delle Provincie d'Italia, *Sul progetto di legge per l'assistenza agli esposti e all'infanzia abbandonata* (Rome, 1908), pp. 47–48.

39. ACS, *Sanità*, 1882–1915, b. 1076.

40. A 1911 short story by Pirandello, "La balia," turns on the play, more or less conscious, of this association between wet nurse and prostitute (*Novelle per un anno* [Verona, 1956]).

41. A 1905 report by the Prefecture of Milan about an epidemic of syphilis in a village speaks of the "great reluctance on the part of the female population of that area to ask for advice from physicians, so much so that diagnoses were first ascertained for the children and then, more or less by induction, for the women, who studiously avoid the confirmation of their condition of health by the physician," (ACS, *Sanità*, 1882–1915, b. 1076).

"A woman cannot ask advice from the health official for her child affected with syphilis, since turning to the health official is equivalent to admitting that she is a prostitute" (*Relazione e proposte* of the "R. Commissione per lo studio delle questioni relative alla prostituzione e ai provvedimenti per la morale e igiene pubblica" [Florence, 1885], p. 94).

42. R. W. Taylor, *On the Question of the Transmission of Syphilitic Contagion in the Rite of Circumcision* (New York, 1873).

43. Ackerknecht, *Anticontagionism*, which casts light on the relationship between anticontagionist positions and liberal interests in politics and in the economy.

44. M. Douglas, *Purity and Danger: An Analysis of Concepts of Pollution and Taboo* (London, 1966), and its Italian translation, *Purezza e pericolo* (Bologna, 1975); and *Natural Symbols* (London, 1970).

45. See Civico Spedale di Mantova, *Istruzioni*, p. 17, and the instructions given to the wet nurses by the foundling hospital of Rome, reproduced in D. Albini, *La questione degli esposti e il brefotrofio di Roma* (Rome, 1896), pp. 84–87.

46. This is what the foundling hospital of Saluzzo was forced to do in 1909, because "the women are afraid of contagious diseases" (pref. di Cuneo, in ACS, *Opere Pie*, Serie 10, b. 32).

47. The foundling hospital of Bologna, which was extremely reluctant to assume the expenses for the care of a syphilitic wet nurse, still had to pay an average of 4,000 lire a year during the period 1872–96, for syphilis insurance for the wet nurses (as emerges from a prospectus appended to the account of the health inspection of 1901, found in ACS, *Sanità*, 1882–1915, b. 1076, and which hereafter I will cite as *Relazione Pavone*).

48. A. Titomanlio, "Sulla sifilide ereditaria nei principali brefotrofi d'Italia in

rapporto ai regolamenti sanitari in vigore," *Riforma medica* 9, part 4 (1893): nn. 280, 281; Grassi, *Relazione* (1891), p. 65.

49. Two types of health certificates were filed: one for the wet nurses who worked at the charitable institutions, like the foundling hospitals, for whom were required only "the main and indispensable notices on the health of the woman" and those for the wet nurses who would go into private wet-nursing, for whom was required "the greatest number of notices possible" (see the ordinance from the Prefecture of Rome of January 25, 1903, in ACS, *Sanità*, 1882–1915, b. 1076). There were, therefore, two categories of wet nurses: one controlled very strictly for middle-class children and one, only loosely controlled, for wretched, miserable foundlings, offspring of wretched, miserable parents.

50. Examples of these forms are found in Civico Spedale di Mantova, *Istruzioni*, and in Ospizio per l'Infanzia abbandonata del Circondario di Genova, *Relazione sull'andamento morale ed economico 1911–1915* (Genoa, 1916).

51. G. Profeta, *Trattato pratico delle malattie veneree* (Palermo, 1888); on Profeta, see *Biographiches Lexicon*, 2: 1257. On the so-called Profeta law, see A. Pazzini, *Storia della medicina* (Milan, 1947), 2: 462–64.

52. The ramifications and functions of this metaphor in nineteenth-century medicine have been reconstructed by Charles Rosenberg, "The Bitter Fruit: Heredity, Disease, and Social Thought," in *No Other Gods*, pp. 25–53. This metaphor had perhaps, in nineteenth-century medicine, a role analogous to that of the metaphor of organization in the biology of the same period (see K. Figlio, "The Metaphor of Organization: An Historiographical Perspective on the Bio-Medical Sciences of the Early Nineteenth Century," *History of Science* 15 [1976]: 17–53).

53. G. Pini, *La sifilide negli esposti* (Bologna, 1901), pp. 3–4.

54. In the 1881 statistics on the causes of death among illegitimate children during the first year of life, the cause listed most frequently was "congenital weakness and immaturity" (91.3 out of 1,000), followed by "gastritis, diarrhea, enteritis" (61.5) and "respiratory diseases" (33.2) (see Min. dell'Agric. Ind. e Commercio, Direzione Gener. della Statistica, *Statistica della causa delle morti avvenute in 281 capoluoghi di provincia, di circondario e di distretto* [Rome, 1882]). Raseri, "Fanciulli illegittimi," p. 24, for a reflection of these statistics in the opinion that the majority of deaths among illegitimate, compared with legitimate, children was caused by "a hereditary bad constitution."

55. Many parts of the semiannual statistical records on the foundling hospitals (ACS, *Sanità*, 1910–20, b. 600) are incomplete regarding the causes of death, which in general do not ever correspond to the number of deaths.

In Bologna, in the 1901 inspection of the foundling hospital, comparison between the clinical records and the death certificates suggested, in the words of the inspector, that the physician for the ward had "more or less exaggerated in the diagnosis of immaturity, pronouncing dead due to immaturity some children who, probably, had died of gastroenteritis from the artificial nursing" (*Relazione Pavone*).

56. M. Oro, *Sulla sistemazione del servizio di profilassi della sifilide da baliato nella SS. Casa dell'Annunziata* (Naples, 1904), p. 4.

57. G. Guidi, "Della utilità della reazione del Wassermann nei brefotrofi," *Rivista di clinica pediatrica* 10 (1912).

58. ACS, *Sanità*, 1910–20, b. 599.

59. P. Pennato, *La reazione di Wassermann nel brefotrofio*, (Venice, 1913): "Why not admit that we are a little too eager to see hereditary syphilis in certain skin and mucous manifestations on the child?"

60. Grassi, *Relazione* (1901), pp. 68–69.

61. "R. Commissione per lo studio delle questioni relative alla prostituzione," p. 92.

On mortality from syphilis, see De Berardinis, "Statistica sanitaria," pp. 452–54: in a population of 10,000, the mortality (mostly among infants) was about 0.74 in 1895, about 0.65 in 1900, about 0.56 in 1905, about 0.53 in 1915.

62. The history of science shows, however, that very rarely do the quantitative data resulting from experimentation lead, on their own, to the immediate rejection of the theory with which they are in contradiction: see T. S. Kuhn, "The Function of Measurement in Modern Physical Science," *Isis* 52 (1961): 161–93.

It is also significant in this context that there was almost immediate controversy regarding the definitive diagnostic value of a negative Wassermann result, and only later regarding that of a positive result. The possibility of a positive reaction in the absence of syphilis was accepted for the first time at the international medical conference in Copenhagen in 1928; see J. H. Stokes, H. Beerman, and N. R. Ingraham, *Modern Clinical Syphilology* (Philadelphia, [n.d.]), p. 71.

63. "Voti expressi dal convegno nazionale dei direttori e amministratori dei brefotrofi ed istituti congeneri," Rome, September 19–20, 1917, in ACS *Sanità*, 1910–20, b. 599.

64. De Berardinis, "Statistica sanitaria," pp. 421–22.

65. At the end of the nineteenth century, there was a reversal in the traditional medical opinion that pregnancy would have mitigated the course of tuberculosis. See L. Acconci, "Tubercolosi e gravidanza," *Clinica moderna* 1 (1895): no. 5.

On abortion and contraception in general, see, for example, the opinions of Bossi, *Malattie utero-ovariche e malthusismo* (Rome, 1909).

66. G. Poppi, *L'allattamento misto* (Bologna, 1904), p. 1.

67. ACS, *Sanità*, 1882–1915, b. 1076.

68. F. Garofalo, *L'Istituto di S. Rocco delle partorienti e delle celate* (Rome, 1949).

69. Archivio di Stato di Roma, *Prefettura*, Serie 3, Opere Pie, b. 4028, fasc. 8. In Mantua the nursing subsidies were introduced in 1877 (S. Magrini, *La soppressione dei brefotrofi e la riforma del servizio esposti nel mantovano* [Mantua, 1914], p. 28); in Milan in 1890 (Grassi, *Relazione* [1901], p. 12); in Bologna in 1896 (G. Poppi, *L'assistenza agli esposti nel brefotrofio di Bologna durante il triennio 1901–1904* [Bologna, 1905], p. 5); in Genoa in 1902 (*Resoconto morale per l'anno 1913*, pp. 27–30).

70. In Mantua, for example, the wet-nurses received a salary of 20 lire the first year, 12 the second, 10 the third, and so forth, in decreasing amounts, until the child's tenth year. The mothers, instead, received 25 lire the first year, 20 the second, and 15 the third, but then the subsidy stopped completely (see Magrini, *L'assistenza all'infanzia illegittima nel mantovano durante la guerra* [Mantua, 1919], p. 116).

71. Grassi, *Relazione* (1901), pp. 38, and 40.

72. Poppi, *L'assistenza agli esposti*, p. 19.

73. Poppi, *Opere pie*, Serie 10, b. 32.

74. E. Modigliani, "Per la riforma del brefotrofio," *La tribune* 108 (April 19, 1917). On Modigliani, see *Biographisches Lexicon*, 2: 1052.

75. ACS, *Sanità*, 1910–20, b. 600.

76. R. D., February 11, 1923, no. 336: "Approvazione del regolamento generale per il servizio d'assistenza degli esposti" (*Gazz. uff.*, March 16, 1923, no. 63) art. 18, c. 1. It did not mean a lot, naturally, that the law spoke of "discreet inquiries," or that still in 1930, for example, a circular from the Opera Nazionale Maternità e Infanzia—established in 1925—invited the foundling hospitals to "protect the secret of unwed motherhood" (circ. no. 46, April 25, 1930). In 1930 ONMI responded unfavorably to the proposal to render compulsory by law the acknowledgment and

the nursing of illegitimate children by the mother. Such a rule, they argued, would have increased the number of criminal abortions and would have encouraged the spread of contraception (see the communication of ONMI to the minister of the interior, July 31, 1930, in ACS, *Min. int., Gabinetto, Assistenza figli illegittimi e infanzia abbandonata*, 1930–33, b. 1).

77. On the "investigation into paternity," see the bibliography in Bachi and Modigliani, *Maternità*, pp. 105–9.

78. On this mortality, see E. Modigliani, "L'assistenza alla prima infanzia illegittima," in *Atti del IX Congresso pediatrico italiano* (Trieste, 1920).

79. The medical literature that supports this theory is endless; see, for example, F. La Torre, "L'allattamento in campagna: mortalità infantile, cause e provvedimenti," *Clinica ostetrica* 4, fasc. 2–3 (1902). On La Torre, see *Biographisches Lexicon*, 2: 869.

Once again, while the frequency of gastrointestinal illness among foundlings was coming to light, other things remained in the shadow. For example respiratory illness, another important element in the statistics on causes of death among foundlings, is treated much more briefly in the medical literature than the other group of illnesses. (But see E. Mensi, "Sulla frequenza della broncopolmonite e sue complicanze come causa di mortalità degli episodi," *Rivista di igiene e sanità pubblica* 14 [1903].)

80. Douglas, *Purity and Danger*, esp. pp. 35–40.

81. See S. Somogyi, "L'alimentazione nell'Italia unita," in *Storia d'Italia*, vol. 5: *I documenti* (Turin, 1973), t. 1, pp. 841–87, on the stability of the eating conditions of the urban lower classes in this period.

82. In Rome, in 1917, the year of the reform, 33 percent of the children were acknowledged, in 1918 51.23 percent, and in 1919 51.42 percent (see D. Albini, "Brefotrofio di Roma: I risultati del biennio 1918–19," *Bollettino della Federazione Nazionale tra i brefotrofi* 2, no. 3 [June 1920]: 15). In Mantua, instead, for example, the acknowledgments that before the reform (1914) averaged 15 percent, rose during the same year to 92 percent, only to rise again to 97.96 percent in 1918 (see Magrini, *Assistenza*, pp. 1–10, 25, 119).

83. E. Modigliani, *Relazione sul primo quinquennio di funzionamento dell'Opera Assistenza Materna* (Rome, 1924), p. 53 (hereafter Modigliani, *Relazione*).

84. Ibid., pp. 7, 53.

85. ACS, *Sanità*, 1910–20, b. 602, containing the reports on the early years of activity of the agency that were sent to the director of health. In general, on the welfare institutions of the years right after the war, see G. Tropeano, *Le opere e le istituzioni di assistenza e previdenza sociale della maternità e dell'infanzia esistenti in Italia nel 1922* (Naples, 1922).

86. The directors of the maternity hospitals of Rome were present at the meeting preparatory to the establishment of the agency as were the medical director of the foundling hospital of Rome and a physician representing the director of health. The pediatrician Enrico Modigliani (see n. 74) had a decisive role in developing the initiative.

On the relationship between women's philanthropic activities and medicine, see L. Gordon, *Woman's Body, Woman's Right: A Social History of Birth Control in America* (Harmondsworth, 1977).

87. I have worked with two sets of forms: the first group (57) are "life histories" reproduced extensively in Modigliani, *Relazione*, and they go back, therefore, to the period 1918–23. A second group of 123 forms, still from Maternal Assistance, but covering the years 1936–67, however, were found among the papers of Mrs. Modigliani, and were put at my disposal, with great generosity, by Dr. Claudio Modigliani. In 1932–33 Professor Roberto Bachi and Mrs. Modigliani were planning a work on unwed motherhood, based on the forms collected up to that point by Maternal As-

sistance, already amounting to over 4,000, To this end, an inquiry was undertaken with new home visits to those women who were helped during the early years after the war and there were thus reconstructed, to use the words of the authors, more than 4,000 "little monographs." The publication of this work was hindered by racial laws; only the first volume (*Le fonti*, here cited in n. 1) appeared. I have tried in vain to find the "monographs" of Maternal Assistance: it seems that the material has disappeared or been destroyed during the move to the ONMI archives. Here I cite the forms of the first group (1918–23) with the original numbering as it appears in Modigliani, *Relazione*; I have instead given progressive numbers to the forms found among the papers of Mrs. Modigliani, and I cite them as Carte Modigliani (CM) with corresponding numbers in my transcription.

88. For example see instead the first-person experiences of maternity narrated in M. Llewelyn Davies, ed., *Maternity: Letters from Working Women* (London, 1915).

89. Pausing over the inspection reports of the female visitors during the period 1918–23, out of the 1,060 women who took part, 13 percent slept in the same room with two other people, 26 percent with three, 21 percent with four, 16 percent with five, 12 percent with six, 5 percent with seven, 4 percent with eight. Of all the rooms, 52 percent contained only one bed (see Modigliani, *Relazione*, pp. 105–6).

90. Ibid., S. 73.

91. Ibid., S. 145.

92. Ibid., S. 375.

93. CM, S. 123. Annita was sent to Rome to become a maid; here a soldier made her pregnant and abandoned her.

94. A statistical table on the professions of the women helped between 1918 and 1923 shows that 50 percent were domestics; following were housekeepers, peasants, seamstresses, workers, laundresses, clerks, typists, and a variety of other professions, from porters to beggars (Modigliani, *Relazione*, pp. 33–35).

95. Ibid., S. 1044.

96. For the years 1918–23 we have a table of the occupations of the unwed fathers; here it emerges that 82.24 percent are of "proletarian status" and 17.76 percent of "bourgeois status" (Modigliani, *Relazione*, pp. 45–48).

97. CM, S. 30, 43, 37, 106.

98. Modigliani, *Relazione*, p. 68.

99. For example, the history of a forty-year-old woman, who lost her father at age three and was in school until age sixteen; she has a son born to her when she was twenty-eight, whom she acknowledged and nursed for eighteen months. In the information forms she speaks at length of her son: "He has completed the third level of vocational training. He was enrolled at Balilla at age seven and has always done very well. This year he will go to summer camp. He has a very good character and is very affectionate and he appreciates the great sacrifices made for him" (CM, S. 104).

100. R.D.L. May 8, 1927, no. 798 "Ordinamento dei servizi di assistenza dei fanciulli illegittimi abbandonati e esposti all'abbandono" (*Gazz. uff.*, June 1, 1927, no. 126).

101. ACS, *Min. int., Gabinetto, ONMI*, b. 1: ONMI material marked "situazione illegitimi: Appunti per il Duce."

The assistance from ONMI took the form mainly of monetary subsidies of variable duration and amount. From the forms from Rome of 1936–37, it appears that the subsidy was usually 60 lire a month, independent of the number of children in the woman's care; and, again from the forms, we see that a woman also had to pay 120 lire each month for a wet nurse, or 90 lire to sublet a room. In 1941, we see in an ONMI account (ibid.) that in only five provinces were the subsidies to the mothers "such as to assure, at least in theory, the conditions necessary for the life and development of the child"; in all the other provinces the subsidies were laughable.

102. This was the guarantee, for example, in a letter to the secretary-general of Partita Nazionale Fascista (PNF) from the director of one of these agencies (Infantiae Salus "La Nutrice") (ACS, *Opere Pie*, Serie 10, b.4).

103. Regarding the instruction given to the female visitors, see, for example, PNF, Federazione provinciale dei Fasci Femminili di Torino, *Lezioni al corso per visitatrici fasciste e patronesse ONMI* (Borgo San Dalmazzo, 1937). Only five lessons treat medical and hygenic material, and only very generally; for the rest, the instructional material describes the health organizations and charitable institutions, the health policies of the Fascist regime, and l'Opera Nazionale Balilla.

104. CM, S. 6.

105. One of the foundling hospital physicians with whom we are concerned, Odorico Viana, noted with disapproval at the end of the 1930s that the young physicians paid attention only to the laboratory diagnoses, glossing over the compilations of clinical sheets and assigning them to the hospital personnel (O. Viana, "Per la riabilitazione della casistica: la cartella nosografica," *La clinica ostetrica* [1937]).

106. T. W. Adorno, "Tipi e sindromi," in *La personalità autoritaria* (Milan, 1973), pp. 355–56 ["Types and Syndromes," in *The Authoritarian Personality* (New York, 1950), p. 747].

For a reevaluation of the biography from the point of view of its usefulness for the social sciences, see J. Clifford, "Hanging Up Looking Glasses at Odd Corners: Ethnobiographical Prospects," in *Studies in Biography*, ed. D. Aaron (Cambridge, Mass., 1978).

107. G. Deledda, *La chiesa della solitudine* (Rome, 1936).

Designed by Martha Farlow
Composed by NK Graphics, Baltimore, in Stempel Garamond
Printed by Edwards Brothers, Inc., on 50-lb. Glatfelter Natural